Psychohistory
and
Religion

PSYCHOHISTORY
AND
RELIGION

The Case of YOUNG MAN LUTHER

Edited by ROGER A. JOHNSON

With Contributions by
Roland H. Bainton   William Meissner, S.J.
Lewis W. Spitz   Roger A. Johnson
Paul W. Pruyser   Clifford J. Green

FORTRESS PRESS

Philadelphia

"Psychiatry and History: An Examination of Erikson's *Young Man Luther*" by Roland H. Bainton first appeared in *Religion in Life*, XL, 4 (Winter, 1971), pp. 450–478, and is reprinted by permission of Abingdon Press.

"Psychiatry and History: The Case of *Young Man Luther*" by Lewis W. Spitz first appeared in *Soundings: An Interdisciplinary Journal*, LVI, 2 (Summer, 1973), pp. 182–209, and is reprinted by permission of the original publisher.

"From Freud to Erikson: Developments in Psychology of Religion" by Paul W. Pruyser first appeared as "Erikson's *Young Man Luther*: A New Chapter in the Psychology of Religion" in *The Journal for the Scientific Study of Religion*, II, 2 (April, 1963), pp. 238–242, and is reprinted by permission of The Society for the Scientific Study of Religion.

Quotations in chapter 5 from *Images of Faith: An Exploration of the Ironic Imagination* (Notre Dame: University of Notre Dame Press, 1973) by W. F. Lynch, S.J., are used by permission of University of Notre Dame Press.

Quotations in chapter 7 from *Dietrich Bonhoeffer* by Eberhard Bethge (original German edition © 1967 Chr. Kaiser Verlag, Munich; English translation © 1970 William Collins Sons & Co., Ltd., London, and Harper & Row, Publishers Inc., New York) are used by permission.

Quotations in chapter 7 from Martin Luther, *A Commentary on St. Paul's Epistle to the Galatians* © 1953 James Clarke & Co. Ltd., Cambridge, England, are used by permission.

Quotations from the works of Erik H. Erikson, *Young Man Luther: A Study in Psychoanalysis and History* (New York: Norton, 1958), *Gandhi's Truth: On the Origins of Militant Non-Violence* (New York: Norton, 1969), and *Identity: Youth and Crisis* (New York: Norton, 1968) are used by permission of W. W. Norton & Co.

Library of Congress Catalog Card Number 76–007870
ISBN 0–8006–0459–8

5782H76   Printed in U.S.A.   1-459

CONTRIBUTORS

ROGER A. JOHNSON is Professor and Chairman of the Department of Religion and Biblical Studies at Wellesley College. He is the author of *The Origins of Demythologizing* and the coauthor of *Critical Issues in Modern Religion*.

ROLAND H. BAINTON is Professor Emeritus of Ecclesiastical History, Yale University Divinity School. Among his numerous publications on Luther and the Reformation are *Here I Stand*, *Reformation in the Sixteenth Century* and *Women of the Reformation*.

LEWIS W. SPITZ is Associate Dean of the School of Humanities and Sciences, Stanford University, and Professor of History. He is a director of the Center for Reformation Research. Among his publications are *The Renaissance and Reformation Movements* and *The Northern Renaissance*.

PAUL W. PRUYSER teaches at the Menninger Foundation and is a past president of the Society for the Scientific Study of Religion. He is the author of the major psychoanalytic psychology of religion, *A Dynamic Psychology of Religion*. His latest volume is *Between Belief and Unbelief*.

WILLIAM MEISSNER, S.J., M.D., has taught psychiatry at the Harvard Medical School and psychoanalysis at the Boston Psychoanalytic Institute. He is coauthor of the text in psychiatry for medical students, *Basic Concepts of Psychoanalytic Psychiatry*. His other publications are *Foundations For a Psychology of Grace* and *Group Dynamics in the Religious Life*.

CLIFFORD J. GREEN is a professor in the Department of Religion and Director of the Professional Ethics Program at Goucher College. He is the author of *Bonhoeffer: The Sociality of Christ and Humanity* and coauthor of *Critical Issues in Modern Religion*.

Contents

Contributors   v

1. Introduction   ROGER A. JOHNSON   1

HISTORICAL STUDIES

2. Psychiatry and History: An Examination of
   Erikson's *Young Man Luther*   ROLAND H. BAINTON   19

3. Psychohistory and History: The Case of
   Young Man Luther   LEWIS W. SPITZ   57

PSYCHOANALYTICAL STUDIES

4. From Freud to Erikson: Developments in
   Psychology of Religion   PAUL W. PRUYSER   88

5. Faith and Identity   WILLIAM MEISSNER, S.J.   97

RELIGIOUS STUDIES

6. Psychohistory as Religious Narrative:
   The Demonic Role of Hans Luther in Erikson's
   Saga of Human Evolution   ROGER A. JOHNSON   127

7. Bonhoeffer in the Context of Erikson's Luther Study
                                   CLIFFORD J. GREEN   162

   Bibliography: Reviews of *Young Man Luther*   197

1. Introduction

Roger A. Johnson

YOUNG MAN LUTHER AND PSYCHOHISTORY

In his presidential address to the American Historical Association in December 1957, Walter Langer challenged historians
to embrace the theory of psychoanalytic psychology as an appropriate tool for their study of the past. He noted the fruitful
uses of psychoanalysis in a variety of other social sciences and
deplored the fact that "historians have for the most part approved of the iron curtain between their own profession and
that of the dynamic psychologists."[1] He pointed out that history was, after all, the scene of human actions and not just
"impersonal historical forces." Since historians were "as much
or more concerned with human beings and their motivations
than with impersonal forces and causation," how could it be
that they had failed to utilize the insights of psychoanalysis?[2]

At the same time that Langer issued his challenge, but
wholly independent of it, Erik Erikson was completing the
manuscript for a new book on Luther. Published in 1958,
Erikson's *Young Man Luther: A Study in Psychoanalysis and
History* was quickly recognized by historians as a powerful
example of the kind of psychoanalytic exploration of the past
for which Langer had argued. As a result, Erikson's book
quickly became the subject of an intense and prolonged controversy concerning the viability of psychoanalysis as an ally
of historical inquiry.

Some historians heralded Erikson's work as a major break-

1. William L. Langer, "The Next Assignment," *The American Historical
Review* 63, no. 2 (January 1958):288.
2. Ibid., p. 286.

through in their field.[3] Like Langer, they appreciated psychoanalysis as a theoretical framework for exploring the complexities of human motivation. They also valued Erikson's
particular kind of psychoanalysis because of his epigenetic
theory and his psychosocial perspective. The former assigned
developmental significance to adult stages of life as well as
earlier childhood stages; the latter incorporated cultural sym-
bols and social institutions within the dynamics of human
development. Taken together, both provided a psychological
theory more amenable to the purposes of historical inquiry;
for in Erikson's theory, the public data of adult life and social
institutions become expressive of, and inseparably bound up
with, the inner depths of the psychic.

Other historians, however, highlighted the deficiencies of
psychoanalytic theory as a historical tool.[4] At its best, psychoanalysis appeared to be limited to the realm of biography,
with little to offer the social, economic, or political historian.
At its worst, even Erikson's modified style of psychoanalytic
history was still sufficiently preoccupied with childhood events
and intrapsychic conflicts to lead the historian from the public
realm of known data into the private domain of the nursery
or neurosis. Since only the analyst with a live patient had

3. For example, Cushing Strout, "Ego Psychology and the Historian," *History
and Theory* 12, no. 4 (1968):281–97; Donald B. Meyer, review article, *History
and Theory* 1 (1960–1961):291–97; anonymous review article, *Daedalus* 92
(Winter 1963):178–87; Sudhir Kakar, "The Logic of Psychohistory," *The
Journal of Interdisciplinary History* 1, no. 1 (Autumn 1970):187–94; H. Stuart
Hughes, *History as Art and as Science* (New York: Harper, 1964), pp. 59 ff;
Bruce Mazlish, ed., *Psychoanalysis and History* (Englewood Cliffs, N.J.:
Prentice-Hall, 1963); Fred Weinstein and Gerald M. Platt, "History and
Theory: The Question of Psychoanalysis," *The Journal of Interdisciplinary
History* 2, no. 1 (Spring 1972):419–34.
4. Frank E. Manuel, "The Use and Abuse of Psychology in History," *Daedalus*
(1971):187–213; H. Stuart Hughes, *The Sea Change* (New York: Harper,
1975), pp. 226 ff; Fred Weinstein and Gerald M. Platt, *Psychoanalytic Sociol-
ogy: An Essay on the Interpretation of Historical Data and the Phenomenon
of Collective Behavior* (Baltimore: Johns Hopkins University Press, 1973),
esp. pp. 12–13, 68; Dietrich Orlow, "The Significance of Time and Place in
Psychohistory," *Journal of Interdisciplinary History* 5, no. 1 (Summer 1974):
131–38; Frederick Crews, "Reductionism and Its Discontents," *Critical Inquiry*
1 (March 1975), esp. 546–49; Philip Pomper, "Problems of a Naturalistic
Psychohistory," *History and Theory* 12 (1973):367–88.

access to that kind of data, the psychohistorian ran the risk of becoming lost in a labyrinth of speculative claims which could neither be confirmed nor negated by hard data.

In addition to the debate concerning the legitimacy of psychoanalytic modes of historical inquiry, Erikson's *Young Man Luther* also provided the catalyst for the emergence of the new discipline of psychohistory. Practicing psychohistorians were less inclined to argue about the general methodological issues raised by Erikson's book, and more occupied with the task of refining those methods by using them in relation to specific historical subjects.[5] As a result of their activity new journals have been founded, new professional associations have been formed, and an increasing array of articles and books, modeled on Erikson's Luther study, have been published.[6]

Because Erikson's book occupied such a prominent position in both the debate concerning psychoanalytic modes of history and the prolific new literature of psychohistory, it would seem reasonable to expect that *Young Man Luther* was the subject

5. For an example of such methodological refinement see John Demos, "Developmental Perspectives on the History of Childhood," *Journal of Interdisciplinary History* 2 (Autumn 1971).

6. *The Journal of Interdisciplinary History* (founded 1970) and *The History of Childhood Quarterly: The Journal of Psychohistory* (founded 1973) reflect the strong psychohistorical concerns of their founding editors. The Group for the Use of Psychology in History of the American Historical Association publishes several newsletters a year reviewing psychohistorical literature and issues; the Group for Psychosocial Interpretations in Theology of the American Academy of Religion provides a yearly forum for papers utilizing Erikson, Gestalt, and comparable approaches to religious subject matter. Indeed, three of the essays in this book—those by William Meissner, Clifford Green, and myself—were originally presented before this AAR working group. In addition, a variety of local Groups for Applied Psychoanalysis have provided the original context for much of the psychohistorical and psychosocial literature. For a bibliographical survey of recent literature see Robert M. Crunden, "Freud, Erikson, and the Historian: A Bibliographical Survey," *The Canadian Review of American Studies* 4, no. 1 (Spring 1973):48–64; Robert Coles, "Shrinking History," *New York Review of Books*, Feb. 22, 1973, and March 8, 1973; and *The Journal of Modern History*, June 1975, a special issue on psychohistory. For a bibliography of psychohistorical religious studies see Donald Capps, "Psychohistory in Religious Studies," *Group for the Use of Psychology in History Newsletter* 3, no. 2 (Spring 1974):4–8; see also an essay by Capps on this same subject in a forthcoming volume edited by Peter Homans.

of considerable critical scrutiny. But such was not the case. The new psychohistorians were too eager to ply their own trade to devote much attention to the problems of Erikson's book. The debate concerning the legitimate role of psychoanalysis within a historian's portfolio tended to focus on the large methodological issues, with little attention to the specific historical claims of Erikson's Luther book. As a result, there is no more agreement today concerning the reliability of Erikson's account of Luther than there was when the book was first published.

In addition, the quality of discussion of *Young Man Luther* has suffered from the lack of dialogue between the relevant secular disciplines and their religious counterparts. The most prominent participants in the debate were psychoanalysts and historians. And, as a cursory reading of their reviews of *Young Man Luther* indicate, they were not familiar with the discussion of the book developed in the relevant religious disciplines—Reformation studies, psychology of religion, and theology. To complicate matters further, Erikson has chosen, for his own reasons, not to reply in print to his critics—a decision he reaffirmed in choosing not to respond to the essays in this volume. Unlike other provocative and controversial books, *Young Man Luther* never enjoyed the benefit of a sustained public dialogue between its author and critics through which conflicting claims could be resolved and points of confusion clarified.

For all these reasons *Young Man Luther,* in spite of—or is it because of?—its prominence in the context of psychohistory, has survived its years of fame and notoriety with most of its ambiguities and complexities intact. And the prominence of the book cannot be confined to the past tense, for it continues to play a vital intellectual role, both as a teaching text in a variety of disciplines and as the definitive paradigm to which aspiring psychohistorians allude. The task, therefore, of delineating a critical assessment of the book's strengths and weaknesses seems imperative, both for the sake of its future readers and for the sake of the several disciplines which continue to draw on its insights. To do this, however, it will be necessary to examine the book in a context larger than that of the psychohistory debate, with attention to specific claims rather than general methodological issues, and from the perspective of religion and theology as well as that of history.

It is the collective aim of the individual essays in this volume to serve this purpose. Thus Roland Bainton and Lewis Spitz, both Reformation historians, provide a detailed and documented critique of Erikson's historical claims. While neither Bainton nor Spitz ignores the methodological issues posed by psychohistory, it is apparent from the abundance of Luther quotations in their essays that their primary subject of inquiry is the life and theology of Martin Luther. Paul Pruyser and William Meissner are both practicing and teaching psychoanalysts; however, they combine their psychoanalytic expertise with a disciplined study of the psychological dimensions of religious phenomena.[7] Pruyser locates Erikson's book in the context of the history of the psychology of religion, with special attention to the advances of Erikson beyond his Freudian predecessors. Meissner, who earlier elaborated a psychospiritual formulation of Erikson's epigenetic theory, examines in this essay some of the psychospiritual ambiguities of ideology.[8] For both authors, the appropriate context for *Young Man Luther* is not psychohistory but psychology of religion.

In a somewhat similar manner, the essays by Clifford Green and myself locate *Young Man Luther* in a theological context. Green concentrates on Erikson's work as an example of historical theology: the understanding of past theologies by means of an exploration of a significant crisis in the life history of

---

7. Paul Pruyser, *A Dynamic Psychology of Religion* (New York: Harper, 1968), and *Between Belief and Unbelief* (New York: Harper, 1974). William Meissner, *Foundations for a Psychology of Grace* (Glen Rock, N.J.: Paulist Press, 1966) and a series of articles in *The Journal of Religion and Health:* "Prolegomena to a Psychology of Grace," 3 (1964):209–40; "Notes on Monotheism," 6 (1967):269–79, 7 (1967):43–60, and 7 (1968):151–63; "Notes on the Psychology of Faith," 8 (1969):47–75; "Notes toward a Theory of Values," 9 (1971):123–37, and 10 (1971):77–97; "Toward a Theology of Human Aggression," 10 (1971):324–32; and "Notes on the Psychology of Hope," 12 (1973):7–29, 120–39.

8. Meissner, "Prolegomena to a Psychology of Grace."

the theologian. In a case study of Dietrich Bonhoeffer, Green tests Erikson's model by exploring the changing shape of Bonhoeffer's theology in relation to one critical turning point in his life. In my essay I focus on Erikson's role as a constructive theologian, or—if that term is too laden with confessional particularity—a proponent of a particular religious and ethical view of the past, present, and future. From this theological perspective the worst historical errors of *Young Man Luther* appear, not as a result of Erikson's psychological methods or historical ignorance, but as telling witnesses to the particular shape of his religious vision.

From this brief synopsis it should be clear that the issues of psychohistory are very much present in the several essays of this volume, even if the context for discussion has been expanded beyond the limits of the psychohistory debate. Indeed, these issues are so present that we will need to clarify some of them in a preliminary manner in this introduction. And the following comments offer not an exhaustive analysis of the psychohistorical issues of *Young Man Luther,* but a rough map of the shape of those issues as they emerge in the following essays.

PSYCHOHISTORICAL ISSUES IN *YOUNG MAN LUTHER* AN EMERGING CONSENSUS AND ABIDING CONFUSIONS

Understandably enough, psychohistorical issues appear most prominently in the two essays by Roland Bainton and Lewis Spitz. As a result, my interpretive comments in this section will refer primarily to these two essays. Three broad areas will be considered: first, the points of disagreement between Bainton and Spitz concerning their evaluation of psychohistory in general and Erikson's work in particular; second, those points on which Bainton, Spitz, and other Reformation historians agree concerning the historical errors of Erikson's account of Luther; and third, the points at which Bainton or Spitz are either confused concerning Erikson's concepts or fail to come to terms with his arguments. This last venture, while not customary for the introduction to a collection of essays, seems required in this instance because of Erikson's role as a silent partner. Otherwise the reader would be left with the impression that all of the objections raised by Bainton and Spitz were valid, and, as we shall soon see, this impression would be far from adequate.

While Roland Bainton and Lewis Spitz are both Reformation historians, their assessments of the role of psychology in historical studies and the contribution of Erikson's book differ considerably. Bainton, in general, regards the application of psychology to the past as a dubious venture. While he acknowledges a few specific aspects of Luther's life that might be illumined by a psychiatric approach, his stress falls on the extreme difficulty of such a path of inquiry. "The dead cannot be interviewed."[9] Similarly, Bainton acknowledges that Erikson offers "some valid insights," but in general these are limited to the kinds of insights previously articulated by Reformation historians.

Spitz, in contrast, has clearly a high regard for the theoretical complexity of Erikson's psychoanalytic position and his willingness to "seek out the awkward data . . . especially when these create difficulties for theory."[10] More important, however, Spitz accepts the fundamental claim of the psychohistorians, namely, the necessity for some comprehensive and systematic psychological theory in the exploration of the past —not just for a few points in the life of Luther but for the reconstruction of Luther's total life history.[11] As a result, in the conclusion of his essay Spitz offers his own psychological account of Luther, one that is drawn primarily from Oscar Pfister with his stress on the "fear motivated piety" dominant in Luther's parents, his surrounding culture, and Luther's early life history.[12]

While Bainton and Spitz disagree in their evaluation of

9. Below, p. 19.
10. Below, p. 83.
11. Below, p. 58.
12. For a comparison of the psychoanalytic interpretations offered by Pfister and Erikson, see Paul Pruyser's essay.

Erikson's contribution and the legitimacy or necessity of psychological inquiry, they strongly agree in rejecting totally Erikson's characterization of Luther's childhood and his parents. Without repeating the details of their arguments and evidence, their critique may be summarized as follows. The data for the reconstruction of Luther's early childhood is too limited; sources used by Erikson are not reliable, for example, occasional sayings from Luther in his old age about childhood experiences with his parents, comments copied by student boarders and never reviewed by Luther himself, and accusations circulated by Luther's enemies; translations are confused; the fundamental claim concerning Luther's father as a murder suspect is contradicted by known evidence; and the total picture of the childhood and parents appears sharply distorted when set against the known data. In summary, had Erikson entitled his book *Child Martin and His Parents* it would have long ago disappeared from our intellectual horizon as nothing but a very shoddy piece of speculation. And on this point there is a clear consensus among Reformation historians.[13]

Several explanations for Erikson's historical errors have been offered. Some, like Bainton, clearly regard these distortions as evidence of the methodological deficiencies of psychohistory. You cannot psychoanalyze the dead. Others, like George Lindbeck, view Erikson's errors as an accurate expression of the state of Luther scholarship in the early 1950s.[14] Lindbeck points out that Erikson is not a Reformation historian and necessarily depended upon the best available secondary sources. Since the Catholic-Protestant polemic concerning

13. In addition to Bainton and Spitz see Heinrich Bornkamm, "Luther and His Father," to appear in English translation in Peter Homans, ed., *Childhood and Selfhood: Essays on Religion and Modernity in the Thought of Erik Erikson*, forthcoming from Bucknell University Press; the German original is "Luther und sein Vater," *Zeitschrift fur Theologie und Kirche* 66 (1969): 39–61. See also Mark Edwards, "Erikson, Experimental Psychology, and Luther's Identity," also in the Homans volume; George Lindbeck, "Erikson's *Young Man Luther*: A Historical and Theological Appraisal," *Soundings* 56, no. 2 (Summer 1973):213 ff; and A. G. Dickens, *Martin Luther and the Reformation* (London, 1967), pp. 13 ff.
14. "Erikson's *Young Man Luther*," p. 212.

Luther was still in force when Erikson wrote his book, he felt free to draw equally from both sides of this battle.[15] In my own essay I offer yet another explanation. Hans Luther, around whom so many of the worst historical distortions cluster, plays a prominent role in Erikson's cosmic drama of good and evil. And Hans may have become such a pure villain in Erikson's version of Martin's life in order to dramatize those evils which Erikson finds stalking our modern world. Whether or not any or all of these explanations are accurate, it is certainly clear that Erikson's claims concerning Luther's childhood and parents do not stand the test of historical scrutiny.

Having stated this common critique of Erikson as strongly as possible, let me hasten to add that the consensus I have described is limited to the areas of Luther's childhood and parents. It does not include Erikson's portrayal of Luther's young manhood or his theology. At these points, specific objections have been raised; for example, Spitz objects to Erikson's interpretation of "the fit in the choir" as an acute experience of identity crisis, and to Erikson's dating and description of the "tower experience."[16] But there appears to be agreement, expressed by silence if not explicit consent, that Erikson's portrait of Luther's personality during the years of his young manhood is basically accurate. George Lindbeck summarized the qualitative gap which he finds between these two segments of Erikson's book by saying, "As far as I can see, Erikson's account of Martin's childhood must be adjudged almost entirely speculative. The treatment of his young manhood, in contrast, is on the whole historically unobjectionable, despite some questionable details."[17] Lindbeck goes on to point out that even Erikson's distortions of Luther's childhood do not invalidate the later segments of his narrative.

15. Lindbeck's explanation may be somewhat too generous. Erikson's most prominent sources—Scheel, Denifle and Reiter—were all published before World War II; the scholarship of the Luther Renaissance, beginning with Karl Holl's publications in the late 1930s, is notably absent from Erikson's book.

16. See below, pp. 77, 80–81.

17. "Erikson's *Young Man Luther*," p. 213.

> It would seem, oddly enough, that virtually nothing need be changed in the basic outlines of Erikson's portrait of the young man. . . . And this is true even if the childhood were radically different, even if the parents were not unusually harsh. . . . Erikson could be right about the psychological factors involved in Luther's entrance into the monastery, his ascetic and moralistic extremism, and his reformatory breakthrough, and still be wrong about his childhood.[18]

Since the central focus of Erikson's book is not "child Martin and his parents" but "young man Luther and his theology," the historical critique of Erikson's work summarized above can in no way be construed as a repudiation of his book as a whole. Individual historians who have focused on Erikson's distortion of parental figures may wish to utilize these errors as grounds for dismissing the whole book, but this judgment is not based on evidence or arguments marshaled thus far.[19] Indeed, if Erikson had only utilized a strict chronological principle in organizing his work, with childhood and parental materials confined to chapter one, it would have been a simple task to warn the reader to ignore this chapter and proceed to the substance of the book. As it is, however, childhood references and the figures of Hans and Margareta run throughout the whole of the book.

Being a psychoanalyst and not a Reformation historian, Erikson has made his share of mistakes. But the difficulties of interdisciplinary dialogue are not limited to the psychoanalytic side; historians also, in responding to Erikson's book, have made their share of mistakes in understanding Erikson's concepts or his arguments. Since Erikson has chosen not to respond to his critics, it does seem appropriate for the sake of a balanced dialogue to indicate some of these errors.

First, Erikson consistently repudiates any intention of explaining adult behavior as caused by childhood experience.

18. Ibid., p. 216.

19. The titles of essays by Erikson's historian critics suggest the specificity of their focus, for example, Bornkamm's "Luther und sein Vater." Bainton's essay in this volume was published in a modified form in German with the titles "Luther und sein Vater," *Zeitwende* 6 (1973):393–404, and "Luther und seine Mutter," *Zeitschrift der Luther-Gesellschaft* 44 (1973):123–30.

This kind of reductionism, associated with early Freudianism, is regarded by Erikson as the fallacy of "originology—a habit of thinking which reduces every human situation to an analogy with an earlier one, and most of all to that earliest, simplest, and most infantile precursor which is assumed to be its 'origin.' "[20] Because he so consistently repudiates the older Freudian version of psychohistory, Erikson tends to avoid any kind of causal language. He does not claim, for example, that childhood oedipal conflicts are the cause of Luther's religious message. Rather, Erikson views any significant human event as a recapitulation of multiple meanings from both past and present. Like an archaeologist, his purpose is to elucidate the varying levels of meaning in any event, not to claim that the chronologically oldest referent is the "real" cause.

In sharp contrast with this stated purpose, Bainton frequently depicts Erikson as if he were assigning causes, as if he were explaining adult behavior by reference to childhood experiences. Thus, Bainton notes that Erikson connects Luther's experience of being punished in school at the end of each week for any lapses in German with his later anxiety concerning forgotten sins.[21] To this point Bainton responds, "There is here, indeed, an interesting parallel, but there is absolutely no need to assume any causal connection."[22] With this objection Erikson could only agree, since he proceeds in the same paragraph quoted by Bainton to note another experience contributing to Luther's intense sense of guilt, "the experience of learning that nothing was ever good enough for teacher or father, and that any chance to please seemed always remote."[23] This latter experience is no more a cause for Luther's preoccupation with conscience and guilt than is the experience of punishment at school, but both may have contributed to Luther's adolescent crisis and his theological quest. In any case, Erikson's purpose is to elucidate the complex religious

20. *Young Man Luther*, p. 18.
21. Below, pp. 52–53.
22. Ibid.
23. *Young Man Luther*, p. 79.

phenomena of Luther's later life in such a way as to include earlier experiences from family or school, not to offer causal explanations.

A second point of confusion concerns the psychoanalytic understanding of human motivation. Two issues need clarification here. First, it is axiomatic for Erikson, as it is for the entire psychoanalytic tradition, that human actions express both unconscious needs and conscious aims. From this theoretical perspective the psychoanalytic historian is not likely to limit the evidence for determining the motivation of a historical agent to what that agent says about his or her own behavior. Other factors also need to be considered: what the person actually did, the psychological style or characteristics of the person's action, and long-range personality trends. Explicit statements of motives by historical subjects may be relevant for resolving the question of motivation, but they certainly cannot be sufficient. Second, it is equally axiomatic for Erikson that human behavior is always "overdetermined"; that is, people do what they do not for a single reason but for a multiplicity of motives. As a result the psychoanalytic historian is likely to be suspicious of any narrative of human action which assigns behavior to a single motive or system of motives. And it does not matter whether that one simple system of motives be psychological, economic, or religious. Thus any "either/or," monocausal theory of human motivation is alien to Erikson's psychoanalytic perspective. Some motives may be known, some may be unknown; some motives may be in conflict with each other, and some may be in contradiction with what is said; but in any case, the psychoanalyst assumes a rich, complex, and diversified palimpsest of motives present in any single act.

On the issue of motivation, Erikson's historical critics are simply confused. Their discussion of Luther's decision to become a monk may illustrate this confusion. Why did Luther enter the monastery? Because he made a vow to Saint Anne at the time of the thunderstorm? Because he was afraid of death? Because he wanted to please God? Because of the strict discipline and whipping by his mother?[24] Luther, at varying times, cites all of these reasons, and the psychoanalytic historian has no difficulty accepting all of them as valid. Bainton, however, is not happy with such a mixture of motives, and dismisses Luther's suggestion that his mother's discipline drove him into the monastery, because "this statement is at variance with Luther's authentic statement of what drove him into the cloister."[25] But how does Bainton, or any other historian, know which of these statements is the "authentic" one? Beyond personal preference for an unstated assumption about the psychological consistency of human behavior, what evidence can the historian appeal to? At this point, the psychoanalytic openness to a plurality of motives appears more congenial to the historian's task, even if this task be defined by the most stringent historiography.[26]

To complicate further the question of Luther's motives for entering the monastery, let us add an additional reason that Erikson proposes, namely, that Luther entered the monastery in order to seek a moratorium. At this point, lest there be any confusion, let us be quite clear that Erikson does *not* hold that Luther entered "the monastery in the thought that it would offer a moratorium," to use Bainton's phrase.[27] Bainton rejects this notion, as Erikson would also. *Moratorium* is, after all, a term created by Erikson to describe behavioral patterns of contemporary youth. Whatever his faults as a historian, he does not usually assign the language of modernity to the intentionality of actors from the past. Therefore, the appro-

24. See below, respectively, pp. 78, 37, 39, 30.

25. Below, p. 30. But contrast Bainton's response with Spitz: "Luther's mother . . . with her excessive discipline . . . led him to the monastery, just as Luther said" (below, p. 85).

26. H. Stuart Hughes identifies the affinity between psychoanalysis and history at this point as follows: "For both [history and psychoanalysis], plural explanations are second nature. The former speaks of 'multiple causation'; the latter finds a psychic event 'overdetermined.' Indeed, for both of them the word 'cause' is admissable only if defined with extreme flexibility: most of the time they prefer to express their interpretations in terms more clearly suggesting the possibility of alternative ways of looking at the matter" (*History as Art and as Science*, p. 47).

27. Below, p. 39.

priate question is not what Luther thought about his monastic decision, but rather, Is Erikson's admittedly modern concept of moratorium appropriate to, and illuminative of, Luther's behavior during the early monastic years? In order to answer this question Erikson describes in some detail a variety of psychological conditions which he has found in his clinical experience to be characteristic of young persons during "moratoria" of their lives.[28] He also describes, on the basis of his historical knowledge, characteristics of both the medieval monastic system and Luther's behavior during his early monastic years. It is his judgment that there is a striking degree of convergence between these two disparate sets of data, and so he describes this period of Luther's life as also a "moratorium."

Neither Bainton nor Spitz replies to Erikson's multifaceted assertion concerning Luther's moratorium; rather, both dismiss the notion of a moratorium as an inappropriate description of the activity of a person engaged in religious and theological struggles. Spitz says, "Luther's time in the monastery was not basically a moratorium for identity crisis resolution but a period of soul-struggle in a religious sense."[29] Bainton comments, "His struggle in the monastery was religious and theological."[30] It is as obvious to Erikson as it is to Spitz and Bainton that Luther's struggle in the monastery was religious and theological. Erikson never claimed that Luther's monastic experience involved nothing but the resolution of an identity crisis; he only claimed that during the monastic years Luther was also engaged in a profound and painful struggle with an overbearing negative conscience and for a new identity. This assertion, whether true or false, does involve a rich mixture of historical data and judgments. Perhaps Erikson was mistaken in his description of medieval monastic life, or at least the life of the Augustinian monastery which Luther joined. Perhaps he was mistaken in the data which he cited as the

28. *Young Man Luther*, pp. 100–104.
29. Below, p. 81; also pp. 79, 85.
30. Below, p. 47.

basis for his psychological interpretation of Luther's struggle in the monastery. But if Erikson's data or judgments are wrong, the historians do not help us gain a more adequate understanding of this segment of Luther's life. For the either/ or bias of pre-Erikson Protestant historians reappears as the principle of explanation for Luther's behavior: either his struggle was religious or it was psychological, but it cannot have been both. To this dogmatic assertion no reply is possible.

A third point of confusion between the historians and psychoanalysts concerns the interpretation of pathological symptoms as part of Luther's total life and thought. Erikson is quite specific in identifying the various forms of pathology that characterize the whole of Luther's life. There were the serious depressions in early youth, which reappeared as severe depressive episodes both in middle age and old age.[31] In the early monastic years there were clear patterns of obsessive-compulsive behavior.[32] Later there were repeated outbursts of anger and abuse in the vituperative attacks against enemies, be they Papists, peasants, or Protestant opponents. Still later were the stomach ailments, both constipation and diarrhea, coupled with the persistent use of anal imagery.[33] Finally there was Luther's quasi-paranoid reaction to "evil forces," in the form of both Satan and the Jews. While much of this behavior may be paralleled in some of Luther's peers, Luther's own life displayed such a quantity of symptoms, an intensity of affect, and a recurrence of symptoms throughout the whole span of his life as to set him apart from others of his own age.

For Erikson the question is not, Is Luther neurotic?—but rather, How shall his neurotic symptoms be interpreted? Erikson rejects the psychiatric and priestly versions of Luther, which reduce this great man to nothing but a bundle of neuroses. In a similar way, Erikson is sharply critical of John Osborn's play *Luther*, purportedly based on Erikson's book,

31. Erikson, *Young Man Luther*, p. 243.
32. Ibid., pp. 61, 137–38.
33. Ibid., pp. 244–47.

precisely because it portrays Luther as if he were a patient in
a mental hospital. At the same time, Erikson also rejects the
tendency of Protestant theological professors to dismiss
Luther's pathological symptoms as irrelevant, since Luther
was "nothing but" a religious personality, a vehicle for God's
gracious revelation. To be sure, Erikson is clear concerning the
religious forms through which Luther's neurotic tendencies
found expression. His sadness "was the traditional *tristitia*, the
melancholy world view of the *homo religiosus*."[34] But it was
not only that, for "he later abandoned this melancholic mood
altogether for occasional mood swings between depression and
elation, between self-accusation and the abuse of others."[35] Similarly, his obsessive-compulsive behavior was channeled
through the rituals of the monastic confessional. But here also
his scrupulosity exceeded the bounds of the religious rituals
provided, so that he found himself rebuked by his superiors.[36]
Again, Luther coped with the destructive drives within himself by projecting them onto the figure of Satan, conveniently
provided by the religious culture of his age. But here also the
obstinacy and the intensity of Luther's struggle with Satan,
in his later years, did not fall within the range of typical
medieval behavior.[37]

In summary, Luther's neurotic tendencies did find expression in religious forms, but pathology by any other name is
still pathology. And we may no more dismiss Luther's pathology from the historical record than we may claim that his
religious insights are invalidated by his pathological symptoms.

The genius of Erikson's contribution at this point is to place
Luther's pathology in the service of his creativity and, eventually, in conflict with the reigning theology of his time. Luther's
preoccupation with guilt and sin, his depressions and obsessive-
compulsive scrupulosity, were both expressive of and reinforced by the dominant cultural portrayal of a wrathful, de-

34. Ibid., p. 40.
35. Ibid.
36. Ibid., p. 156.
37. Ibid., p. 249.

manding God. For Erikson, Luther's passionate quest for a gracious God was driven both by the psychic disorders of his personal life and the ideological disorders of medieval religiosity. Similarly, Erikson finds the salient features of Luther's theology to express simultaneously a resolution of his personal anguish and a reformulation of the excessively foreboding belief-system dominant in his age. The freedom of the Christian conscience from the terror of law, the radical distinction between the theological functions of law and gospel, grace and works, and the new status of the believer as *simul justus et peccator*—these are not peripheral but central elements in Luther's theology, and Erikson has with considerable persuasion related all of them to the particularity of young Martin's life history.

Erikson thus takes Luther's pathology seriously, not so as to undermine his theological creativity but rather to reinforce it. As Paul Pruyser observes, the distinctive characteristic of Erikson's genius appears in his ability "to interweave healthy and unhealthy processes, . . . constructive and destructive alternatives . . . , in a continuum of health and illness."[38] Erikson's model of human existence is thus a paradoxical one. He does not believe in any state of pure health or pure illness, but portrays individual lives as moving from the one to the other and always incorporating some of both. In many ways his psychological model of the human person is strikingly similar to Luther's theological anthropology. For Erikson, as for Luther, man is *simul justus et peccator*. And just as Luther could claim that even Satan serves God, so Erikson claims, in Luther's case, that even pathology can serve creative purposes.

And what is the response of the historians to Erikson's clinical insights concerning Luther's pathology and the paradoxical model of human creativity which he proposes? Very little. Bainton and Spitz agree that Luther's depressions must be acknowledged, for Luther spoke of them so frequently. However, they also agree in refusing to take these depressive episodes seriously as symptoms of a psychological disorder.

38. Below, p. 91.

For once again we meet the familiar refrain of the either/or: Luther's depressive episodes are purely religious and not psychological. Bainton says that "those later despondencies were of a religious character. Presumably, then, the earlier ones had the same quality."[39] Spitz comments, "In later life Luther recalled that from youth on he had suffered depressions like those that plagued him in old age, and those depressions may well have been religious in content."[40] Other pathological episodes in Luther's life history are simply not mentioned by the historians, except for Bainton's suggestion that Erikson may have characterized Luther's monastic years as an "overreaction" simply because of Erikson's own antiascetic bias.[41]

The hard parts of Luther's story, those pathological episodes with which Erikson has wrestled to incorporate in his account of a great man's youth, those symptomatic outbursts which may yet prove embarrassing to all who claim Luther as one of their spiritual ancestors, the historian critics of Erikson have chosen to ignore or dismiss as "nothing but" religious.[42] And so, we must probably wait for yet another version of Luther's life which both takes seriously the clinical data discussed by Erikson and also avoids the historical errors in his book.

39. Below, p. 36.
40. Below, p. 85.
41. Below, p. 43.
42. Lindbeck's position differs considerably from the either/or posture described above: "No objections [to Erikson's account] need be raised from the theological side. Luther at least would probably have denied that there is any necessary incompatibility between explanations in terms of divine agency and psychological causation. 'Natural' and 'Supernatural' were not mutually exclusive categories for him, in contrast to medieval scholastics or modern fundamentalists. God uses all kinds of profane things to terrorize guilty consciences, why not also displaced fear of one's father? The vehicles of God's grace and inspiration are innumerable, why not also the successful surmounting of an identity crisis? There is no particular reason in principle, as far as I can see, why Luther could not add the whole battery of Freudian psychic mechanisms to his list of the *larvae dei*" ("Erikson's *Young Man Luther*," pp. 216–17).

2. Psychiatry and History: An Examination of Erikson's *Young Man Luther*

Roland H. Bainton

Psychiatry is the next frontier of history. Such in essence was the judgment of Professor Langer of Harvard in his presidential address before the American Historical Association in 1958. In that same year Erik Erikson applied psychiatry to historical biography in the case of Luther. His was a serious attempt to discover how a great man passed through adolescent turmoil and was able so to get himself in hand that he could deploy his powers. The attempt is worth making but exceedingly difficult. The dead cannot be interviewed. We are compelled to rely only on literary sources, and since the men of the past did not employ our categories and vocabulary we have to scrutinize their asides and translate their terminology. To do this with any measure of success requires a thorough acquaintance with the man's entire output. In the case of Luther the material for his later life is overwhelmingly abundant; for the earlier, disconcertingly slight. Acquaintance with the man does not alone suffice. Granted that human nature is essentially unchanged over the centuries, human behavior is drastically conditioned by environmental factors. Consequently one must master the milieu of the subject of the biography. Nor does the milieu suffice. One must be familiar also with what preceded. Out of his own past what did the man select? How did he combine and rework what went before? When it comes to Luther one must be thoroughly familiar with the Bible. He continually used its language without specific reference, and only one versed in Scripture will recognize the source of his terminology. Then, too, the man's influence must be assessed.

19

Why did his word take hold? Does the appeal to others throw light on the origins within himself? When all of the material is amassed and critically sifted, lacunae appear. They can be abridged only by conjecture. The psychiatrist may well contribute to understanding by conjecture, but a surmise is not to be treated as a fact and used as the basis for another surmise. One who constructs a pyramid of conjectures may be compared to God who made the world out of nothing.

Erikson's *Young Man Luther* has some valid insights. He points out that Luther's doctrine of justification by faith amounts to a turning away from God as a father-judge to God as a nursing mother who suckles her child without any reference to desert, and the child in perfect trust simply receives.[1] This is a thoroughly Lutheran insight, but he who perceives it is not to be denied his mead of gratitude. Luther, seeing his little Martin at the breast, commented: "The enemies of that child are the pope, the bishop, Duke George, King Ferdinand and all devils, and the dear child pays no attention to any of them, no matter how many they be and what mighty lords with ill intent, but sucks on the teats with joy, looks happy, smiles and lets them rage as long as they like. Truly Christ said we must become as little children."[2]

There is another insight in the chapter entitled "The Meaning of 'Meaning It,' " that is to say meaning something intensely, passionately. "Truth," comments Erikson, "is only that which one means with one's whole being and lives every moment."[3] Absolutely right. This insight suggests another which I wish he might have seen fit to explore because it is very important for the understanding of Luther's relation both to his God and to his parents and needs to be borne in mind before these points are discussed. One might phrase this additional insight as "the meaning of 'not meaning it.' " Luther

---

1. Erik H. Erikson, *Young Man Luther* (New York: Norton, 1958), p. 198.
2. Luther's *Tischreden* (Table Talk), vol. 2, no. 1631 (hereafter cited as TR) in the Weimar edition of Luther's works, *D. Martin Luthers Werke. Kritische Gesamtausgabe* (Weimar: Hermann Bohlaus Nachfolger, 1883–) (hereafter ctied as *WA*).
3. *Young Man Luther*, p. 209.

cites three biblical passages to show that when God appears to reject us, we must not allow ourselves to believe that he really means it. Here are the passages.

The first is that of the Canaanite woman, who besought Jesus to cure her daughter. He told her that he was sent only to the lost sheep of the house of Israel and that it was not fair to take the children's bread and throw it to the dogs. "Yes," she answered, "but even the dogs eat the crumbs that fall from their master's table." And Jesus, marveling at her faith, did as she asked.

Luther commented:

> This is written for our comfort and instruction that we may know how deeply God hides His grace from us and that we must not think of him according to our ideas and feeling, but only according to His Word. Here we see that though Christ speaks harshly he does not give a final judgment, an absolute "no." All his answers sounded like "no." He did not say that she was a dog. Nevertheless the "no" sounded stronger than the "yes." Yet there was a "yes," deep and secret. This shows the state of our heart when sore pressed. Christ in this story behaves the way the heart feels, for it thinks the answer is "no" when in reality it is not. Therefore the heart must turn away from its feeling and lay hold of the deep secret "yes" under the "no," with firm faith in God's Word.[4]

The second example is the case of the marriage feast at Cana when the wine gave out and Mary came and told Jesus. He answered, "Woman, what have you to do with me?" Then she said to the servants, "Do whatever he tells you." Here is Luther's commentary:

> How roughly Jesus rebuked the humble remark of his mother, who was concerned about the guests! Just see what this did to faith. What was there to believe in? Utter nothingness and darkness—no help in sight—God estranged and hostile—nothing whatever left! This is what happens to us when in our consciences we feel sin and the lack of righteousness and when in the hour of death we feel life slipping and the horror of hell grips us and the hope of blessedness fades. Then in all humility

4. *WA* 17^{II}, p. 202.

we ask and knock, beg and seek, that we may be delivered from sin, death, and despair. But Christ acts as if sin would win and death remain and hell never cease, just as he treated his mother and by his rebuff made her distress greater than it had been before. At such a time it seems as if all is lost. Faith then is sorely assailed, but see what his mother does and learn from her. No matter how gruff he sounded she would not believe that he was angry and ill-disposed. Had the mother allowed herself to be repelled by these harsh words she would have done nothing, but when she told the servants to do what he said, she showed that she had surmounted the rebuff and expected from him only sheer kindness. From this we learn that we should regard God as kind and gracious even though all our senses and feeling indicate the contrary. Then feeling is killed and the old man destroyed to be replaced simply by faith in God's goodness.[5]

The third example is that of Jacob wrestling with the angel. He thought it was an angel, says Luther, but his opponent really was God. Jacob having tricked his brother Esau and run away was now returning with wives and children to an encounter with his brother who might destroy him. The worst of it was that God, who allowed Esau to wax strong, might have decided to give him the inheritance and go back on the promise to Jacob. God appeared to be saying, "Jacob, you shall perish." And Jacob answered, "No, I shall not."

Were ever yes and no so sharply set over against each other? This was not a fight against flesh, blood, the devil, a good angel, but against God appearing in hostile guise. What a paroxysm of anguish, with faith saying over and over "No, no, no! God commanded, God called, God sent me that I should return to the land of my fathers. I will not believe you. Even though God slay me, yet shall I live." When faith is weakest, then is it strongest. When the smouldering flax barely smokes, then is it ready to burst into flame.[6]

These passages abundantly illustrate the point that man in relation to God must go beneath the apparent *nay* to the

5. *WA* 17[II], pp. 63–64. For fuller references see my *Luther's Meditations on the Gospels* (Philadelphia: Westminster Press, 1962), pp. 43–46.
6. *WA* 44, pp. 99–101.

everlasting *yea*. This applies also in human relations, as we shall see.

Now let us examine the evidence adduced by Erikson as the basis for the application of psychoanalysis to Luther's early days. My critique here is threefold. The first is that the evidence is scant, late, and flimsy; the second, that the projections from childhood to adolescence and maturity are sometimes false, sometimes unnecessary, and sometimes implausible. The third is that the motives attributed to Luther are invalid.

The evidence on which Erikson largely builds his case consists of three sayings taken from Luther's *Table Talk*, spoken when he was fifty years of age, recorded by students, often in discordant versions and never seen by Luther himself. This does not mean that such material is to be automatically rejected, but it must be corroborated by firsthand evidence, and the exact language cannot be pressed. The three sayings have reference to harshness on the part of Luther's teachers, his mother, and his father. They lie in the general context of humanist educational reform, and much of the sort was said by Erasmus, who, the illegitimate son of a priest, may never have seen his father.

One must also remember that in protesting against severe corporal punishment Luther was commenting on two biblical texts. The first was Col. 3:21, "Fathers, do not provoke your children lest they become discouraged" (Luther: *kleinmütig*). The other is from Eph. 6:4, "Fathers, do not provoke your children to anger" (Luther: *Zorn*). To illustrate these texts Luther adduces personal experiences. Once he was beaten by his mother, once he was beaten by his father, once he received fifteen strokes in one day from his teachers. In each case he could remember only one instance.

Let us begin with the reference to the teachers, which calls for the least discussion. The reason for fifteen strokes in one day was that the boys were punished for speaking German instead of Latin on the playing field. One boy each week was appointed as the *lupus*, the "wolf," to report any infractions. At the end of the week each demerit received a whack. Luther

called for the abolition of the whole system,[7] but he carried
from the experience no personal resentment against his
teachers.[8]

Erikson's treatment of this passage illustrates his method of
projection. He tells us that because Luther was required to
speak Latin and to inhibit German, therefore in later life he
was so voluble in German.[9] But he was just as voluble in Latin.
If one reads his reply to Erasmus, the *De Servo Arbitrio*, in
Latin, out loud and fast, one will feel the torrential flow of his
eloquence.

When it comes to Luther's relations to his parents Erikson
assumes a love-hate ambivalence. On the love side in the case
of the mother the inference is that Luther must have been
drawn to her because "nobody could speak and sing as Luther
later did if his mother's voice had not sung to him of some
heaven."[10] The love side of the ambivalence is then an inference from the way in which he later spoke and sang. It is a
possible inference. But is it a necessary inference? Might he not
have loved music because he loved music? Might he not have
sung because he was gifted with a splendid voice? If a love of
song must of necessity have been engendered by the hearing of
music and song in infancy, need the singer have been his
mother? Why not a nurse?

With regard to the hate side Erikson makes another inference. "Nobody would discuss women and marriage in the way
he often did who had not been deeply disappointed by his
mother."[11] What he said about women and marriage is open
to verification. What did he say? Yet even his sayings do not
settle the point as to whether he must have been disappointed
in his mother. One needs to ask whether his sayings were sufficiently at variance with current attitudes to require a personal
explanation.

7. *WA*, TR 3, no. 3566a, b.
8. Roland H. Bainton, *Here I Stand* (Nashville: Abingdon Press, 1950), p. 25.
9. *Young Man Luther*, p. 57.
10. Ibid., p. 72.
11. Ibid., p. 73.

For centuries controversy had been going on as to the rating of women and the estimate of marriage. The twelfth century marked the crisis in European mores. The Church imposed clerical celibacy, the Cathari rejected all sexual relations as evil, while the courts of love exalted womanhood and denigrated marriage. There followed a continuing literary conflict between the defenders and the detractors alike of woman and of marriage.[12]

In this controversy Luther was on the side of the defenders of marriage and of women. "Marriage," said he, "is the highest estate after religion,"[13] instituted by God, approved by Christ, and practiced by the patriarchs and apostles.[14] "My father slept with my mother and enjoyed her. They did not come together specifically for progeny. They did not know they were going to have a Dr. Martin Luther."[15] "They were godly folk and so were the married patriarchs and prophets."[16] "No one can sufficiently praise marriage."[17] Erikson himself recognizes that Luther "said deep, sweet, humorous and novel things about marriage."[18]

There were in fact three stages in Luther's advocacy of marriage. In the first he was inveighing vehemently against the obligatory celibacy of the clergy. "This," said he, "is responsible for the almost universal practice of clerical concubinage. God has not commanded celibacy. Nature forbids it. Sexual life is as natural as eating and drinking. The few on whom the gift of chastity has been conferred can live without marriage like Jesus, Mary and John the Baptist. But to impose the exceptional upon mankind in general is to invite looseness." Yet Luther himself in his early period had no thought of marriage. If anyone had told him at the Diet of Worms that in

12. Émile V. Telle, *L'Oeuvre de Marguerite d'Angoulème Reine de Navarre et la Querelle des Femmes* (Toulouse, 1937).
13. *WA*, TR 4, nos. 4138, 1814, 1786.
14. Ibid., no. 3983.
15. *WA*, TR 4, no. 4773; 2, no. 1658.
16. *WA*, TR 3, no. 3181b.
17. *WA*, TR 4, no. 4873.
18. *Young Man Luther*, p. 237.

seven years he would be married and a father, he would have laughed him to scorn. When, as he was in hiding at the Wartburg, the news came that not only priests but also monks were marrying, he ejaculated, "Monks too! They won't give me a wife."

But when in 1525 he did marry, there was a shift in emphasis. The home became the successor of the monastery as the sphere in which to suffer hardship in the service of the Lord. The bearing and rearing of children for the wife and feeding them for the husband were deemed vastly more taxing than any ascetic exercises in the cloister. All of the strains of married life made it preeminently the school for character. In the third period Luther saw the home as the substitute for the monastery in another sense, as the area above all others for the practice of the gentler Christian virtues of self-sacrifice, self-effacement, yielding, sharing, forgiving, reconciling. The love of the husband and the wife has the quality of the love of Christ and the Church, and the attitude of the parents to the children is a mirroring of the love of God for man.[19]

Here are a few excerpts from Luther's encomia of marriage. "Nothing is more sweet than harmony in marriage and nothing more distressing than dissension. Next to it is the loss of a child. I know how that hurts."[20] "Marriage offers the greatest sphere for good works, because it rests on love, love between the husband and the wife, love of the parents for the child, whom they nourish, clothe, rear and nurse. If a child is sick the parents are sick with worry. If the husband is sick the wife is as concerned as if it were herself. If it be said that marriage entails concern, worry and trouble, that is all true, but these the Christian is not to shun."[21]

---

19. Lilly Zarncke, "Der Begriff der Liebe in Luthers Äusserungen über die Ehe," *Theologische Blätter* 10, no. 2 (1931):45–49; "Der geistliche Sinn der Ehe bei Luther," *Theologische Studien und Kritiken* 106 (1934):20–39; "Luthers Stellung zur Ehescheidung und Mehrehe," *Zeitschrift für systematische Theologie* 12 (1934):98–117; "Die naturhafte Eheanschauung des jungen Luther," *Archiv für Kulturgeschichte* 25 (1934–35): 281–305.

20. *WA*, TR 1, no. 250.

21. Erlangen edition of Luther's works, vol. 3, pp. 513–14.

Youthful infatuation does not last, just as at the wedding at
Cana, attended by Christ, the wine gave out. There was no
beer and the bridegroom stood there like a beggar. Mary then
went to Jesus and told him the wine was emptied. He answered
as it were, "Do you have to drink water, that is do you have
trouble in the outward man and is it bitter? See then, I will
make it sweet and turn the water into wine. I will not pour
out the water. It will have to stay. But I will perfect it. I will
not take the vexation out of marriage. I may even increase it.
It will turn out wonderfully, as they only know who have
tasted it."[22]

When a friend suddenly lost his wife after seven hours in
labor, Luther wrote saying that no one breaks up so many
marriages as God. He brings together and he sets asunder. In
the morning the wife sleeps beside her husband. In the evening
she rests with God. "Oh how it hurts when married couples,
who love each other, are divided!"[23]

With respect to women and their place in society Luther
said that a preacher who reviles women will come to a bad
end. Honor should be given to the female sex, responsible as
it is for the bearing and rearing of children. He who holds it in
despite despises God.[24] Though the weaker sex, woman has the
glory of motherhood.[25] Women are more fervent than men in
prayer.[26] They are prone to mercy. Woman is a joyous life
companion. "When depressed flee solitude. Eve got into
trouble when she walked in the garden alone. Seek company,
convivial company, female company." Among the cures for
despondency are faith in Christ, a good fit of anger, and the
love of a woman.[27] The company of a charming young lady is
not to be despised (*elegantis puellae das ist auch gut*).[28]

As for the sphere of women, Luther believed, along with

22. Sermons on John 2:1–11 in *Dr. Martin Luthers Evangelienauslegung*
(Göttingen, 1954), p. 14.
23. *WA*, TR 4, no. 4209.
24. *WA*, TR 6, no. 6797.
25. *WA*, TR 4, no. 4138.
26. *WA*, TR 2, no. 1858.
27. *WA*, TR 1, no. 833.
28. Ibid., no. 141.

his generation, that they should confine themselves to the home. He selected biblical texts as a warrant: Gen. 3:16, that because of the fall Eve should be subject to Adam; 1 Cor. 14:34, that women should keep silent in church; 1 Tim. 2:12, that no woman is to teach or have authority over men.[29] Luther quite overlooked the prophecy of Joel 2:28 that your sons and your *daughters* shall prophesy. But he did recognize exceptional cases. When a duchess introduced the reform into her territories and the bishop told her that women should keep silence in church, she replied that if churchmen failed of their duty others might step in. Right, said Luther, women and children might step in.[30] He would deny to women any role in politics, war, and law.[31] God gave women large hips that they might stay at home and supervise the household.[32]

But within the domestic sphere he jokingly referred to his wife as not "My Lady," but "My Lord." He began to be worried that he relied more on her than on Christ.[33] "In domestic affairs," said he, "I defer to Katie. Otherwise I am ruled by the Holy Ghost."[34] "The eyes of the wife cook better than the maid, the man, the fire and the coals."[35] Women speak wisely on household matters. Their eloquence exceeds that of Cicero, and what they cannot accomplish by words they achieve by tears.[36] He was willing to knuckle under to Katie provided she did not let him down with too hard a thump.[37] He liked to tease her and suggested in view of her talkativeness that before opening her mouth she should say the Lord's Prayer, though he recognized that she could teach an Englishman German much better than he.[38] He remarked, perhaps ruefully, perhaps jest-

29. *WA*, TR 6, no. 6567.
30. *WA*, TR 3, no. 3813.
31. *WA*, TR 1, no. 104; 5, no. 5210; 6, no. 6567.
32. *WA*, TR 1, no. 55; 2, no. 1975.
33. *WA*, TR 1, no 980; 2, nos. 1352, 2458.
34. Albrecht Thoma, *Katharina von Bora* (Berlin, 1900), p. 71.
35. Ernst Kroker, *Katharina von Bora* (Leipzig, 1906), p. 194.
36. *WA*, TR 1, no. 1054.
37. *WA*, TR 2, no. 2789b.
38. Ibid., no. 1975.

ingly, that the only way to get an obedient wife is to carve one
out of stone.[39] Sometimes he threw out a jibe at the women in
his congregation. In expounding the story of the Visitation of
Mary to Elizabeth, he pointed out that Mary "went with haste,
not like our women who stop every five paces to strike up a
conversation."[40] But this quip may have been nothing more
than the trick of a medieval preacher who, when attention
lagged, would raise a laugh against some segment of the audi-
ence—readily distinguishable because the professions were dif-
ferently attired and in those days women could be distinguished
from men by their costumes!

Luther's sober tribute to the housewife is contained in his
translation, or one might better say paraphrase, of the thirty-
first chapter of the book of Proverbs.

> Where will one find a virtuous wife? She is rare and more
> precious than a pearl. Her husband leans on her and entrusts
> to her everything. She makes him glad and troubles him not
> all her life long. He will not lack for victuals. She busies her-
> self with flax and wool and enjoys working with her hands.
> She is like a merchant bringing wares from afar. She rises early
> and breakfasts her family and assigns to the maids their tasks.
> She buys a farm and lives by the fruit of her hands. She plants
> a vineyard and tends it with joy. Her hand is upon the distaff
> and her fingers on the spindle. She opens her hands to the poor
> and neglects not the needy. Her household fears not the snow
> for they have warm underwear. The roof does not leak. She
> makes quilts. Silk and purple are her garments and she is not
> slovenly. She opens her mouth with wisdom and on her tongue
> is good counsel. She instructs her children in God's Word. She
> eats not her bread in idleness. Her sons rise up and praise her
> and her husband does her honor. Many daughters bring riches
> but a virtuous wife outdoes them all. She will be famed for the
> fruit of her hands and her works shall praise her in the gates.[41]

If this evidence .disposes of the assumption that Luther
must have been deeply disappointed in his mother, we must
now proceed to inquire whether there is any proof that he was.

39. Ibid., no. 2034.
40. *WA* 27, p. 230.
41. *WA*, TR 4, no. 4783.

What do we know about his mother and his relationship to her? Admittedly our information is scant. She shared the folk belief that if a stone were thrown into a certain lake the devils would stir up a tempest.[42] She sang the ditty:

> If folks don't like you and me
> The fault with us is like to be.[43]

Erikson infers from this, as other have done, that she was not liked, but the point is simply that *if* one is not liked one has only oneself to blame.

Then comes the saying which is the keystone of the argument for the love-hate ambivalence, this time on the hate side. "My mother once whipped me for stealing a mere nut till the blood came. Her strict discipline caused me to go into the cloister and become a monk, though she meant it well."[44] Erikson declares that in the German version Luther says that his mother's severity drove him not into the monastery but into monkery—that is, extreme asceticism. But the German text does say explicitly *dass ich darnach in ein Kloster lief und ein Mönch wurde.*[45] But either way the statement is at variance with Luther's authentic statement of what drove him into the cloister. One wonders whether the explanation given in this saying may not have been an addition of the note-taker.

The main point is that Luther's mother treated him with severity. She drew blood. There is no indication that she meant to. She treated him in this fashion *once*, just once. Her intentions were good. Luther's complaint was not that she thrashed him but that the punishment was out of proportion to the offense. It would have been entirely in order to beat him for stealing money, a coat, or a chest, but not for stealing an apple, a pear, or a plum.

What further do we know about the mother? She did not

42. *WA*, TR 3, no. 3841.
43. *WA* 38, p. 338.
44. *WA*, TR 3, no. 356a, b.
45. Ibid., p. 416.

approve of his entering the monastery.[46] Luther did not invite her to his first Mass, but no women were invited. He sought the consent of his parents to his marriage though at the time he was forty-two years old. He informed a friend that he was inviting his "dear father and mother" to his wedding banquet.[47] He named one of his daughters after his mother and during her last illness wrote her a fine letter of consolation. Here is a translation, slightly condensed:

> Grace and peace in Christ Jesus, our Lord and Savior, Amen. My dearest mother, I have received the letter of my brother James about your sickness. It makes me very sad, especially because I cannot be with you as I wish I were. But with this letter I am with you personally and assuredly in the spirit, together with all our house. I trust that you have been abundantly instructed and thank God His comforting Word dwells in your heart. Though you have many preachers and comforters, still I would add my part to show that I am your child and you are my mother. God made us both and bound us together so that I may increase the number of your comforters.
>
> Dearest mother, be assured that your illness is God's gracious and fatherly rod and a very little rod compared with that with which he visits the ungodly and sometimes His own dear children whom he suffers to be beheaded, burned and drowned so that we must all sing, "For Thy sake we are slain all the day long."[48] So you must not mourn or be troubled by your sickness but thank God and recall how little is your suffering compared with that of His dear Son, our Lord Jesus Christ, which he suffered not for himself like us but for our sins.
>
> Secondly, dearest mother, be assured that the main ground of your blessedness, on which your comfort rests, in all extremities, is the "chief corner stone," Jesus Christ, who will not fail us nor suffer us to fall. . . . He says, "Be of good cheer. I have overcome the world."[49] If he has overcome the world he has also overcome all the princes of the world and their power and what is in their power if it be not death? . . . But now

46. Otto Scheel, *Dokumente zu Luthers Entwicklung* (Tübingen, 1929), no. 417.

47. In *WA*, Luther's *Briefwechsel* (Letters) (hereafter cited as Br), vol. 3, nos. 890, 897, 900.

48. Ps. 44:23; Rom. 8:36.

49. John 16:33.

he has overcome sin and death and given us this comforting word. We are to accept it with joy and thanksgiving. If any would affright us we are to say, See, see, see my soul, what are you doing? Death, dear sin, how do you live and frighten me? Don't you know that you have been overcome and you, death, are dead. Don't you know the one who has said, "I have overcome the world"? We are not to be terrified but hear the word of the Savior, "Be of good cheer. I have overcome the world."

St. Paul says, "Oh death, where is thy sting? Oh hell, where is thy victory?" "You, death, cannot scare me with a wooden skeleton. You have no power over me. You can show your teeth but you cannot bite. God has given us the victory over you through Jesus Christ, our Lord." . . . Comfort yourself with these thoughts, dearest mother, and be thankful that God has delivered you from the papist error that we can be saved through our own works and those of the monks and the error that Christ is not a comforting Savior but a cruel judge and tyrant from whom we should run to Mary and the saints. We know that Jesus Christ is our Mediator, our throne of grace, our bishop in heaven before God, who continually intercedes for those who believe in him.

You have the letter and seal, namely the gospel, baptism and the sacrament of the altar and preaching. Be thankful for such grace. Hear the words of Christ, "I live and you shall live and no one shall take your joy from you."[50] May the Father and God of all comfort, give you His holy Word, a firm, joyous and thankful faith that you may taste and experience the truth when he says, "Be of good cheer. I have overcome the world." All of the children pray for you and my Katie. Some weep. Some eat and say, "Grandma is very sick." May God's grace be with us all. Amen.[51]

Now let us see the use to which Erikson puts his assumption about Luther's relation to his mother. Because he was deeply disappointed in her, we are told that he dethroned the Virgin Mary, and her cult disappeared in Lutheran lands, though to be sure, adds Erikson, he attacked the cult rather than Mary herself.[52] Well now, if the cause was disillusionment with respect to his mother, what point was there in

50. John 14:19; 16:22.
51. *WA*, Br 6, no. 1820, condensed.
52. *Young Man Luther*, p. 71.

attacking only the cult and not primarily the Virgin? And in what sense was she dethroned? Only in the sense that she was stripped of every title not accorded her in the New Testament. Luther does not call her the Queen of Heaven, the Queen of the Sea, and the great intercessor with her Son. But every honor accorded to her in the Bible he renders with the utmost devotion. He has the Angel Gabriel tell her that no woman has ever lived on earth to whom God has shown such grace. "You are the crown among them all."[53] He praises her humility that she was ready to do maid service for her cousin Elizabeth, and that she, who might have been attended by legions of angels, trudged her weight on foot over the snow from Nazareth to Bethlehem for the birth of her child. The artists, says Luther, show her riding on a donkey. The Gospels do not mention a donkey. "I think she walked."[54] Did Luther take the donkey away from her because he was deeply disappointed in his mother? If that is the explanation, how explain his treatment of the Wise Men? Luther tells us that they were not necessarily three. Scripture does not give the number. They may have been a dozen. And they were not kings. That they were is a legend which crept in through the liturgy. They were simply wise men.[55] Did Luther dethrone the Wise Men because he had had one tilt with his father?

Let us now turn to the father-son relationship. What do we know about the father? Erikson tells us that the father, Hans Luther, *apparently* had a towering temper and was in fact *supposed* to have killed a shepherd before coming from Möhra to Mansfeld. Because he wished to maintain his status in the new environment he contained his "native fury" in public and gave vent to his rage at home.[56] He had "a driving economic ambition. [He certainly did hope that his son would be able to care for him and his wife in their old age], which was threatened by something (maybe even murder) done in the

53. *WA* 52, p. 626.
54. *WA* 10$^\text{I}$, pp. 62–63.
55. Ibid., pp. 555–72, 602–3; *WA* 17$^\text{II}$, p. 364.
56. *Young Man Luther*, p. 57.

past, and by a feeling close to murder which he always carried inside. Martin seems to have sensed on more than one occasion that the father, behind his disciplined public identity, was possessed by an angry, and often alcoholic, impulsiveness which he loosed against his family (and would dare loose *only* [italics Erikson's]) under the pretense of being a hard task-master and righteous judge."[57]

What is the source of the charge that Luther's father had killed a shepherd while at Möhra before coming to Mansfeld? It emanates from Witzel, who belonged to the company of Luther's virulent detractors and wished to discredit him by besmirching his parent. If the father was in danger before the law he would not have moved from Möhra to Mansfeld, which lay in the same political jurisdiction. If he had killed the peasant and was not in danger from the law, he must have been exonerated. How much credence can be placed in rumors is evident when one recalls that according to another story, father Hans was a Bohemian heretic, and again that he was a changeling begotten by the devil.[58] This point has not been medically confirmed.

What ground is there for saying that the father was an alcoholic? Only a single saying, the point of which was precisely the opposite. Luther was rebuking an alcoholic nephew and told him to abstain from liquor as from poison. "There are some," he added, "who may imbibe rather freely because, when a bit affected, they are gay and affable. They sing and joke like my father."[59]

And what do we know about bursts of temper at home? There is just one saying about a beating at the hands of the father.[60] Luther said, "One ought not to flog children too hard. My father once whipped me so that I ran away and felt ugly toward him until he was at pains to win me back." This is the

57. Ibid., p. 66.
58. Julius Köstlin, *Martin Luther* (Berlin, 1903), vol. 1, pp. 14–15.
59. *WA*, TR 4, no. 5050.
60. *WA*, TR 2, no. 1559.

translation which I gave in my life of Luther, *Here I Stand.*[61] Erikson thinks a more accurate rendering would be, "I fled him and became sadly resentful toward him till he gradually got me accustomed or habituated to him again."[62] The German reads *"dass ich ihn flohe und ward ihm gram, bis er wieder zu sich gewoehnte."* The key word in the first half of this sentence is the word *gram*, which I translated as ugly. I would not hold out for the word. I would be quite willing to substitute resentful, estranged, alienated, turned off, but not *sadly.* This meaning cannot be extracted from *gram.* The way to find out what it means is not to consult a modern German dictionary. Words change their meanings in the course of four centuries. One must find out what the word meant in Luther's day and more particularly what it meant for him. Luther said, "That the Papists are *gram* against me and hate me is no wonder."[63] "The pope is *gram* against me."[64] "It is sad when severe punishment causes children to be *gram* against their parents and to hate their teachers."[65] "He who prates about [the details of the life to come] is a big ass. I am exceedingly *gram* against him."[66] *Gram* does not mean *sadly* resentful.

Then there is the other half of the sentence which I rendered that the father was "at pains to win me back." Erikson translates, "until he gradually got me accustomed or habituated to him again." The German word is *gewoehnen*, which does means to accustom, climatize, adapt. It certainly cannot mean that the father got the son used to being thrashed. It must mean that he took the initiative to undo the hurt, to overcome the estrangement, alienation, or resentment, and to recover rapport. I still think that "win me back" best conveys the meaning, though I would not quibble over a word. But I

61. *Here I Stand*, p. 23.
62. *Young Man Luther*, p. 64.
63. *WA*, TR 3, no. 292b.
64. Ibid., no. 3838.
65. Ibid., no. 3566b.
66. *WA*, TR 5, no. 5672. Cf. Ph. Dietz, *Wörterbuch zu Dr. Martin Luthers Deutschen Schriften* 2 (Leipzig, 1872).

would insist that the word *gradually* has been inserted by Erikson. There is no indication of how long the process may have taken.

But if there was no trace of sadness in Luther's resentment, might not this support the thesis that the father was a brutal tyrant? It might, were it not for the statement that the father himself undertook to repair the damage. Once again one must stress the word *einmal*, once. Luther could recall only a single example of such behavior. The closest relation continued between the father and the son during this period.

But there was a considerable period of estrangement because of the son's religious development. Old Hans wanted Martin to prosper sufficiently to care for his parents in their old age.[67] Martin should take a degree in law and marry an honorable and opulent wife.[68] The father presented the son with a copy of the *Corpus Juris* and addressed him deferentially with the polite form of speech rather than with the familiar *du.*[69] Luther was pursuing the course mapped out for him. There is not the slightest indication that he was unhappy over it. He did say in later life that from his youth he had known depressions like those which plagued him later. These later despondencies were of a religious character.[70] Presumably, then, the earlier had the same quality. Luther went home from the university to see his parents. Why did he go? We do not know. Erikson says, "It stands to reason that Hans demanded an accounting," seeing that steps had already been taken to secure a wife.[71] That we do not know. The father wanted the son to marry *early*. That we do not know. Luther, we are told, was resisting these plans. That we do not know. The father demanded a showdown. That we do not know. Was there any other reason why Luther might have gone home? we are asked. Certainly! He might have gone home

67. Scheel, *Dokumente zu Luthers Entwicklung*, no. 536, p. 204.
68. Ibid., no. 47, from *WA* 8, pp. 573 ff.
69. Ibid., no. 420, p. 153; no. 508, p. 184.
70. Ibid., no. 48. *WA*, TR 3, no. 3893.
71. *Young Man Luther*, p. 91.

for the simple reason that he wanted to. People did make long journeys to see others because they wanted to. Matthew and Katherine Zell made a round trip of six hundred miles from Strasbourg to Wittenberg because they wanted to see Luther. And not all children are so withdrawn from their parents that they go home only when summoned.

Erikson continues that Luther, unwilling to comply with his father's demands and in consequence deeply troubled, started back for the university. On the way he was caught in a violent thunderstorm. In panic he vowed that he would become a monk. Erikson does not say that he made the vow deliberately to get himself off the hook with his father, but the vow served that purpose. If he did not consciously seek the monastery as an escape from parental authority, what was the reason for the vow? Erikson agrees that it was not to get away from the mother who had once thrashed him, but rather because of the fear of death. Luther said so.

At this point Erikson introduces from Huizinga a passage on the cult of death in the late Middle Ages. Quite right! But we need to consider the transformation which had taken place in the cult of death by Luther's time. Huizinga observes the change and Tenenti elaborates.[72] After the Black Death of 1348, which is assumed to have taken off something like half the population of Europe, the cult of death luxuriated in the macabre. But man cannot live on horror. The terror was attenuated. Huizinga notes that when the demand for burial in the cemetery of the Holy Innocents in Paris was so great that corpses had to be disinterred to make room for others and were then stacked in charnel houses; in front of the very cadavers, shops were erected, feasts were held, and prostitutes strolled. Tenenti observes that for the humanists, such as Erasmus, the way to die well was to live well and trust to the mercy of God.[73]

72. Johann Huizinga, *The Waning of the Middle Ages* (London, 1924), pp. 134 ff.
73. Alberto Tenenti, *Il Senso della Morte e l'Amore della Vita nel Renascimento* (Torino, 1957).

Why was Luther, then, not blasé with respect to death?
Why was he not content to live well and trust to the mercy
of God? Erikson suggests that Luther was more inclined to
primitive superstitions about malevolent forces because his
father was a miner in "constant danger of being crushed by a
mere squeeze of the earth's insides."[74] But Erasmus in his
youth was also petrified by the thought of death,[75] and his
father was not a miner but a priest, whom, as we have noted,
the bastard son may never have seen. Erasmus and Luther
both experienced the terror though for different reasons. Erasmus feared that he would not be able to complete his life's
work and that he would not be prepared for the vision of God.
Luther feared what came after death, the judgment.[76] He said
that he had been terror-stricken by the portrayal of Christ as
the implacable judge. Well might he have been stupefied by
the woodcuts of Christ seated on a rainbow, a sword protrud-
ing from one ear signifying wrath and a lily from the other
symbolizing mercy. Below, the dead were being hurried into
paradise or harried into hell. There was one depiction even
more appalling because from each ear protruded a sword, with
no lily. Below, a saint, presumably Peter, carries under his arm
a soul. A devil has lassoed the foot of this soul and, bracing
himself against Peter's rump, is tugging hellward. Such a prospect drove Luther to desperation.

Yet he had no thought of fleeing from the wrath to come by
taking the cowl. Not even the contemplation of death and
judgment had driven him to take a vow on an earlier occasion
when he had been confronted by imminent death. Why, then,
this time did he take the vow? Because this time he was convinced that God had issued a command. There was no pretense of having seen a vision or heard a voice. Yet God was in
that storm. Of this Luther was thoroughly convinced. God
was laying on him a command which he was loath to obey. He
did not welcome the monastery as an escape from his father.

74. *Young Man Luther*, p. 58.
75. Erasmus, *Erasmi Epistolae* 3, no. 867, pp. 167–68.
76. Scheel, *Dokumente zu Luthers Entwicklung*, no. 522.

The vow, said he, was coerced and unwilling.[77] He regretted it afterward, but felt obligated to carry through. "I entered the monastery," said he, "to please God."[78]

Erikson thinks that the monastery offered Luther an opportunity for a moratorium until he had thought himself through. He knew that he could easily get out of the monastery, as did Erasmus. Yes and no. He could leave at the end of the year of novitiate before he had taken the vows. But not easily afterward. Erasmus was relieved only of the obligation of residence and of wearing the habit of his order. He was not released from his vow of poverty, chastity, and obedience. Those who did simply break away like Butzer and Oecolampadius had to take refuge for protection in the fortress of Franz von Sickingen. In any case Luther did not enter the monastery in the thought that it would offer a moratorium. It may have served that purpose. Indeed, he said afterward that during the first year in the monastery the devil is relatively quiet.[79] But he said the same thing about the first year of his marriage twenty years later.[80] Did he need a second moratorium? In any case Luther testified abundantly that he had no thought of treating the monastery as a device for a moratorium. He gathered a few friends for a farewell party, and because they were disconsolate, played for them the flute. He told them that they would never see his face again. He was dead to the world.[81]

Only after the step had been taken did Luther notify his parents by letter. Erikson thinks he was cowardly not to have faced them in advance. What a scene that would have been! Luther's mind was made up. The father's mind was made up. The mother disapproved. The father was infuriated, dropped the polite form of address, called his son *du* and disowned him outright.[82] But Luther refused to believe that his father meant

77. Ibid., no. 47.
78. Ibid., no. 523.
79. Ibid., no. 50.
80. *WA*, TR 1, no. 141.
81. Scheel, *Dokumente zu Luthers Entwicklung*, no. 423; *WA*, TR 4, no. 4207.
82. Scheel, *Dokumente zu Luthers Entwicklung*, no. 508.

it and sought to win him back. The situation was now reversed. The father had tried to reestablish rapport with the son whom he had alienated by the thrashing. The son now undertook to recover the confidence of the father whom he had hurt by the vow.

One is not to infer that Luther was tormented by guilt over what he had done. Disobedience to parents in order to enter the religious life was the one form of defiance to parental authority countenanced by the society of that age. St. Francis had resisted his father, who for a time locked him up and then dragged him before the court of the bishop. Francis stripped and handed over his clothes, saying that hitherto he had known as his father Pietro Bernadone, now only the Father in heaven. And Francis was canonized.

Luther was not conscience-smitten but he was grieved because he had hurt his father. Certainly he could not have done otherwise without disobedience to God, but to have to choose between the earthly and the heavenly father was of the essence of tragedy. Yet not ineluctible tragedy. The breach could be healed. The father really did not mean what he said.

An opportunity for a gesture of reconciliation came with the saying of Luther's first Mass. During the novitiate he had so far commended himself to the brethren that they had received him into the order and further had ordained him as a priest. His father was invited to attend the first Mass and the date was set to suit his convenience.[83] The father, in the meantime, had grudgingly subdued his indignation. When two other sons were taken by the plague, friends persuaded him that this was a divine visitation punishing him for his unwillingness to give his firstborn to the Lord. He bowed, cowed and still inwardly resentful. But now, receiving the invitation, he resolved to do the handsome thing and came riding with twenty horsemen and brought a present of twenty gulden for the monastery.[84] Luther's mother was not invited, for this was only a man's affair.

83. Ibid., nos. 303, 515, 543.
84. Ibid., nos. 47, 508.

Luther now confronted the stupendous moment when by the consecration of the elements he would bring the presence of God bodily to the altar. He related the occasion many times with variations. Here is the fullest account:

> To talk to God is terrific. His speaking to us is tremendous, but for us to speak to Him is harder. Then our weakness and our unworthiness hold us back and we think, "Who am I that I should dare to lift up mine eyes and raise my hands to the divine majesty?" Angels surround Him. At His nod the earth trembles and shall I, poor little creature, say, "I want this. I want that"? The horde of monks and priests do not know what it is to pray. Those who are genuinely religious may overcome these thoughts, but it is extremely difficult, for I, dust and ashes and full of sin, am talking to the living, eternal and true God. No wonder that he who prays should tremble and flee, as I once did when I was a monk and came to the words in the Canon of the Mass, *Te igitur clementissime Pater* (Thee, O most merciful Father) and again *Offerimus tibi vivo, vero, aeterno* (We offer unto Thee, the living, true, eternal [God]). I was stupefied and horror stricken by these words. I thought, "With what voice shall I address such Majesty, seeing that only with dread should one approach the presence of an earthly prince or king?"[85]

Commentators have pointed out that Luther ought not to have been so terrified by the words "most merciful Father." He explained that he was aghast at approaching even the most merciful save through Christ as mediator.[86]

There are two points in his recital. One is the terror of the creature appalled by the majesty of the Creator. The other is the abject shrinking of the wrongdoer before the face of the All Holy. Utterly limp, Luther came from the ordeal to the banquet for the joyous celebration of the event. He sat next to his father and, having trembled before the Father in heaven, now sought consolation from the father on earth. Deeper than all was the hope that the resentment was now genuinely past and the father at one with the son. "Dear father, why were you

85. Ibid., nos. 450, 420; indexed under *Primitz*.
86. Ibid., no. 343.

so contrary to my becoming a monk? And perhaps you are not quite satisfied even now. The life is so quiet and godly."

This was too much for old Hans, who was magnanimous enough to bring a present of twenty gulden but could not bring himself to endorse his son's step. He flared up before all the doctors, masters, and guests. "You learned scholar, have you never read in the Bible that you should honor your father and your mother? And you have left me and your dear mother to look after ourselves in our old age. We had expected comfort and help from you, because I had spent so much on your education. And you went into the cloister against our will."[87] "But father," answered Luther, "I can do more for you by my prayers in the cloister than if I had stayed in the world. Besides, I was called from heaven in the thunderstorm."[88] "God grant," replied old Hans, "it was not a delusion of the devil."[89] "He told me," said Luther, "that I had disobeyed one of the ten commandments. That word hit me in the bowel as nothing ever did in all my life."[90]

Immediately following his encounter Erikson places a legend that when Luther was seated in the choir and the passage was read from the Gospel about the exorcising of a deaf and dumb demoniac, Luther screamed, *"Non sum, non sum!"* ("I'm not! I'm not!"). That is, "I'm not the demoniac," and fell swooning to the floor.[91] The story is poorly authenticated. It received distribution through Cochlaeus, whose virulent misrepresentations of Luther have poisoned the Catholic attitude toward him until recently refuted by the Catholic scholar Adolf Herte.[92] Cochlaeus wrote later than, and presumably was dependent on, Dungersheim, who took the tale from Nathin, who appears to have derived it from the Bishop of Mansfeld. Thus we get it at fourth hand. But in itself it is not incredible.

87. Ibid., no. 536, p. 204.
88. Ibid., p. 205.
89. Ibid., nos. 46, 508.
90. Ibid, nos. 46, 47, 303.
91. Ibid., no. 533.
92. Adolf Herte, "Die Lutherkommentare des Johannes Cochlaeus," *Reformationgeschichtliche Studien und Texte* 33 (1935).

Luther did believe in demoniacal possession and said that he had once seen a devil expelled.[93] In a fit of depression he might well have wondered whether he might not be himself possessed. This was the common assumption in that period with regard to an opponent. Might it not also be true of oneself?

But if the incident occurred at all, it does not fit here. The problem posed for Luther by his father was not whether the son was possessed of a devil but whether the thunderstorm conveyed a message from God or was a delusion of the devil. This was an old medieval problem. The monks sailing in quest of the earthly paradise saw on the horizon a verdant isle. When with joy they made closer approach the vision of delight evaporated in a gust of smoke. When St. Martin was confronted by Christ resplendent he scrutinized him minutely and asked, "Where are the nail prints?" The apparition vanished. Where are the nail prints? Was it of God? Was it of the devil?

Luther then plunged into extreme mortification of the flesh, discarded clothes till he nearly froze to death,[94] reduced on food till his cheek bones protruded. Erikson calls this overreaction. For one who presumably looks upon any asceticism as pointless, of course it is overreaction. But one must proceed on the basis of Luther's assumptions. How was he going to assure himself that God and not the devil had driven him into the cowl? And if he had been deluded, was he forever damned? Eternity was at stake. "I castigated myself in order to make God friendly to me."[95] Here we have it again. He would not believe that God really meant to reject him. He would elicit God's recognition by doing the uttermost that any man can render. He would wrestle with the angel till the break of day, even though, having received a blessing, he should forever after like Jacob move with a limp.

So, too, was it also with the father. Luther would not give up. But the father could not be brought beyond sullen acquiescence until after the son had broken with monasticism. Let us

93. Otto Scheel, *Martin Luther* (Tübingen, 1917), vol. 1, p. 27, n. 45.
94. Scheel, *Dokumente zu Luthers Entwicklung*, nos. 514, 528.
95. Ibid., nos. 425, 155.

jump ahead to complete the data on the relationship with the father and then come back to the wrestlings with God.

When Luther was placed under the ban of the Church and the empire at the Diet of Worms, he was secreted for a year at the castle of the Wartburg. News then reached him that not only priests but even monks were marrying at Wittenberg. His judgment was asked. He searched the Scriptures and came to the conclusion that monastic vows were not binding. A treatise followed with a dedicatory letter to his father, in which he said in essence:

> God spoke to me through you when you questioned whether God was commanding me in the thunderstorm to disregard my duty to father and mother. We were both ignorant. You would have kept me out of the cowl but God wished me to be a monk that by experience I might know the deficiencies of monasticism. And now God and not you has taken me out of monasticism. You may feel that I should now abandon the cowl and go back to your previous program for me. As far as the cowl is concerned, that means nothing to me, but God's authority is above yours and He has called me to a pastoral ministry.[96]

In other words, the father and the son were now on the same level. Each acted according to his lights. Each was mistaken. Both were led by God to a salutary outcome.

Erikson thinks the son has succumbed to the father's wish and values. But he still was not fulfilling his wish. That came only in part with Luther's marriage. To take care of an escaped nun he took her to wife, but only after going home at the age of forty-two for the consent of his parents. They were enthusiastic. Luther gave as the reasons for the marriage that it "would please his father, rile the pope, make the angels laugh and the devils weep and would seal his testimony."[97] Both parents were present at the wedding banquet.[98] As Luther was to name a daughter after his mother, so also a son

96. *De Votis Monasticis, Luthers Werke,* ed. Clemen (Bonn, 1912), 2:188–92. English in Theodore G. Tappert, "Luther: Letters of Spiritual Counsel," *Library of Christian Classics* 18 (1955):258–63.

97. *WA,* Br 3, nos. 892, 900, 911.

98. *WA,* TR 1, no. 623; 2, no. 2129a.

after his father. The parents made several visits to Wittenberg to visit the growing family.

Erikson sees in all this an adoption by the son of the father's values. Rather the reverse! The father wanted him to marry an opulent wife. He took an indigent nun. The father wanted him to be prosperous. In giving he was as prodigal as St. Francis. The son's last letter to the father indicates that the father had come to agree with the son:

> Dear father, my brother James has written me that you are seriously ill. Since the air is bad and the season perilous I am worried about you. Although God has given you a strong, tough body, still your age gives me concern. Since we cannot be sure of the hour of our lives I would very much like to be with you but my friends have advised against it and I realize that I should not tempt God by rushing into danger, for you know that the nobles and the peasants are hostile toward me. We would have the greatest joy if you and Mother could come to us. My Katie wishes it with tears and so do we all. We do hope you can come. That is why I have sent Cyriacus to see whether you are equal to it. Whether it be God's will that you live or die, I would love to be with you in person and show how grateful I am to you and give you the service of a son according to the fourth commandment.
>
> So I pray with all my heart that the Father who made and gave you to be my father through His boundless goodness, will enlighten your spirit and keep you that you may know with joy and thanksgiving the blessed teaching of His Son, our Lord Jesus Christ, to which through His grace you have been called and have come out from the abominable former darkness and errors and I hope that His grace, who has given you such knowledge, will bring to fruition that which He has commenced in you both in the life here and in the joyous future of our Lord Jesus Christ.
>
> In your sickness, then, lift up your heart and be comforted for we have in that life with God a sure and true helper Jesus Christ, who for us has overcome sin and death and now sits for us in heaven and oversees us with all angels and awaits us that when we set forth we need not worry or fear. . . . He has promised and cannot deceive us. There can be no doubt about that. "Ask," he says, "and it shall be given unto you. Seek and ye shall find. Knock and it shall be opened unto you." . . . I want to say this in writing that I may share your

faith, your struggle and your comfort and thanksgiving to
God for His holy Word which He has so richly, powerfully
and graciously given us at this time.

If it is His will to keep you longer from that blessed life
and cause you, together with us, to suffer, see and hear calamity may He give you grace to bear it willingly and obedi-
ently. This accursed life is nothing other than a real vale of
tears and the longer one is in it the more does one see the
sin, evil, plague and calamity. There is no end to it till this
mortal puts on immortality. Then it will cease and we can
sleep in peace in Christ till he comes to wake us with rejoic-
ing. Amen.

I commend you to Him who loves you more than you love
yourself and has shown His love in that He has taken your
sin upon Himself. . . . Let God worry. He has already done
more than we can comprehend. May the Lord and Savior be
with you and grant that here or there we may see each
other happily again. Our faith is strong and we doubt not
that we shall surely see each other with Christ because for
God the distance from this life is not as great as that between
Mansfeld and Wittenberg. It is only an hour's sleep and then
all will be changed.

I am sure your pastor will instruct you richly and you don't
need my admonitions but I must excuse my physical absence
which distresses me greatly. The family greet you and pray
for you, my Katie, Hänschen, Lenchen and Mumme Lena and
the whole house. Please greet my dear mother and all the
friends. God's grace and power be and abide with you forever. Amen.

Your dear son
Martin Luther[99]

After the father's death Luther wrote to Melanchthon:

Hans Reinecke wrote me that my dearest parent, Hans Luther,
has departed from this life. . . . His death has shaken me as
I recall not only the tie of nature but also the tenderest love,
because my Creator gave me from him whatever I am or have.
And although I am consoled by what you write that he died
quietly, strong in the faith of the Lord Jesus, nevertheless
compassion and the memory of the sweetest converse have so
struck me in the bowels that scarcely ever have I so despised

99. *WA,* Br 5, no. 1529, pp. 238–41. English in Tappert, "Luther: Letters of
Spiritual Counsel," pp. 29–32.

death. . . . I won't write any further of my grief. It is right and godly for me as a son to mourn such a parent through whom the Father of mercy has brought me into being and by his sweat made me whatsoever I am. I rejoice that he lived in these days that he should see the light of truth. Blessed be God in all His deed and counsels forever.[100]

Now we can come back to Luther's development. His struggle in the monastery was religious and theological. Erikson disavows competence in theology but nevertheless essays to review the history of Christian thought from the New Testament to Luther in about three pages. In so doing he contrasts the world views of the Middle Ages, the Renaissance, and the Reformation. In his judgment the religion of the Middle Ages was vertical, directed toward God. That of the Renaissance was horizontal, extending outward to man. In the Renaissance he points to two aspects which he regards as complementary, the one practical, the other theoretical. On the practical side we have the emergence of the Titans, colossal men, endowed with almost superhuman energy, ability, and power; despots, poets, artists, animated in life by a lust for dominance over their kind and an immortality of fame thereafter. They differed from the robber barons of the Middle Ages in their elegance and magnificence. This is the type long ago described by Symonds as the Faustian man.

On the theoretical side we have the revival of Neoplatonism with its doctrine of the dignity of man. Pico in his treatise with that title said that man is the "maker and molder of his destiny." This could be taken to mean that man has the capacity to master all disciplines, acquire all knowledge, discover all lands, and look upon uncharted seas from the heights of Darien. If it were so interpreted, it was misinterpreted. This is not what Pico meant.[101]

He pictured man at the center of the great chain of being, able to descend to the level of the beasts or ascend through the hierarchies of angels until united in ecstasy with the Ineffable.

100. *WA*, Br 5, no. 1584.
101. Charles Trinkaus, *In Our Image and Likeness*, 2 vols. (University of Chicago Press, 1970).

The way of ascent lay in an emancipation from the trammels of the senses. Such a view tended toward the renunciation of the world with its sensual delights. That Pico, before his death, should have wished to enter a monastery is by no means the anomaly that Erikson assumes, but the logical outcome of his philosophical and religious position. The disparagement of the physical, the corporeal, the sensory might lead even to a discarding of all pictorial representation. Hence it was that Michelangelo in the end esteemed his life's work to have been in vain because brush and chisel cannot capture the Ineffable. Pico's religion is the very antithesis of the pattern of the Titan who behaves like Machiavelli's prince.

Now where does Luther fit into this pattern? Erikson must of course regard him as medieval in that his religion was vertical, but at the same time he is described as one of the Titans not only in his amazing genius and astounding energy but also in his lust for dominance, marked by "an almost criminal egotism" and showing the "exhibitionist grandeur" of Renaissance man. On what evidence does this characterization rest? We are told Luther rebelled "first against his father to join the monastery; then against the Church to found his own church."[102] This statement is simply wrong. We have seen that he did not enter the monastery because of rebellion against his father. He did not rebel against the Church. As a loyal son he protested against abuses. Against his will he was cast out of the Church. He did not set out to found a church of his own. For a year after the condemnation at Worms he was hiding at the Wartburg. Then he came back to Wittenberg not in order to found a new church but because summoned by the town council to allay disorders among his followers. Luther knew full well that if he came out of hiding he might be burned. The Elector had told him that in such case he could give him no protection. Luther replied that he was not asking for protection. At vastly greater risk than ever he had ventured at Worms, he now stepped out into the open in order to curb the violence of his disciples, though in all likelihood he would go to the stake—

102. *Young Man Luther*, pp. 74, 77, 157, 194, 232, 262.

and he would have, if the Emperor had not been diverted by wars with the French, the Turks, and the pope.

Is there any other ground for the statement that Luther was consumed by an "almost criminal egotism"? Yes, we are told that he had "a fanatic preoccupation with himself."[103]

"Fanatic" may be taken to mean an undeviating devotion to a position with which the speaker does not agree. But the point is right that Luther was preoccupied with the question of how he stood in relation to God, or, if you like, whether he was in harmony with the cosmos. The answer to this question had to be individual and personal. Luther said that no man can die for another. No man can believe for another. And would not Erikson have to say that no young man can achieve his identity save for himself? Later on, Luther was vastly concerned for others and often quite worried lest an error on his part would imperil their souls. The convulsion which shattered the external framework of Christendom had its inception in the desperate struggle of one individual to get right with God.

Luther was an individual not only over against God but also over against the Church and society. He was himself deeply troubled by the question of singularity. Why was it that he felt so strongly about God's wrath while others were blasé? Why was he in anguish over what appeared to be God's injustice when others blithely accepted the promises of his mercy? Why was he not satisfied with macerations of the flesh and the consolation of the confessional? Could it be that he alone was so plagued? He explained his difficulties to his confessor, Staupitz, who commented, *Ich verstehe es nicht,* "I don't understand it." If, then, an experienced confessor did not understand him, was he different from all others? Delivery from this desperation came through reflection on the words of Christ, "My God, hast thou forsaken me?" Christ forsaken! He, too, then felt alienation from God, and Luther was not the only one in all history, for Christ was tempted in all things even as we are.[104]

103. Ibid., p. 148.
104. Bainton, *Here I Stand; WA,* TR 2, no. 1347.

But then singularity took on another form. How could it be
that Luther was right in what he was saying when so many in
the Church disagreed with him? To him alone had insight been
given as to the meaning of Scripture? Were not only popes but
also councils wrong? And after Luther had been pronounced a
heretic by both the Church and the empire, could it be that he
alone was right? *Bist Du allein klug? Tu solus sapis?* "Are you
alone wise? Do you alone know?"[105]

This was the problem of knowledge, and here two traditions
lay side by side in Christian history. The one stemmed from
the Greeks, who assumed that truth must be hammered out by
the matching of minds in dialogue. Witness the dialogues of
Plato. An emergent consensus has a claim to be regarded as
true. So Aristotle. This is the basis of the doctrine of natural
law, that law which is recognized by all peoples as valid, and
of the doctrine of natural theology, for that which is univer-
sally believed, such as the existence of God (it was then) may
be assumed to be true. But truth in the Hebrew tradition is
given by revelation and the revelation may be granted to only
a single individual, a Moses who received the tables of the law
on the mount, or a prophet who stood alone in his generation.
In the New Testament, Jesus said, "I thank thee, Father, Lord
of heaven and earth, that thou hast hid these things from the
wise and prudent and revealed them unto babes."[106] And the
babes were not numerous.

But in time the traditions fused. The Church grew. The
babes became the bishops, and then the consensus of the bishops and, by and by, of the councils was regarded as having
the supreme claim to the truth. But Luther had come to regard
the bishops, the councils, and the popes as the "wise and prudent" to whom the revelation had not been given. He was one
of the babes. This conclusion drove him to the deduction that
the minority is always right.[107]

105. *WA*, TR 1, no. 300; 3, no. 3593; *WA* 8, p. 412 (Scheel, *Dokumente*, no.
51).
106. Matt. 11:25.
107. *WA* 7, p. 317.

But if the minority is right, does it not have an obligation to proclaim the truth to the majority as once did the prophets? Here Luther increasingly passed from preoccupation with himself to responsibility for the salvation of others. A new form of anxiety then assailed him. Was he perhaps leading others astray? And then a new temptation. If he alone were really right, might he exalt himself and fall into the chiefest of all sins, pride? If he assumed that God had made him a vehicle of truth and salvation, was he not guilty indeed of "almost criminal egotism"? Luther fought the implication. He was embarrassed by glory and disclaimed hotly the assumption that he was an authority. He did not care about a reputation and would be glad to see all of his books perish to be replaced by better works.[108] He had no itch for the footlights and rejoiced in the contributions of others. He was often not in a state of elation but of despondency because of his shortcomings.

But was Luther's disclaimer of pride genuine? If he referred to himself as the German prophet, did he not have a very high evaluation of himself? Was he not after all an exhibitionist after the manner of some in the Renaissance? Luther himself had an answer to that question. He quoted the words of the Virgin Mary, "Behold from henceforth all generations shall call me blessed." "Was that humble? Certainly it was. It was the truth. Humility does not consist in denying the truth. If any one says to me, 'You have beautiful hands,' in order to be humble have I got to say, 'I beg your pardon, sir, they are hoofs'? There is no humility in denying one's gifts. But remember they are gifts. Praise God for whatever He has given you and use it in His service."[109]

Therefore one will find in Luther no affected self-depreciation but a frank recognition that God was using him and a deep awareness that only God could do anything with so weak an instrument. There is a remarkable essay by Karl Holl on Luther's image of himself. And Karl Holl was the greatest Luther scholar of our century. His conclusion was that Luther

108. Scheel, *Dokumente zu Luthers Entwicklung*, no. 571.
109. See my *Luther's Meditations on the Gospels*, p. 29.

"wished to conceal his person completely behind his work. He was so completely different from the men of the Renaissance that he fought fame as something from which Christians should only recoil with horror."[110]

We have observed that the picture of the Renaissance extrovert was not supported by the theology of Pico. This view of religion also was not congenial to Luther. It assumed that man can ascend to God. Luther held that God must descend to man. There is no self-help when it comes to salvation.

Let us now return to the course of Luther's inner struggle. First he tried macerations of the flesh, as already observed, but from these he could never derive satisfaction. The question was always, had he done enough? Then he turned to the sacramental system of the Church devised not for saints but for sinners. The supreme sacrament in this respect was penance divided into three parts. The first was contrition, but who could be sure that he was genuinely contrite and not merely fearful of punishment? The third was satisfaction, but no one could make adequate satisfaction. The second was confession, and this was possible, or so it seemed at first. But Luther discovered that many sins elude memory. After confessing for six hours he would go out and then recall something overlooked. He would then return until the confessor snapped, "Look here. If you expect Christ to forgive you come in with something to forgive—parricide, blasphemy, adultery—instead of trotting in with these dolly's sins." But Luther's question was not whether his sins were big or little but whether each and every one had been enumerated and absolved.

Then came a still more disconcerting discovery. There are sins which man does not even recognize. Here Erikson introduces again his projection thesis.[111]

Luther was applying to the confessional the residue of his experience in school when he had been whipped in one day fifteen times for talking German on the playing field. He

110. Karl Holl, "Martin Luther on Luther," *Interpreters of Luther: Essays in Honor of Wilhelm Pauck* (Philadelphia: Fortress, 1968), an English translation of an essay published in German in 1921.
111. *Young Man Luther*, p. 79.

would not even remember that he had done it. There is here, indeed, an interesting parallel, but there is absolutely no need to assume any causal connection. Luther found the point where he found everything else, in the Bible. Adam and Eve, after tasting the fruit of the forbidden tree, went blithely for a walk in the cool of the day. Jonah fleeing from the Lord's command to preach repentance to the people of Nineveh was soundly asleep in the hold of the ship and would never have been troubled in conscience had he not been wakened and disclosed as the cause of the storm by the casting of lots.[112] One may say, of course, that a childhood experience opened Luther's eyes to the significance of these passages. True, but there is no need for this assumption. Who is there, who when some remark of twenty years past has been brought to mind, has not winced and said, "How could I ever have said something so unkind?"

After despairing of himself Luther began to despair also of God. Erikson says that Luther projected onto God the image of his arbitrary, tyrannical father and therefore hated God.[113] We have already seen that this picture of the father is the figment of a fertile imagination. But granted that it be true, still there is no need for such a projection. Luther need only have accepted his father's picture of God. For did not the father believe that to punish his unwillingness to have Martin take the cowl, God had caused the deaths of two other sons? Who wouldn't hate such a nasty God?

But Luther never mentions this as a problem. The psychiatrist will probably say, "Of course not. He wouldn't even be conscious of what he was doing." Luther does tell us, however, what he believed to have been the problem. It was the doctrine of predestination, that God chose some for bliss and some for eternal damnation before ever they were born. Was not this manifestly unjust? "More than once," said Luther, "have I by this doctrine been cast into the very abyss of desperation."[114] Why not take Luther at his word? The doctrine

112. Bainton, *Here I Stand*, p. 55.
113. *Young Man Luther*, p. 58.
114. *WA* 18, p. 719.

of predestination was in the works he was studying. It was in
the Bible. It was in Paul. It was in Augustine, the saint for
whom his own order was named. "If God does this," thought
Luther, "he is grossly unjust. I hate him."

Luther eventually found his way out by positing two aspects
of God, almost two gods. Perhaps the psychiatrist might throw
some light on this. There is the hidden God responsible for
disaster in this life and predestination as to the next. His ways
are past finding out. We are not to measure him by our standards. We will not say that he is unjust, but we shall not see
how he is just until beyond the grave. The other God is the
revealed God, revealed in Christ and especially in the cross of
Christ. The behavior of God which transcends all the compre-
hension of the natural man is his amazing mercy in that he did
not wipe out the rebellious race of men, but instead sent his
Son to die upon the cross for their redemption. Christ's merit
makes up for all of their demerits. And they have only to
accept that which has been done for them. Let them cease their
striving to get right with God by fulfilling all his demands.
They can never do it. Let them in humility accept his gift in
faith and thanksgiving. Erikson rightly sees that this reliance
solely on God's mercy is like the receptiveness of a child at
the breast. Nevertheless he suggests that Luther's deliverance
lay in the identification of himself, once estranged from his
father, with Christ forsaken by God. In order to enter into the
suffering of Christ, Luther had an itch for martyrdom. That
he did not. The cross, said Luther, is neither to be evaded nor
sought. He was emancipated from the asceticism of monks and
mystics. The point for him was that the suffering of the Son
emanated from the love of the Father.[115]

And now a word about a theme of which Erikson makes
much, anality and scatology in Luther. There is no doubt that
he used language which today gives offense to those over
thirty. But several points should be borne in mind. Luther was
not peculiar in his generation in this regard. Witness a scato-

115. *Young Man Luther*, p. 198.

logical passage in More's reply to Luther.[116] Even more to the point is Luther's indebtedness to the medieval tradition. Biblical texts brought scatology into the exegesis of the scholastics. One such text was the word of Paul (Phil. 3:8), "I have suffered the loss of all things and count them but dung that I may win Christ." The other was Psalm 113:7, "He lifteth me out of the dunghill." One must also bear in mind the many passages about the bowels of Christ, the bowels of mercy, the bowels of compassion. The modern vernacular translation would be "guts." A recent historian of the late Middle Ages has pointed out that while such expressions were commonly allegorized, still the actual latrine was regarded as the devil's peculiar seat of operation.[117]

Luther interpreted sin as sinfulness. Consequently man has within himself a dunghill. But this also becomes the seat of Christ's operation, for when man recognizes what he is and becomes utterly humble, renouncing all self-justification, then Christ begins to operate and lift him out of his dunghill.

One other point is that Luther was in no wise tinged with Neoplatonic dualism with regard to the body as an impediment to the spirit. For him the person was a whole man, *totus homo,* and every physical function presented an analogy to the counterpart in religion. When once he was befouled by a babe on his lap he remarked, "O how much does our Lord God have to put up with in us, much more than a mother with a child."[118]

The historian of the late Middle Ages, to whom reference was made above, remarks that if a psychiatrist essays to apply his discipline to history, he should work in collaboration with a historian. But even if he did, could he still apply his discipline to the past? Only with difficulty, as was observed at the outset. But I have already suggested a number of points at

116. Thomas More, *Responsio ad Lutherum,* ed. John Headley (New Haven: Yale University Press, 1969), vol. 5¹, p. 311.
117. Heiko Obermann, "Wir sein Pettler. Hoc est verum," *Zeitschrift fur Kirchengeschichte* 78 (1967):232–52.
118. *WA,* TR 3, no. 3203b.

which a psychiatrist could at least tell us whether the inner torments of a man of the sixteenth century belong only to him and his period or to all mankind. I have indicated three aspects of the problem of singularity which might be illumined. Luther at first feared that he was singular, in fact unique, and that no one in all history had experienced such a sense of alienation from God. The observation that Christ himself exclaimed, "My God! my God! why hast thou forsaken me?" dispelled this torment. Another form of singularity arose from the conviction that he was right when so many said he was wrong. This doubt has plagued many in modern times who have opposed popular wars. Luther reassured himself by referring to the authority of Scripture, but then he was asked how he could be sure his interpretation was right. This is the philosophical problem of knowledge, but it becomes psychological when a man is led to doubt his own capacity for knowing. A third form arises from actual singularity in the case of a genius. How does he adjust to living with people less gifted? This is partly an ethical question. How shall he avoid arrogance and pride? But it is partly psychological. How will he make a social accommodation?

These are areas for exploration. The first step is to make the utmost effort to get the facts straight.

3. Psychohistory and History:
The Case of *Young Man Luther*

Lewis W. Spitz

Among early twentieth-century intellectuals who made a major impact upon the modern mind, Sigmund Freud was the "towering figure of the era."[1] He might well have taken his inspiration from Shakespeare's line in *Measure for Measure*, "Let your reason serve to make the truth appear where it seems hid." For the great achievement of psychoanalysis was a fuller and more systematic examination of the unconscious in mental life. His theories of hysteria and madness, the interpretation of dreams, and the psychopathology of everyday life have trickled down into the thought patterns and vocabulary of common men all through Western society. Now that leading psychology departments are disdainful of Freudianism and medical doctors incline more to chemical cures and psychosurgery, historians have discovered the affinity of psychoanalysis to their own discipline in theory and practice, and are making fascinating applications to great men and the masses of time past. The most eminent proponent and practitioner of psychohistory, that paradigm or even discipline emerging in the area of overlay between history and psychoanalysis, is Erik Erikson, whose career has spanned the Atlantic and whose exceptional mind has bridged a seemingly even greater intellectual chasm.

PSYCHOHISTORY AND HISTORY

Two centuries ago the historian Wegelin (1721–91) asserted the necessity of understanding the psychology of rulers

1. H. Stuart Hughes, *Consciousness and Society* (New York, 1958), p. 19. I wish to thank my colleagues Dr. Paul Robinson and Dr. Margot Drekmeier for their critical reading of this paper and many helpful suggestions.

and the psychological bond with their people, the need to get at their obscure wishes and passions.[2] Historians from Herodotus to the present, in fact, have operated with certain intuited psychological presuppositions about their subjects. Psychoanalysis promises a more coherent pattern of explanations than the casual and amateurish psychological observations often ventured by historians. Both in history and in the theory and practice of psychoanalysis the "how" and the "why" are inseparable questions. In the search to understand individuals and groups the deepest inquiry is concerned with motives.[3] Both probe the past, for, as Freud stated in his paper "On the History of the Psychoanalytic Movement," "It appeared that psychoanalysis could explain nothing current without referring back to something past."[4] In both, facts are significant only in a context of interpretation.[5]

Distrusting surface explanations, both probe the past, and individual or collective memory, and reconstruct in detail the circumstances surrounding an event. Both require sensitivity, imagination, and a feel for the significance of seemingly insignificant detail. They probe the consciousness of the individual person, the springboard for human action in a single life and in history on the collective plane. Case histories are used to arrive at understanding. The aim of both is human self-knowledge, to understand the past in order to liberate man from the burden of the past and enable him to gain strength from the experience and understanding of the past with which to shape the future.

Psychohistory appears in two varying modalities. Historical

2. Hans W. Gruhle, *Geschichtsschreibung und Psychologie* (Bonn, 1953), pp. 23, 46, 134, 139, 168.
3. H. Stuart Hughes, "History and Psychoanalysis: The Explanation of Motive," *History as Art and as Science* (New York: Harper, 1964), p. 42, an excellent statement of the parallels between psychoanalysis and history in aim and method.
4. Sigmund Freud, "On the History of the Psychoanalytic Movement" (1914), *Collected Papers*, vol. 1, cited in Fritz Schmidl, "Psychoanalysis and History," *Psychoanalytic Quarterly* 31 (1962):532.
5. Hans Meyerhoff, "On Psychoanalysis as History," *Psychoanalysis and the Psychoanalytic Review* 49, no. 2 (1962):8.

psychology involves a study of the psychology of people who are not great men, the psychology of groups. From the school of Lucien Febvre has emerged one of the finest examples of this approach, Robert Mandrou's *Introduction à la France moderne (1500–1640): Essai de psychologie historique.*[6] Psychological history studies the psychology of great men, the event-makers, the experiences of unique individuals without whom history might have been markedly different.

In literary, artistic, political, and religious biography and criticism, the value of psychoanalytical insights has been recognized for some time. In *Richard II*, after all, Shakespeare had probed beneath the surface of the mind:

> My brain I'll prove the female to my soul;
> My soul the father; and these two beget
> A generation of still-breeding thoughts,
> And these same thoughts people this little world.

Psychoanalysis has proved of value in exploring the modes of subjectivity and stream-of-consciousness in the modern novel.[7] Freud with his peculiar Leonardo and pathetic Woodrow Wilson had set a precedent in the artistic and political realms.[8]

6. Robert Mandrou, *Introduction à la France moderne (1500–1640): Essai de psychologie historique* (Paris, 1961), especially chapter 3, "L'Homme psychique: Sens, sensations, émotions, passions." Alain Dufour, "Quelques Réflexions sur l'historiographie du VXIe siècle," *Histoire politique et psychologie historique* (Geneva, 1966), pp. 9–35, advocates "historical psychology."

7. See Leon Edel, *The Modern Psychological Novel* (New York: Grosset & Dunlap, 1964); *Literary Biography* (New York, 1959), pp. 91–122; and *Henry James* (New York, 1953), a case study.

8. Lewis J. Edinger, "Political Science and Political Biography: Reflections on the Study of Leadership (1)," *The Journal of Politics* 26 (May, 1964):423–39, recognizes the need to understand the event-makers in political history. A disciple of Wilhelm Dilthey (the founder of the modern *Geisteswissenschaften*), Georg Misch, professor of philosophy at Göttingen University, in his epochal *Geschichte der Autobiographie* (Leipzig and Berlin, 1907) explored the psychological differences of Greeks, Romans, and patristic authors as reflected in their autobiographies. One of the most fascinating psychoanalytic studies, of tremendous political relevance, is that of Arnold Künzli, *Karl Marx: Eine Psychographie* (Vienna, 1966), opening with the telling lines from *Die deutsche Ideologie:* "Es zeigt sich, dasz . . . die Geschichte eines einzelnen Individuums keineswegs von der Geschichte der vorhergegangenen und gleichzeitigen Individuen loszureiszen ist, sondern von ihnen bestimmt wird."

Freud's *Totem and Taboo* (1913) and *Moses and Monotheism* (1939) were hardly his most substantial pieces, but in daringly arguing that religious phenomena are to be understood on the model of the neurotic symptoms of the individual he provided a text for a materialistic psychology of religion. Historians struggled long and hard to transcend the confines of traditional political and military history to a new history which would include economic, social, and intellectual subjects. But they were slow in coming to the analysis of the psychological dimension either of individuals or of groups, except for the attention paid to the pathological behavior of mobs or the hysterical behavior of sects. The call to the "newest history" was issued by William L. Langer in his 1957 presidential address to the American Historical Association in which he referred to "the urgently needed deepening of our historical understanding through exploitation of the concepts and findings of modern psychology." He was speaking not of classical or academic psychology but of psychoanalysis and its later developments and variations, all included in the terms "dynamic" or "depth psychology."[9]

Charles Poore, in a review of a Civil War book in the *New York Times* the week after Langer's address, reconstructed a conversation which might well become commonplace among historians and biographers:

> "Have you read the new Freudian biography of Sitting Bull by Pottawatomie Jones of Lewis Nichols University?"
> "No. But I've been helping to read proofs on the Adlerian version by Socrates Robinson, who holds the Kenneth Campbell chair of history at Princeton."
> "That should be interesting."
> "It is, in a measure."
> "Why the reservation?"
> "Because it's taking an awful lot of time from my own

9. William L. Langer, "The Next Assignment," *The American Historical Review* 63, no. 2 (January 1958):283–304. Langer's address is republished in Bruce Mazlish, ed., *Psychoanalysis and History* (Englewood Cliffs, N.J.: Prentice-Hall, 1963). Cf. also Langer's foreword to *The Psychoanalytic Interpretation of History*, ed. Benjamin B. Wolman (New York: Harper, 1971).

three-volume history of the Black Hawk War, you know. Particularly since I'm following Jung throughout."

He suggested Lytton Strachey's *Queen Victoria* as an appropriate annual prize in the field.[10]

PSYCHOLOGICAL ASSESSMENTS OF LUTHER

In his address Langer spoke of the case of the greatest of the reformers, Martin Luther, who reflected clearly the reaction of the individual to the somber situation of late medieval culture. He spoke of his abnormally strong sense of sin and of the immediacy of death and damnation. He suggested that Luther's trials were typical of his time and argued that it was inconceivable that Luther should have evoked so great a popular response unless he had succeeded in expressing the underlying, unconscious sentiments of large numbers of people and in providing them with an acceptable solution to their religious problem. Luther wore his heart on his sleeve and his volubility has made him a ready object for psychological analysis. The historiography of the problem has already reached formidable dimensions.

As early as 1837 Joseph Spriszler, a Roman Catholic priest, applied to Luther Aristotle's saying on genius in the words on Seneca: *"Nullum umquam magnum ingenium sine admixtione furiae fuit."* No doubt Luther was a man of outsized intellect verging on genius in creativity, brilliance, and versatility. He was a heroic type, but notable more for constancy and faith than for the bravado of a Renaissance man. "We know that genius is incomprehensible and unaccountable and it should therefore not be called upon as an explanation until every other solution has failed," wrote Freud. "Everything new must have its roots in what was before. Few tasks are as appealing as inquiry into the laws that govern the psyche of exceptionally endowed individuals."[11] But attempts to understand

10. Charles Poore, "Books of the Times," *The New York Times*, Thursday, January 2, 1958.
11. David Bakan, *Sigmund Freud and the Jewish Mystical Tradition* (Princeton: Van Nostrand, 1958), p. vi. On Spriszler see Heinrich Bornkamm, *Luther im Spiegel der deutschen Geistesgeschichte* (Heidelberg, 1955), pp. 258–61.

Luther in terms of genius have indeed added little by way of explanation, inclining either toward extremes of adulation or denigration.[12]

Early in our century polemical Roman Catholic historians, following the lead of Cochlaeus, Luther's dedicated defamer, portrayed Luther in unflattering terms. A Dominican, Heinrich Denifle, working in the Vatican archives, proposed what the ecumenical Father Sartory has labelled the pansexual interpretation of the Reformation.[13] Denifle defamed Luther as a lust-ridden monk, given to secret vices, driven by overpowering sexual urges to oppose celibacy and to break with the Church. Denifle's associate, Albert Maria Weiss, O.P., in a supplementary volume on Luther's psychology, revised Denifle's judgments and clarified his argument with less acerbity, and Catholic historians subsequently abandoned the thesis of Luther's moral corruption.[14] But Denifle's text provided many an uncritical Freudian with material for a libidinous interpretation of Luther. If Denifle was overheated, the Jesuit Hartmann Grisar accorded Luther a cold trial, relating his dogmatic deviation to a pathological manic-depressive psychology.[15]

12. Hagiographic in nature is Bruno Markgraf, *Der junge Luther als Genie. Beitrag zur Luther Psychologie* (Leipzig, 1929). Demeaning in nature is Wilhelm Lange-Eichbaum, *The Problem of Genius* (London, 1931). Of interest in connection with this general problem is Edward Hitschmann, *Great Men: Psychoanalytic Studies* (New York: International Universities Press, 1956).

13. Heinrich Denifle, *Luther und Luthertum in der ersten Entwicklung, quellenmässig dargestellt*, I, 1 and 2 (Mainz, 1904). Adolf Herte, *Das katholische Lutherbild im Bann der Lutherkommentare des Cochläus*, 3 vols. (Münster in Westfalen, 1943) shows how Cochlaeus's vitriolic fabrications have poisoned the whole stream of Catholic, and some other, historiography down to the time of the new ecumenical era in church history.

14. Albert Maria Weiss, O.P., *Lutherpsychologie als Schlüssel zur Lutherlegende* (Mainz, 1906), *Ergänzungen zu Denifles Luther und Lutherthum:* "Denifle was a historical researcher of the first rank, but as a historical writer Denifle was not the equal of the researcher" (p. 42). J. Paquier, who translated Denifle into French (*Luther et le Lutheranisme*, 4 vols. [Paris, 1910–1916]), in an article in the *Dictionnaire de Théologie Catholique* (15 vols. [Paris, 1899–1950], vol. 9, 1, col. 1168), described Luther as a "very complex pathological case."

15. Hartmann Grisar, *Luthers Werden*, 3 vols. (1911–12) (English translation *Luther* [London, 1913–1917]), and *Martin Luthers Leben und sein Werk*, 2d ed. (Freiburg i. Br., 1927). The pioneer ecumenical Catholic history of the Reformation rehabilitating Luther as a person and as a sincere religious charac-

The medical doctors, too, were intrigued by Luther, of whom Søren Kierkegaard had spoken in his diary as "a patient of exceeding import for Christendom." In an undistinguished biography of Erasmus, John Joseph Mangan, M.D., introduced a chapter in consideration of Martin Luther in which he assembled evidences of Luther's murderous father, his demonology, sexual drives, physical ills, and disturbed psychology.[16] He was sharply refuted by John Alfred Faulkner, M.D., in an article entitled "An American Doctor Looks at Luther."[17] The most exhaustive examination of Luther's physical ailments, however, was that of Wilhelm Ebstein, who noted that Luther was an accurate observer and acute diagnostician of his own ills. Although Luther observed how in his own case worries caused bodily sickness, Ebstein found that in each instance a physical illness precipitated a period of psychological depression, including that of 1527.[18] His depressions lasted two or three days at the most and did not impair his writing or academic work.

The psychologists and psychoanalysts, too, have been drawn to this unusual man who incorporated a delicate spiritual constitution in a robust physique. Ernst Kretschmer of Marburg and Hubert Rohracher of Vienna, with their peculiar theories correlating personality and body types, have identified Luther

ter was Joseph Lortz, *Die Reformation in Deutschland*, 2 vols. (Freiburg i. Br., 1939–40; 4th ed. 1962). Lortz had predecessors in this rehabilitation, less influential than he, such as F. X. Kiefel, "Martin Luthers religiöse Psyche, Zum 400-jährigen Reformationsjubiläum," *Hochland* 15, no. 1 (1917–18): 7–28; and S. Merkle, "Gutes an Luther und Übles an seinen Tadlern," *Luther in ökumenischer Sicht*, ed. Alfred von Martin (Stuttgart, 1929), pp. 9–19.

16. John Joseph Mangan, *Life, Character, and Influence of Desiderius Erasmus of Rotterdam*, 2 vols. (New York, 1927).

17. John Alfred Faulkner, "An American Doctor Looks at Luther," *Princeton Theological Review* 26 (1928):248–64.

18. Wilhelm Ebstein, *Dr. Martin Luthers Krankheiten und deren Einflusz auf seinen körperlichen und geistigen Zustand* (Stuttgart, 1908). Ebstein's analysis is confirmed by a recent retrospective diagnosis, Annemarie Halder's *Das Harnsteinleiden Martin Luthers* (Trier, 1969), on his stones in the bladder and urinary tract between 1537 and 1546. Luther's observation on psychosomatic illness is in *Tischreden*, vol. 5, no. 6024, p. 445 (hereafter cited as TR), in the Weimar edition of Luther's works, *D. Martin Luthers Werke. Kritische Gesamtausgabe* (Weimar: Hermann Böhlaus Nachfolger, 1883–) (hereafter cited as *WA*): *"Ubi animus est aeger, ibi sequitur corpus languidum."*

with the cyclothemic temperament and a typical pyknic
physique, qualified by melancholic and schizothymic characteristics.[19] The heretical Freudian C. G. Jung contrasted
Luther's extroverted type with Zwingli's introverted spiritual
type and related the difference to their position on the sacrament.[20] A great professional historian but very amateurish
analyst, Preserved Smith, in 1913 published an article on
"Luther's Early Development in the Light of Psychoanalysis."[21]
Smith delivered a primer of "Freudian" observations complete
with an alcoholic father, oedipal rage, obsession with the
demonic, repressed elementary sexual life, harsh home discipline, preoccupation with concupiscence, and depressions. He
argued that the dogmas of the bondage of the will and justification by faith were not attained by logical deduction from
biblical or any other premises but were merely interpretations
of his own subjective life, though the horizon began to clear
with his first call to Wittenberg in 1508, due in a measure to
the affection and help given by the Vicar General, Johannes von
Staupitz, and he began to sublimate his sexual impulses to professional and intellectual interests. Combining the Catholic
jaundice of Spriszler and the Danish dourness of Kierkegaard,
the psychoanalyst Paul J. Reiter wrote two massive volumes
on the world about Luther and his character and psychology.[22]
In his analysis of Luther's personality, spiritual life, and sick-
nesses, Reiter was guided by Alfred Otto, S.J., followed
Denifle uncritically in declaring Luther to have been a bad

19. Ernst Kretschmer, *Physique and Character: An Investigation of the Nature of Constitution and of the Theory of Temperament* (New York, 1936),
pp. 225, 227, 239, 250, 256, and *The Psychology of Men of Genius* (London,
1931), pp. 155–56, "attacking the father image in the form of the Pope."
Rohracher lectures on *Charakterkunde* at Vienna in basic agreement with
Kretschmer. See also Jean Delumeau, *Naissance et affirmation de la Réforme*
(Paris, 1968), pp. 289–95: "La these psychoanalyste à propos de Luther."

20. C. G. Jung, "Der Abendmahlstreit zwischen Luther und Zwingli. Das
Typenproblem in der Geistesgeschichte," *Gesammelte Werke* (Zurich and
Stuttgart, 1960), vol. 6, pp. 67–69.

21. Preserved Smith, "Luther's Early Development in the Light of Psychoanalysis," *American Journal of Psychology* 24 (1913):360–77.

22. Paul J. Reiter, *Martin Luthers Umwelt, Charakter und Psychose*, 2 vols.
(Copenhagen, 1937–41).

monk, and accepted the worst construction that Grisar had managed to put on things. When Grisar says that Luther was an epileptic, Reiter concedes that that is *gar nicht ausgeschlossen*. Oscar Pfister of Zurich, in contrast, turned attention away from Luther's physical or personal problems to the dimension of deep religious fear and his resolution and the persistence of fear in his theology.[23] And so the literature grows about the man on whom more has been written than about anyone else in the history of the world with the exception of Christ.

ERIKSON'S LUTHER

Far superior to all previous attempts at a posthumous psychoanalysis of Luther is Erik H. Erikson's *Young Man Luther: A Study in Psychoanalysis and History.* "Erikson presides together with the Princess Royal, Anna Freud, and René Spitz over the exclusive but still highly creative world of classic psychoanalysis."[24] Erikson has not simply repristinated Freud but has creatively gone beyond the master to develop on a clinical basis the idea of the life cycle, giving an epigenetic schema which is an elaboration of Freud's theory of psychosexual stages and an extension of it beyond adolescence over the whole span of an individual's life, into old age. He relates the psy-

23. Oscar Pfister, *Christianity and Fear: A Study in History and in the Psychology and Hygiene of Religion* (London: Allen & Unwin, 1948). Pfister much earlier published *The Psychoanalytic Method* (New York: Dodd, Mead & Co., 1917), with an introduction by Sigmund Freud. Pfister was a correspondent of Freud's and the only religionist for whom he had much use. Pfister was also the first clergyman to use psychoanalytic ideas and methods in his pastoral work. To be taken considerably less seriously is Norman O. Brown, *Life Against Death: The Psychoanalytic Meaning of History* (Middletown, Conn.: Wesleyan University Press, 1959), whose fourteenth chapter, "The Protestant Era," is a fabric of questionable value based on a distressing amount of historical misinformation. For an intelligent critique of Brown in comparison with Marcuse see Paul A. Robinson, *The Freudian Left* (New York: Harper, 1969), pp. 223–33.

24. Donald M. Kaplan, "Since Freud," *Harper's Magazine* 237, no. 1419 (August 1968):55–60. The very moving biography by Robert Coles, *Erik H. Erikson: The Growth of His Work* (Boston: Little, Brown & Co., 1970), is a great human document. Chapter 7, pp. 202–54, gives the *Entstehungsgeschichte* and a running resumé of *Young Man Luther.* See also Henry W. Maier, *Three Theories of Child Development: The Contributions of Erik H. Erikson, Jean Piaget, and Robert R. Sears, and Their Applications* (New York: Harper, 1965), pp. 12–74.

chological and biological stages of development, each stage of development having crucial tasks to be done. These stages are normative for every individual, having roots in infancy and childhood, and have a strategic priority at special points in the developmental process. The degree of health of the individual depends upon the degree to which these focal tasks or the crises at each stage have been successfully met. The constructive realization of human potential takes place through and by means of the cumulative achievement of a balance of trust over mistrust, autonomy over shame and doubt, initiative over guilt, industry versus inferiority, and so forth.[25] He thus correlates the strengths and weaknesses that can arise at each stage or phase of life. In Luther's case, Erikson explains,

> The characteristics of Luther's theological advance can be compared to certain steps in psychological maturation which every man must take: the internalization of the father-son relationship; the concomitant crystallization of conscience; the safe establishment of an identity as a worker and a man; and the concomitant reaffirmation of basic trust.[26]

Erikson is surely best known popularly as well as in scientific circles for the concepts of identity and identity crisis— there has indeed been a world-wide identity explosion! As Erikson explains it, "identity formation employs a process of simultaneous reflection and observation, a process taking place on all levels of mental functioning, by which the individual judges himself in the light of what he perceives to be the way in which others judge him in comparison to them and to types that have become relevant to him."[27] This is an unconscious

25. Perry Lefevre, "Erikson's *Young Man Luther*: A Contribution to the Scientific Study of Religion," *Journal for the Scientific Study of Religion* 2, no. 2 (April 1963):248–52, p. 250; the other two statements in this "bibliographical focus" are also worth consulting: Paul W. Pruyser, "Erikson's *Young Man Luther*: A New Chapter in the Psychology of Religion," pp. 238–42, and Philip Woollcott, "Erikson's Luther: A Psychiatrist's View," pp. 243–48. The *textus receptus* is, of course, Erikson's *Childhood and Society* (New York: Norton, 1950), especially chapter 7, "Eight Ages of Man."
26. *Young Man Luther*, p. 213.
27. Erik H. Erikson, *Identity, Youth and Crisis* (New York: Norton, 1968), p. 22. Cf. Richard I. Evans, *Dialogue with Erik Erikson* (New York: Harper, 1967), pp. 35–36: Identity means an integration of all previous identifications and self-images, including the negative ones.

process for the most part, except in cases in which inner conditions and outer circumstances combine to aggravate a painful, or elated, "identity consciousness." In Luther's case Erikson finds a prolonged identity crisis, and because of its prolongation, as well as delayed sexual intimacy, intimacy and generativity were fused in his life. Moreover, the integrity crisis

> which comes last in the lives of ordinary men is a lifelong and chronic crisis in a *homo religiosus.* He is always older, or in early years suddenly becomes older, than his playmates or even his parents and teachers, and focuses in a precocious way on what it takes others a lifetime to gain a mere inkling of: the question of how to escape corruption in living and how in death to give meaning to life. . . . This short cut between the youthful crisis of identity and the mature one of integrity makes the religionist's problem of individual identity the same as the problem of existential identity.[28]

Moreover, Erikson, unlike many psychoanalysts who insist upon keeping their discipline "intrapsychic," is concerned with society, social process, culture, and the interpersonal, matters of great interest to historians. Erikson attempts to deal with a process "located" in the core of the individual yet also in the core of his communal culture. In the case of Luther this means that one cannot separate personal growth from communal change, or the identity crisis in Luther's life from contemporary crises in historical development, because the two help to define each other and are truly relative to each other. In fact, Erikson explains, the "whole interplay between the psychological and the social, the developmental and the historical, for which identity formation is of prototypal signifi-

---

28. *Young Man Luther*, pp. 260–61. The problem of delay in the achieving of identity is related to the need for achieving a moratorium in the monastery. But this delay is especially problematical in view of the possibility that the epigenetic cycle may not have been so constant in times past as it is presently observed to be in the clinical situation. The Dutch psychologist Jan Hendrik van den Berg, *Metabletica über die Wandlung des Menschen. Grundlinien einer historischen Psychologie* (Göttingen, 1960), has a lengthy discussion in chapter 2 showing that during the sixteenth and seventeenth centuries children were assimilated rapidly and prematurely into adulthood. The "cases of stupefying precocity are legion."

cance, could be conceptualized only as a kind of psychosocial relativity."[29]

Finally, Erikson sees development and change in both the subject and the observer. The clinical situation, the therapeutic encounter, is itself a historical situation. By analogy, this historical study of Luther initially involves the sympathy of the observer and serves as a vehicle for testing and clarifying his statement about identity and related psychological phenomena. "In *Young Man Luther*," he tells us, "I attempted to put the suffering of a great young man into the context of his greatness and his historic position. . . . There is often an intrinsic relation between the originality of an individual's gifts and the depth of his personal conflict."[30]

The observer is involved in the process and brings to his observations insight and wisdom gleaned from his clinical experience. Erikson's *Luther* is not the usual applied psychoanalysis, nor is it mere biography, the story of a man in action; it is rather a notable example of psychohistory. Erikson has suggested that the psychohistorian is an artist who works with "disciplined subjectivity." The distinguished historian Sir Maurice Powicke remarked that what we call the facts of history are really judgments about historical events, judgments which have an experiential base in the life and learning of the historian, and that historical generalizations are judgments about judgments. The historian must, however, reject projections (analogous to Freud's "archeological reconstructions") which are mistaken, arbitrary, or improbable. There is a common meeting ground between the psychohistorian and the historian, but the good historian is apt to approach that sacred ground with extreme criticality.

Erikson's work is admirable in trimming away the hagiographic mistletoe which from the days of Mathesius has grown about the Saxon oak, such as the tales of grinding poverty and the rags-to-riches theme. On the other hand, he rejects the slanderous aspersions of Denifle and is critical of many of

29. *Identity, Youth and Crisis*, p. 23.
30. Ibid., p. 249.

Reiter's diagnoses. He offers valid insights into the aspects of Luther's personality either given scant attention by psychologically less sophisticated biographers or not understood in the total context of his personality and environment. His aim is to elucidate those obscure years in Luther's biography which supposedly saw the resolution of his identity crisis. Erikson pays close attention to Luther's immediate family experience and early life and to three major crises, all three legendary in nature, but still intriguing.

ANALYSIS OF THE ANALYSIS

The historian's primary objection to the work of the psychohistorian is almost certain to be that the limited source materials available, especially on the young Luther, do not supply sufficient material to sustain a depth-psychological investigation.[31] There are "grave difficulties" to psychoanalyzing the dead. The information available to the historian does not really allow for a dynamic demonstration of unconscious motivation as may be true of a living subject. In Luther's case there are only two basic references which shed direct light upon the disciplinary circumstances of his home and school, both from the somewhat suspect *Tischreden* of 1532 and 1537. The historian must also protest if the psychohistorian's projections wander imaginatively too far away from what the sources indicate or even run contrary to other available evidences. Historians are stuck with the *res particulares* and must accept with good humor charges of being idolaters of the letter.

31. It is interesting to note that although the book received much attention from psychologists and religionists, few historians other than Greenslade, Donald Meyer, and Bainton have reviewed it. Roland Bainton has given it repeated attention: "Luther: A Psychiatric Portrait," *The Yale Review* (Spring 1959):405–10, republished in Roland H. Bainton, *Studies on the Reformation* (Boston: Beacon, 1963), pp. 86–92; "Psychiatry and History: An Examination of Erikson's *Young Man Luther*," *Religion in Life* 40, no. 4 (Winter 1971):450–78, and above, pp. 19–56. Of interest also are Bainton's articles "Interpretations of the Reformation," *The American Historical Review* 66 (1960):74–84, and "Luther's Struggle for Faith," *Church History* 17 (1948):193–206, both republished in Lewis W. Spitz, ed., *The Reformation— Basic Interpretations* (Lexington, Mass.: Heath, 1972), pp. 1–10, 200–12.

Martin's Family Environment

Freud laid Sophocles under contribution for the name *Oedipus complex*, since he not only dramatized the myth relating the incest taboo but exposed the suppressed impulse behind it.[32] Erikson sees Luther as the victim of an unhappy home situation in which a severe love/hate relation toward his parents and harsh teachers bred in him a need to rebel. His subconscious hatred of his father and drive to disobedience against his father he transferred to the pope and thus became the leader of the schism in Christendom. Here are a few typical statements from the text: "This early doubt [whether his father was motivated by love and justice rather than by caprice and malice] was projected on the Father in heaven with such violence that Martin's monastic teachers could not help noticing it" (p. 58). "I said that Luther could not hate his father openly. This statement presumes that he did hate him underneath. Do we have any proof of this? Only the proof which lies in action delayed, and delayed so long that the final explosion hits nonparticipants" (p. 65). "Martin took unto himself the ideological structure of his parents' consciences: he incorporated his father's suspicious severity, his mother's fear of sorcery, and their mutual concern about catastrophes to be avoided and high goals to be met. Later he rebelled: first against his father, to join the monastery; then against the Church, to found his own church—at which point, he succumbed to many of his father's original values" (pp. 73–74). "The conversion was necessary so that Martin could give all his power of obedience to God, and turn all his venom of defiance against the Pope" (p. 97).

The idea that Luther's father was harsh with him as a regular thing is based upon one saying in the *Tischreden* of May, 1532, in which Luther cautions against disciplining children too severely and says that he does not intend to punish his

---

32. See the sprightly essay of Edmund Wilson, "Philoctetes: The Wound and the Bow," *The Wound and the Bow* (Cambridge, Mass.: Houghton Mifflin, 1941),p. 290. Wilson relates genius and disease, superior strength and crippling disability.

son Hans too severely, for, he recalled, *"mein vatter steupt mich einmal also sehr, dass ich ihn flohe und ward ihm gram, bis er mich wieder zu sich gewoehnte"* (My father once whipped me so hard that I fled from him and felt ugly toward him [or, became sadly resentful toward him] until he gradually got me accustomed to him again). Erikson criticizes Bainton's translation of *gram* as "I felt ugly" and argues that "I became sadly resentful" really describes the feeling of a child toward somebody he loves and "reaccustom" could refer only to the purpose of the father of restoring an intimate daily association. Bainton has responded with examples of Luther's use of *gram* as "angry" or "feeling ugly" and denies that it can mean "sadly resentful."[33] But the historian must insist on a closer look at the best available text, in this case Schlaginhaufen's transcript of the *Tischreden*, which reads: ". . . *mein vatter steupt mich einmal also sehr, das ich im floh und das im bang was, bis er mich wider zu im gewenet.*"[34] The preferred translation should read: ". . . my father once beat me so severely that I fled from him and he was anxious until he won me to himself again." This interpretation makes the son the hold-out and the father the one who was anxious and concerned because of the unhappy situation. In any case, *bange* can hardly mean "sadly resentful." It is of some interest to note that Luther said *einmal, once,* which does not suggest a customary thing but rather an exceptional situation. *Einmal* can, of course, merely mean "once upon a time," and a psychiatrist could also argue that *once* was enough to induce a

33. *Young Man Luther*, pp. 64–65; Bainton, "Psychiatry and History," pp. 34–35 above. Both take their reading from Otto Scheel, *Martin Luther. Vom Katholizismus zur Reformation* (Tübingen, 1921), vol. 1, p. 11, which is to be found in Aurifaber's parallel text (*WA*, TR 2, no. 1559, p. 134). Whoever edited FB. 4. 76 (*Dr. Martin Luthers Tischreden oder Colloquia*, vol. 4, ed. Heinrich Ernst Bindseil [Berlin, 1848]) obviously preferred to make Luther angry or sadly resentful, but this was misleading. If the word *gram* is taken as a noun the sentence would then read: "I fled from him and was a grief to him, until he again won me over to him."

34. *WA*, TR 2, no. 1159, p. 134, lines 5–7. Heinrich Fausel (*D. Martin Luther. Der Reformator im Kampf um Evangelien und Kirche. Sein Werden und Wirken im Spiegel eigener Zeugnisse* [Stuttgart, 1955], p. 4, n. 4) gives this reading: ". . . *Mein Vater stäupte mich einmal so sehr, dasz ich vor ihm floh und dasz ihm bange war, bis er mich wieder zu sich gewöhnt hatte.*"

lasting trauma. But it should be clear that this passage can hardly be used to create a picture of a tyrannous or cruel father. Father Hans took the initiative in winning Martin back and there is no hint that this was done in a sentimental or unmanly way. Erikson, summarizing the father-son relationship, writes succinctly (p. 66):

> I have so far mentioned two trends in the relationship between Hans and Martin: 1) the father's driving economic ambition, which was threatened by something (maybe even murder) done in the past, and by a feeling close to murder which he always carried inside; and 2) the concentration of the father's ambition on his oldest son, whom he treated with alternate periods of violent harshness and of habituating the son to himself in a manner which may well have been somewhat sentimental—a deadly combination.
>
> I would add to these trends the father's display of righteousness. Hans seems to have considered himself the very conception, the *Inbegriff,* of justice. After all, he did not spare himself, and fought his own nature as ruthlessly as those of his children. But parents are dangerous who thus take revenge on their child for what circumstances and inner compulsion have done to them; who misuse one of the strongest forces in life—true indignation in the service of vital values—to justify their own small selves. Martin, however, seems to have sensed on more than one occasion that the father, behind his disciplined public identity, was possessed by an angry, and often alcoholic, impulsiveness which he loosed against his family (and would dare loose *only* against his family) under the pretense of being a hard taskmaster and righteous judge.

Such a portrait of Hans, the man who looks out from Lucas Cranach's drawing with such a plain, honest, workworn face, may well impress the historian who knows the sources as the product of insufficiently disciplined subjectivity. The reference to murder, of course, has to do with a story which George Witzel told about Luther's father. Witzel had reverted to Catholicism after a brief period as a Lutheran, and Luther once commented that given enough florins he would turn Lutheran again. In actual fact, a young brother of Hans named Kleinhans was a ne'er-do-well and drunkard who once threatened a shepherd with a dagger. There is no evidence that he killed him, and it seems unlikely indeed, since in moving from

Moehra to Mansfeld he remained in the same legal jurisdiction.
Erikson inexplicably transfers this incident to Hans, writing
(p. 57) that "the very existence of such a brother whom
scandal (maybe even murder) eventually brought to town
must have underlined for Big Hans the danger of losing his
own hard-won position—and this especially because he himself apparently had a towering temper, and was, in fact, supposed to have killed a shepherd before coming to Mansfeld."
Luther occasionally commented that no one could provide
better information on his family than the counts of Mansfeld.
The scattered archives of the counts of Mansfeld do indeed
contain nearly everything that we shall ever know about Hans,
including the story of Kleinhans. They were edited by Walter
Möllenberg decades ago and should be consulted also by the
psychohistorian.[35]

Nor was Luther's father an alcoholic, for the one reference
to his drinking suggests a brighter scene. Luther heard that his
nephew, Hans Pollner, was drinking to excess and admonished
him: "Some when intoxicated are happy and agreeable, like
my father, they sing, joke, but you turn wholly to anger. Such
men should abstain from wine like poison."[36] This father was
elected to the city council and became one of the *Vierherrn* in
a town to which he had immigrated, built up his holdings by
hard work and sober management until he owned part of six
pits and two smelting operations, and left a considerable estate
at the time of his death.

No, Hans Luther was not harsh, drunken, or tyrannous,
but rather tender and pious as well as stern and ambitious for
himself and his son. Hans was inclined to be tender and deeply
moved by suffering. Luther on two different occasions recounts
a story which illustrates the point: "My father was asked at
Mansfeld by a certain neighbor to come and see him, for he
was in mortal agony. Turning on his bed he showed him his

35. Walter Möllenberg, "Hans Luther, Dr. Martin Luthers Vater, ein mans-
feldischer Bergmann und Hüttenmeister," *Zeitschrift des Harz-Vereins für
Geschichte und Altertumskunde* 103 (1906):169–93. For a favorable account
of Witzel see Winfried Trusen, *Um die Reform und Einheit der Kirche, Zum
Leben und Werk Georg Witzels* (Münster, 1956).
36. *WA*, TR 4, no. 5050, p. 636.

posterior and said, 'See, dear Luther, how they beat me!' at
which Father was so shocked and so shaken by those reflections that he nearly died himself."[37]

On one occasion Hans took Martin into a wheat field to
show him the grain ripe for harvest and told him how the
heavenly Father cares for us. The same man who was merry
and humorous when he had belted a few joked with his wife
in bed. Luther relates that his sons respect him just as he
respected his parents, for his father slept with his mother and
joked with her (*mit ihr geschertzt*) just as Luther did with his
wife, and they were nevertheless pious people, just like the
patriarchs and prophets.[38]

Hans was a man of genuine piety and an active churchman.
The Mansfeld relatives recounted that Luther's father prayed
often and earnestly at the bedside of his children. He was
badly shaken when in 1505 he lost two sons to the plague and
reflected that he should perhaps willingly give Martin to the
Lord for service as a monk. He had as a very close friend Jonas
Cemmerer, a priest, and had priests and teachers as house-
guests on occasion. As one of the *Vierherrn* or councilmen he
signed endowments for the church and served as a trustee for
prebends. In 1497, the year in which Luther went away to
Magdeburg to be with the Brethren of the Common Life, Hans,
the priest Johann Ledener, and the Mansfeld citizens won a
sixty-day indulgence from the bishop for all those who attended
mass at the two altars of a Mansfeld church dedicated to
George, Mary, and an assortment of saints. Late in life Luther
commented that his father had opposed his entering a monastery "because he knew the rascality of the monks."[39] There is
no other evidence that he was opposed to monasticism on those
grounds, but it is not improbable, given the opposition between secular and regular clergy and the widespread criticism
of the lazy and ignorant monks on the popular level as well as
among humanists like Hutten and Erasmus even before 1517.

37. *WA*, TR 2, no. 2370, p. 436; no. 1308, p. 36.
38. *WA*, TR 3, no. 3181b, p. 213; *WA*, TR 2, no. 1659, pp. 166–67.
39. *WA*, TR 3, no. 3556, pp. 410–11.

Hans's work ethic and his works-righteous religion dove-
tailed very smoothly. They did not fall out of phase until he
had learned from his son the evangelical way. He died in this
faith in 1530. Luther wrote him a letter of consolation and
held Christ the Redeemer before him. The priest asked him
whether he believed what he had heard and he said, "Of course
I believe it, I would be a knave not to."[40] On June 5, 1530,
Luther wrote to Melanchthon:

> John Reineck wrote me today that my beloved father, the
> senior Hans Luther, departed this life at one o'clock on
> Exaudi Sunday. This death has cast me into deep mourning,
> not only because of the ties of nature but also because it was
> through his sweet love to me that my Creator endowed me
> with all that I am and have. Although it is consoling to me
> that, as he writes, my father fell asleep softly and strong in
> his faith in Christ, yet his kindness and the memory of his
> pleasant conversation have caused so deep a wound in my
> heart that I have scarcely ever held death in such low esteem.
> . . . I will not write more about my grief. It is good and godly
> for me to mourn as a son such a parent by whom the Father
> of mercy created me and by his sweat made me what I am.
> I rejoice that he lived in these days so that he could see the
> light of truth. Blessed be God in all His acts and counsels
> forever. Amen.[41]

Luther loved his mother much as he did his father, "for
they meant well by me." Luther recounts that his mother *once*
beat him until the blood flowed for stealing a nut. Such severity, which made him shy and led him into the monastery, he
recalled, might be reserved for a worse theft such as a coat or
money.[42] Erikson assumes that he must have been deeply disappointed with his mother, for consider what he says about
marriage (p. 73). But Luther elsewhere observed how sweetly
his mother sang, at the age of forty-two he invited her to his
wedding, he named a daughter after her, and when she was

40. *WA*, TR 1, no. 933, p. 470; *WA*, TR 2, no. 1388, p. 81. See also Otto
Scheel, *Martin Luther* (Tübingen, 1917), I, pp. 8–11, 14–15.

41. *WA*, Br 5, no. 1584. See the excellent article by Heinrich Bornkamm,
"Luther und sein Vater," *Zeitschrift für Theologie und Kirche* 66 (1969):
38–61.

42. *WA*, TR 3, nos. 3566a and 3566b, pp. 415–17.

on her deathbed he wrote her one of the finest letters of love
and consolation that can be found in all of literature.[43] And
as for marriage, no one had for a thousand years preached
about and practiced marriage in such a laudable way.[44] The
psychohistorian is mistaken in projecting from an alleged disappointment in the mother Luther's "dethroning of the Virgin
Mary." Luther opposed the cult of Mary because he believed
that the idea of Mary interceding for the sinner with her Son
made Christ seem forbidding, to be approached only through
an intermediary. He denied Mary the extravagant titles, such
as "queen of heaven," not found in the Scriptures. But he continued to cherish Mary as an ideal of womanhood and honored
her as the mother of Christ. He kept an icon of Mary in his
study his whole life and wrote a commentary on the *Magnificat*
that was recently republished by two Catholic publishing
houses. Christ himself rebuked Mary, though Luther did not.
An analyst could perhaps even do something positive with
Luther's fond allegorizing of the beloved Church as a she:

> She is my love, the noble Maid,
> Forget her can I never;
> Whatever honor men have paid,
> My heart she has forever.

In the same passage, Erikson notes that Luther said he had
once received fifteen strokes from the teacher before noon. A
lupus or spy was appointed to report any child who spoke
German instead of Latin on the playground. *Once* Luther had
a particularly bad day. Luther criticized such severity as well
as the boredom of rote learning in school. Erikson declares
with an air of seriousness that it was because Luther was
required to speak Latin and inhibit his German that in later
life he became so voluble in German. But as the translators of
the new fifty-six-volume American edition of *Luther's Works*
know, he was voluble also in Latin. A survey of all the available information suggests that Martin did not have a particu-

43. *WA*, Br 6, no. 1820.
44. See Olavi Lähteenmäki, *Sexus und Ehe bei Luther* (Turku, 1955).

larly unhappy childhood so far as parents and school were concerned.

THREE MAJOR CRISES

Erikson analyzes three events and their ramifications in terms of the struggle to achieve identity, a central feature of his psychoanalytic ego psychology. He appreciates the fact that these occurrences may be only legendary, since the information about them is meager and some of the sources suspect.

The fit in the choir loft. This incident supposedly occurred in Luther's early or middle twenties while the preacher was reading the story of the youth, deaf and dumb, possessed of a devil, being brought to Christ by his father (Mark 9:17). Luther is said to have fallen to the floor of the choir loft and bellowed with a loud voice, *"Non sum! Non sum!"* Erikson finds the *non sum* to be an expression of an identity crisis. The story is told, however, by Luther's archenemy and dedicated defamer, Johannes Cochlaeus (*Rotzleffel,* Luther called him), in his commentary on Luther's life and works published three years after Luther's death, or more than four decades after the event. It is told, moreover, to prove that Luther had secret commerce with a demon. Cochlaeus's whole book is so full of falsehoods that Cardinal Aleander warned against its publication, fearing that the reaction would make it counterproductive. Cochlaeus seems to have derived the story from Dungersheim, another foe of Luther, who is purported to have heard it from Nathin, a teacher of Luther who remained Catholic, who may in turn have derived it from the Bishop of Mansfeld, in whose church it might have happened.[45] Given Luther's supercharged medieval religiosity, preoccupation with the fear of demonic possession would in any case provide a more immediate explanation of Luther's alleged reaction than a vocational identity crisis.

The thunderstorm. During the middle of the spring semester of Luther's first term in the law school at Erfurt in 1505 he

45. Bainton, p. 42 above.

made a trip home, about which we have no further information. On the way back he was caught in a terrific thunderstorm and a bolt of lightning struck so close that in terror
Luther vowed to St. Anne that if he were spared he would
enter a monastery.[46] Once before on the way home he had
been struck in the leg with his own dagger and bled so pro-
fusely he had called on Mary for help.[47] But why did he go
home on this occasion? Erikson says that the father may have
demanded an accounting about his plan to leave law for the
monastery. This is possible, but Luther recalled that when he
entered the father did not know it, and he became a monk
because he was terrified by lightning, feared death, and took
the vow. His father asked, Suppose it was a demon and not
God? Luther recalled, near the end of his life, that his father
had been angry after he wrote that he had entered the
monastery.[48]

When Luther celebrated his first mass in 1507, his father
came with two wagons of twenty friends, brought beer and
other gifts, and gave twenty gulden to the monastery. But at
the banquet on that occasion Hans spoke and asked whether
they had not heard that the fourth commandment enjoins
honoring and obeying one's father and mother. In his *De votis
monasticis* years later, dedicated to his father, Luther recalled
that this thrust of Hans struck home.[49] There was tension,
then, and the strain of going against his father's wishes that he
study law, do well in life, and support his parents in their old
age. Was there evidence of subconscious hate or was his act
motivated by a drive to defy his domineering father? Luther
recalled in later years that he and his father had both been in
error about monkish works serving as the basis for justification
in the sight of God. The motive for Luther's decision to enter

46. *WA*, TR 1, no. 881, pp. 439–40 (related in the first half of the 1530s):
"*Cum Martinus Lutherus inscio patre suo monesterium ingressus esset, ter-
ritus fulmine, aegerrime hoc tulit pater ac rescripsit: Wie, wens ein gespenst
were?*" Cf. Carl Stange, *Luthers Gedanken über die Todesfurcht* (Berlin,
1932).

47. *WA*, TR 1, no. 119, p. 46.

48. *WA*, TR 5, no. 5379, p. 99.

49. *WA*, TR 2, no. 1558, pp. 133–34.

the monastery, conscious and subconscious, seems to have been deeply religious, an expression of fear-motivated piety which Luther had to respond to despite the filial respect and loving concern he felt toward a father who was working so hard to support him in the best schools. His action was predicated upon the structure of the only religious and intellectual paradigm he knew at that time.

The tower experience. The *Turmerlebnis* marked Luther's breakthrough to an evangelical understanding of the concept "righteousness of God." In 1545 he related his struggle to understand St. Paul's meaning in Romans 1:17, "In it the righteousness of God is revealed." He had been taught to understand it as "formal or active righteousness," the righteousness with which God is righteous and punishes the unrighteous sinner. Then, he recalled,

> At last, by the mercy of God, meditating day and night, I gave heed to the context of the words, namely, "In it the righteousness of God is revealed, as it is written, He who through faith is righteous shall live." There I began to understand that the righteousness of God is that by which the righteous lives by a gift of God, namely by faith. And this is the meaning: the righteousness of God is revealed by the Gospel, namely the passive righteousness with which merciful God justifies us by faith, as it is written, "He who through faith is righteous shall live." Here I felt that I was altogether born again and had entered paradise itself through open gates.[50]

There is a massive literature debating the date of this tower experience, ranging from as early as 1512–13 to as late as 1518–19. The tendency now is not to ascribe such great importance to this alleged event, because a close study of the exegetical notes, from the *Dictata* on the Psalms through the commentaries on Romans, Galatians, and Hebrews, suggests a gradual clarification in Luther's mind as to the nature of the

50. This account is known as *Luthers groszes Selbst-Zeugnis* and is found translated as "Preface to the Complete Edition of Luther's Latin Writings, Wittenberg, 1545." *Luther's Works* (Philadelphia: Fortress, 1960), vol. 34, pp. 327–38; reprinted in Spitz, *The Reformation—Basic Interpretations*, pp. 171–79, "Luther's Road to Reformation."

"passive righteousness" which God bestows upon man by grace alone.

In his table talk between June 9 and July 12, 1532, however, Luther described his struggle to achieve clarity about faith and righteousness and said that "the Holy Spirit had given him this understanding in this tower." In one of the three rescripts the words *auff diser cloaca* are added.[51] The phrase looms large in the Catholic-Protestant polemic early in this century and has stimulated analysts to a veritable frenzy of speculation about psycho-physiological relationships, oral-anal release, and the Grand Canal controversy. In fact, however, the east tower room on the second floor of the Black Cloister contained the small library reading room with a large Bible where the monks went to read and meditate. It was not a facility. Two explanations of the phrase *auff diser cloaca* seem far more probable than the defecatory hypothesis. As early as 1919 Ernst Kroker, who had edited these passages in the *Tischreden*, argued in an article in the *Lutherjahrbuch* that the term *cloaca* had to be used in a transferred sense in order to fit the usage of that day. The psychoanalytic explanation is all but untenable in the light of what we now know about the usage of the term by monks, and specifically by Augustinian hermits. In connection with the experience of *accedia*, the *Klosterkrankheit*, the phrase *in cloaca* was used not only with reference to the *locus* but to describe a state of melancholy in a way similar to our colloquial expression "down in the dumps." Thus Luther, troubled in conscience, fearful and anxious, suddenly understands that St. Paul is speaking of the righteousness God bestows on man through forgiveness, and he is lifted out of the depths into the joy of paradise.

There was a long tradition of theologians who "suddenly" perceived the meaning of a fairly common text: Augustine, Thomas Bradwardine, Richard Fitzralph, John Gerson, Andreas, Carlstadt, Contarini, Vadian, Calvin. The medieval

51. *WA*, TR 3, nos. 3232a, b, c. p. 228. No. 3232b reads, "*Dise khunst hat mir der Heilig Geist auff diser cloaca auff dem thorm gegeben.*"

stercus-cloaca tradition of the *humilitas* theology referred to the humility and low estate of the doer of works, not of good works themselves. Only those who have emptied themselves can come with confidence to the covenant for the forgiveness of sins. At the end of his first lectures on the Psalms Luther says literally that it is the beggars who are *latrina et cloaca, quod est verum,* who come for forgiveness. That is the meaning of the very last words which Luther wrote on a small slip of paper found after his death: "Do not try to fathom this divine *Aeneid,* but humbly worship its footprints. We are beggars. That is true" (*Wir sein Pettler. Hoc est verum*).[52]

Once again it is evident that the nature of Luther's struggle and resolution was religious and indeed theological in nature. If the late date is to be preferred for the *Turmerlebnis,* which seems to be the growing consensus of scholarly opinion, then it was a mature man of thirty-four or thirty-five who came to a new understanding of the all-important text. Luther's time in the monastery was not basically a moratorium for identity crisis resolution but a period of soul-struggle in a religious sense.

There are other rather serious questions to be raised about a psychohistorian's use of evidence and projections. Thus the "turnabout" hypothesis concerning Luther's rejection of the peasants in 1525 did not hold. Luther was completely consistent in favoring the peasants and admonishing the nobles before and after the event; but also, before, after, and during the peasant revolt, he opposed violence, anarchy, murder, rape, theft, and the abuse of the Gospel for worldly ends. The Reformation continued afterwards to spread as a spontaneous people's movement in many new areas of the Empire, for the common men seemed to understand Luther's consistency. Where peasant resistance to evangelical preachers was encountered in the back country in subsequent years it was due to the

52. Heiko A. Oberman, "Wir sein Pettler. Hoc est verum. Bund und Gnade in der Theologie des Mittelalters und der Reformation," *Zeitschrift für Kirchengeschichte* 78 (1967):232–52.

conservatism of Catholic peasants against evangelical innova-
tors, not opposition to a "turnabout" or to repressors.[53]

Other matters merit discussion but can only be referred to
here. The anality and scatology in Luther the sweaty realist,
as Huxley dubbed the reformer, poses problems. "Love hath
built its tent," sings Yeats, "in the place of excrement." The
question of singularity and ego development requires further
exploration. The critical theological problem of predestination
and justification, the nature of Staupitz's theology and influence, all deserve detailed study by the historian in dialogue
with the psychohistorian. But rather than attempting to crowd
a diffuse discussion of many points onto the few remaining
pages, more can be gained from suggesting an alternative or
at least modified reading of the evidence.

THE MAJOR TREND

The two most significant recent creations of psychohistory
are surely Erikson's *Luther* and his *Gandhi.* In going beyond
the biological analysis of some Freudians and polemicists to
study Luther's emotional crises in youth and early adulthood
in the familial and social setting against a background of his
own clinical observation of young men today, Erikson offers a
look inside which is more than historical and has the ring of
truth. Of the methodological problems encountered by the
psychohistorian Erikson writes: "A clinician's training permits,
and in fact forces him to recognize major trends even where
the facts are not all available; at any point in treatment he
can and must be able to make meaningful predictions as to
what will prove to have happened, and he must be able to
sift even questionable sources in such a way that a coherent

53. See Franz Lau, "Der Bauernkrieg und das angebliche Ende der Luther-
ischen Reformation als spontaner Volksbewegung," *Lutherjahrbuch* 26 (1959):
109–34. Vadian's famous tract of 1521 entitled *Karsthans* shows how widely
understood it was that Luther opposed fighting and killing and consistently
held to the principle that only constituted authority had the power of the
sword. Cf. Lewis W. Spitz, *The Renaissance and Reformation Movements*
(Chicago: Rand McNally, 1971), pp. 346–47.

predictive hypothesis emerges." In psychoanalytic treatment of a living subject the analyst has certain ways of verifying such a hypothesis. "In biography," Erikson observes, "the validity of any relevant theme can only lie in its crucial recurrence in a man's development, and in its relevance to the balance sheet of his victories and defeats."[54]

Like the psychohistorian, the historian should be able to establish a major trend which will accommodate the known sources and provide a satisfying interpretation without doing violence to any known or even probable evidences. In a well-guarded vault deep beneath the New School is a depository of golden paradigms which serve as the official standard and measurement for behavioral scientists. Whatever facts about any given subject do not fit the paradigm are often trimmed or conveniently forgotten. The great beauty of Erikson's work as a psychohistorian is that he seeks out awkward data and examines them for their heuristic value, especially where they create difficulties for theory. It would be possible, of course, to criticize Erikson's neo-Freudian developmental approach from the position of structural and cognitive behavioral psychology, but the modest aim of this paper has been rather to examine his analysis from the historian's point of view.

. The historian shares the psychohistorian's conviction that Luther was a most unusual young man, brilliant, sensitive, perceptive, tense, articulate, and given from early youth to "ups and downs." A sober psychological assessment based upon the context of his behavior throughout his adult life suggests that he had a cyclothemic personality varying between hyper- and hypothemic levels in mood. At the same time he enjoyed a sthenic fund of initiative, so that no true and lasting synchronized phase of depression and loss of initiative can be shown, not even in the difficult years 1527 and 1528 when he once suffered a depression lasting two or three days. His mood variations created complications for his personal and academic life but left the content of his professional work as a theologian

54. Fritz Schmidl, "Psychoanalysis and History," pp. 537–38.

unaffected.[55] His productivity remained unimpaired at all times. It is time, the German scholar Hans Preuss has suggested, for a major work on the wholesome Luther, now that his personality complications and existential theological depths have been plumbed.

The historian sees a "trend" in Luther's development that makes his behavior explicable in both psychological and theological terms. Luther's biographer Otto Scheel, who asserts that there can be no talk of a particularly unhappy childhood for Martin, devotes a full chapter to the religious life in Mansfeld. That religiosity can best be described as a fear-motivated piety, and this is how Luther remembered it—Christ the stern judge. The full picture of Hans Luther reveals a man tender and pious, solicitous of his son's affection, encouraging in his son by his own religiosity and churchmanship a piety of the intense late medieval kind, which the whole environment lived and breathed. At the same time Hans was ambitious for his own economic improvement and for the success of his eldest son. The conflicting values of an ascetic, fearful religiosity and a secular, assertive ambition eventually collided in Luther's life, for the course of his life led to a steady deepening of the religious dimension, to the point where it demanded his total dedication even though it meant abandoning the career planned for him by his father, and on one level and for a time acquiesced in by the son. *Even though*, not *because*, it meant going contrary to his father's wishes. The father-son relation, so far as the evidence goes, was not of the kind to produce a need for defiance, oedipal rage, or an extra-

55. This is the sensible diagnosis of Eberhard Grossmann, M.D., Th.D., *Beiträge zur Psychologischen Analyse der Reformatoren Luther und Calvin* (Basel, 1958). Grossmann rejects the analysis of Reiter that Luther suffered from an organic endogenous cyclophrenia even in a mild form. On Calvin, Grossmann simply concludes there are a number of personality traits which contribute to the understanding of the uniqueness of Calvin but which cannot be grasped by the mere use of the notions of any constitutional typology. Horst Beintker, *Die Überwindung der Anfechtung bei Luther* (Berlin, 1954), pp. 70–77, discusses the shortcomings of a psychological explanation of Luther's *Anfechtung* or soul-struggle.

ordinarily acute hate/love syndrome. The tension with his earthly father from the time of his decision to enter the monastery until he emerged once again resulted from his conscientious need to be earnestly and exclusively about "his heavenly Father's business." He was, in fact, sorry to grieve his father, and ironically it was in good measure his father's own piety that had contributed so much to his predicament.

Luther's mother perhaps even more, with her excessive moralism and strict discipline, however well intended, led him to the monastery, just as Luther said. His teachers, too, ingrained in him a fear-motivated piety, so that, as he recalled, he turned pale at the mention of Christ the judge. The devil, too, was portrayed so realistically that he became incorporated into Luther's theology not as a superstitious hangover but as a central operative factor.[56] The Brethren of the Common Life at Magdeburg, his teachers at Eisenach, and the atmosphere at Erfurt, a little Rome with its two hundred churches, combined to reinforce the religious impulses of his boyhood.

Given this ideological conditioning, the verifiable events and even the legendary incidents in the life of young man Luther fall into place. In later life Luther recalled that from youth on he had suffered depressions like those that plagued him in old age, and those depressions may well have been religious in content. The fit in the choir loft, if it happened at all, can best be understood as Cochlaeus intended it, as evidence of Luther's fear of demons rather than a clue to an identity crisis as defined in ego-psychology. Fear of death and divine wrath rather than a subconscious urge to defy his father drove him into the monastery, just as he said. The long search in the monastery for certainty was less a moratorium while searching for identity-crisis resolution than it was a struggle to resolve a religious problem acutely felt and critical because he took it and himself so seriously. His resolution was biblical, a product of his exegetical labors, just as other men of that

56. See Hans Martin Barth, *Der Teufel und Jesus Christus in der Theologie Martin Luthers* (Göttingen, 1967).

day. Zwingli, Calvin, Vadian, Carlstadt, Münzer found their
basic answers in the Scriptures in ways analogous to but still
independently of Luther's resolution.

Luther's religious preoccupation and the nature of its resolution explains the break with the papacy. He was an obedient
rebel and a reluctant reformer, for as late as 1520 he "lay
prostrate before the pope" and begged for understanding. He
did not transfer disobedience against his father to the pope,
or hate from his earthly to the heavenly Father. He did not,
after all, break with worldly authorities such as the prince or
emperor, and he remained the leader of a conservative Reformation. His scrupulosity explains why he trembled when he
said his first mass and why he felt struck when his father
quoted a divine commandment against him. The intensity of
his fear-motivated piety explains his religious rapport with the
broad masses of medieval men. The gospel he preached was
an answer to the fear-ridden piety which plagued the conscience
of a whole generation. From 1512 to 1517 Luther gained confidence as a professor of theology, when he felt the platform
firm under his feet and witnessed students taking notes of
what he had to say and thousands buying the books of a *doctor
in biblia*.[57] But even his new confidence and trust came and
went, for in later years he wondered whether he could ever
be so bold again as he had been when in 1521 he took his stand.

Seeing Luther in this light calls into question some of the
central assertions of *Young Man Luther*. But Erikson's book
remains, nevertheless, a great achievement. His explanation
of the problem of creative genius, the nature of historical greatness, the relation of an unusual young man to his familial and
social environment, and the phenomenology of religious experience constitutes a major achievement. Nor does this revised

57. See the precocious essay of Peter G. Sandstrom, "Luther's Sense of Himself as an Interpreter of the Word to the World" (Honors thesis, Amherst
College, 1961). German Luther research has not produced a full-length biography since Julius Köstlin's which was first published in 1875. Heinrich
Bornkamm, who is presently engaged in writing such a work, has taken cog-
nizance of the need for the biographer to take the psychological dimension
seriously in "Probleme der Lutherbiographie," *Lutherforschung Heute* (Berlin, 1958), pp. 20–21.

reading of the evidence subvert completely the assumptions of the psychohistorian about the intimate and delicate relations of father and son, for a father who is a sweet persuader can induce pressures more persistent than one who is overtly gross and hateful. *Young Man Luther* is a marvelous vehicle for relating in a moving parable the way an unusual youth became a great man of history. In fact, historians are in the author's debt for pointing up the great importance for history of a single man and what transpires within the "inner court." For it is the great paradox of history, as Veronica Wedgwood observed in her *Velvet Studies*, that individuals who are like the anonymous waves of the sea, mere grains of sand on the shore of time, infinitesimal dust, nevertheless are the cause of all things.

4. From Freud to Erikson: Developments in Psychology of Religion

Paul W. Pruyser

When Oscar Pfister, the Swiss pastor-psychoanalyst, wrote *Christianity and Fear* in 1944, he appeared shocked to note that Martin Luther, despite having grown up in some ways, nevertheless continued to believe firmly in the concrete reality of the devil, advocated the burning and torturing of witches, recommended the drowning of idiot children, and retained a considerable element of magical thinking in his approach to the sacraments. Pfister saw Luther among the reformers as "the typical sufferer from fear." He was quick to add that this statement is double-headed in that it "tells us very little and a great deal about him." It says little "regarding his creative power, the value of his prophetic gifts, the truth of his view regarding divine grace and the truth of Christ's doctrine of salvation, and the correctness or otherwise of his dogmatic formulations." But it says much "about his psychological development as such, and about the inspired enlightenment which compelled him . . . to rend the net of legalism and asceticism." And it says much also "about his abandonment of the synthetic-symbolical methods of alleviating fear through the sacrament and through stereotyped compulsion ritual, and about his analytical adoption of divine grace."[1]

It is interesting, and I hope enlightening to the psychology of religion, to compare Pfister's study with Erikson's *Young Man Luther*, published fourteen years later. Both writers are psychoanalysts, but each in a unique adjectival way: Pfister is the Protestant minister whose pastoral concerns come through,

1. Oscar Pfister, *Christianity and Fear* (London: Allen & Unwin, 1948), pp. 344–45.

whereas Erikson is an anthropologist practicing in a clinical-psychiatric setting, whose cultural interests and clinical expertise are quite in evidence. Both men see Luther's religious quest as conflict-laden and his religious growth as a process of problem-solving. Both men are interested in Luther's emotions and motivations, though Pfister's study is focused on one special affect, whereas Erikson's tends to assess broadly the whole gamut of feelings and needs. Both men admit that the clinician, in evaluating a historical figure who can no longer be interviewed and whose relatives are no longer accessible to social workers, must make a very prudent use of reliable and questionable pieces of information and circumstantial evidence —yet both have a firm clinical confidence in the psychological validity of the basic data they choose. Both men use standard psychiatric nomenclature when they allude to "compulsion neurosis," "compulsion rituals," "obsessive ruminations," and so forth, in describing some of Luther's tendencies. Both men, finally, commit a rather daring act, rare enough in the history of the psychology of religion, by frankly bringing their hero's systematic or constructive theology under scrutiny. They relate the man to his work and vice versa, apparently feeling free to pursue a psychological analysis of the theological system with the conviction that this too is a psychological datum; that it is need-determined, conflict-laden, symptomatic, wish-fulfilling, idiosyncratic and thematically consistent with its author's dominant personal concerns. But Erikson's book is of a very different order than Pfister's study, despite the fact that both men write from within the mainstream of psychoanalysis. Three factors contribute to this difference.

In the first place, Erikson's clinical procedure is far more explicit and systematized. He tries to come as close as possible to a case study such as one writes about psychiatric patients. Ordinarily in psychiatry this means that one assembles a clinical history from various informants, naturally including the patient himself, complemented by examinational data about the patient which assess him totally and structurally at any opportune cross section in time. In the latter part, the emphasis is on the interrelatedness in the here and now of the patient's perceptions, thoughts, linguistic processes, actions, and emotions; his relations to other people and to himself; his drives, his possessions, his value system, his body, his symptoms, and so forth. Assets and liabilities, strengths and weaknesses are evaluated, and a temporary, transitory diagnosis is formulated which will provide a rationale for treatment. But since psychoanalysis comes closer to a protracted process of diagnosing and self-diagnosing concomitant with treatment of a least activistic kind, diagnostic statements and conclusions tend to be more complex and ad hoc and less typological than those which prevailed until recently in general psychiatry. Now it is obvious that the ideal case study needs modification when it is applied retroactively to historical personages who have long been dead and about whom there is considerable folklore. Certain gaps in the history will have to be tolerated, and direct examinations, which are impossible, will have to be compensated for by inferential statements. Yet it seems to me that Erikson is quite successful in his attempt at case study under such adverse circumstances.

He carefully weighs the relevance of his data by taking a close look at the motives and the observational acumen of his informants about Luther. The earlier commentators on Luther's life, and the testimonies of his contemporaries, are seen as neither wholly right nor totally wrong. By analogy to the parents, siblings, children, and friends of psychiatric patients, they are seen as interacting, involved, having and eliciting positive and negative feelings, engaged in power relations, always and inevitably somewhat distorted in their views, and sometimes more disorganized than the patient himself. Even the unreliable informants are useful; they bring attitudes towards the patient which throw light on both the patient and themselves. For it is precisely from such entangled interactions that, after much sifting and weighing, a picture of the patient emerges, not abstracted from his interactions but imbedded in them. And herein lies one essential difference between clinical case study methods and the work of detectives, prosecution attorneys, or fact-minded (that is, "detectivistic") historians. The latter attempt to isolate the individual as a self-acting agent so as to impute to him the responsibility for certain events or deeds, or to free him from any blame. The clinician preserves under all circumstances the patient's imbeddedness in his milieu, refusing to isolate him, seeing him in incessant reciprocal interaction with everyone and everything that is relevant to him, consciously or unconsciously.

In the second place, application of the case study method to historical persons does not necessarily make the subject a patient, though this might seem so at first sight. Erikson's goal is not to label Luther with a fancy disease name or to prove that he belonged to this or that nosological type. This is what several medical writers early in the twentieth century tried to do with Jesus, to which Albert Schweitzer retorted in kind, with his *The Psychiatric Study of Jesus*,[2] unfortunately using the same outworn psychiatric system which assumed static disease entities. The same preoccupation with disease syndromes mars the otherwise so fascinating work of Anton Boisen. In the psychoanalytic framework, however—and Erikson's book is an excellent example of it—the emphasis is not on disease, but on the interweaving in each person of healthy and unhealthy processes, on constructive and destructive alternatives of behavior, on workable conflict resolutions and the perpetuation of psychological or social problems. The result is a continuum of health and illness, with perpetual fluctuations in the life of the single individual.

Along with this, and undergirded by the dynamic-genetic point of view, the old and the new in the individual's development are not radically opposed to each other, but interpenetrate on a continuum of meanings. Thus Erikson can describe one aspect of Luther's religious quest as a search for the reassuring, maternal theology of Augustine, using with new depth and meaning the classical phrase "the milk of grace," without

2. Albert Schweitzer, *The Psychiatric Study of Jesus*, trans. C. R. Joy (Boston: Beacon Press, 1948).

thereby either infantilizing Luther or keeping his theology a purely intellectual pastime. It allows him to show that in Luther's case the toilet could indeed be a place where insights are generated. This is not vulgarity, nor reductionism, but an acknowledgement of life's multiple continuities which survive the onslaught by social, moral, or rational ordering principles.

In the third place, during the fourteen years which lie between the publication of Pfister's and Erikson's books, many developments have taken place within psychoanalysis itself. Psychoanalytic concepts have become more articulate, richer, more precise, more open to traffic with nonpsychoanalytic concepts. Many ancillary constructs have been incorporated into the psychoanalytic framework, and signs of integration into a comprehensive theory have become apparent. During these years psychoanalysis has evolved from a specialized and somewhat ad hoc psychiatric theory to a general psychological theory. This evolution has mainly taken place in America with such men as, among others, Erikson himself and his colleague David Rapaport at Austin Riggs. The results are conspicuous in Erikson's Luther study and make his work quite different from Pfister's, despite a common early psychoanalytic core in their convictions.

Pfister relies almost exclusively on a scheme of *drive and inhibition* and *anxiety and defense,* characteristic of the early and middle periods of the history of psychoanalysis. It leads him to say that Luther's attitude to fear closed his mind to the implication of free salvation (as in the parable of the prodigal son), that he needed "a regression to St. Paul's doctrine of grace, though in modified form" by the symbolical and ethical action of the sacraments, and that he did not entirely succeed in restoring love to the center in piety. Erikson's analytic apparatus comprises the whole of ego-psychology, commensurate with Rapaport's ten points of view in psychoanalytic theory,[3] and Erikson's own enrichments.[4]

3. David Rapaport, *The Structure of Psychoanalytic Theory* (New York: International Universities Press, 1960).
4. Erik H. Erikson, *Identity and the Life Cycle* (New York: International Universities Press, 1959).

In ego psychology one emphasis is on the person's talents, special cognitive styles, and basic proclivities. For instance, Erikson pays considerable attention to Luther's great vocal and linguistic skills: "his receptivity for the written word; his memory for the significant phrase; and his range of verbal expression (lyrical, biblical, satirical, and vulgar)."[5] It is in part through this gift that Luther found himself (his theology of the Word, his new emphasis on congregational singing, his sublime Bible translation which formalized a native language for a new nation). It helped him to identify with Christ who is the Word. It was involved symptomatically in the voicing of his cry during the fit in the choir; it produced stress when he was faced with the monastic demand for silence; it made his father's injunction against any back talk all the more harsh. It finally was used vengefully in his passionate, grand, and enduring back talk to the Roman hierarchy and papal abuses. This emphasis leads Erikson to conjecture that "nobody could speak and sing as Luther later did if his mother's voice had not sung to him of some heaven," and so this talent became an important mode in his seeking of an identity.

Another stable characteristic is seen in the nature of Luther's conscience, which bore kinship to his father's suspicious severity, his mother's fear of sorcery, and the driving ambition of both. This conscience set the stage for his enduring scrupulosity, for obsessive ruminations during stressful periods; it stimulated doubting and tended to equate, by a genetic principle, wrongness with dirt, thoughts with substances, salvation with cleanliness. Erikson describes these equations in Luther's life in detail and succeeds in linking together Luther's theological innovations and grandeur with his repetitious vulgarity and convincing earthiness. Again, these two products are psychologically not radical opposites nor two Luthers, but tendencies of the *one* Luther which lie on a continuum. Indeed, one might say that the very style of Luther's obsessive thought processes with their recurrent *ifs, ands, buts* and *howevers* was a unique preparation for the dialectical conceptions of

5. Erik H. Erikson, *Young Man Luther* (New York: Norton, 1958), p. 47.

grace in his theology, necessitating paradoxical modes of formulation. How different this is from the steady and coolly logical
thought of a Spinoza!

On the basis of such psychological assessments as these,
keeping both the longitudinal and the cross-sectional view in
mind, Erikson goes deeply into the whys and hows of Luther's
personal and theologically conceptualized beliefs. I see in this
Erikson's major contribution to the psychology of religion,
and I believe that it is a rather novel one, though it has
antecedents in the work of some earlier psychoanalysts whose
works are, however, rarely summarized adequately in the
standard textbooks of the psychology of religion.[6] His emphasis
is not on the traditional topics such as conversion, the nature
of religious feelings and beliefs, types of religious experience,
motivation for the ministry, or the correlation of denomina-
tional background with authoritarian and conservative attitudes. He attempts to show, rather, that in a religious genius
we find a constant act of theologizing which is existential precisely to the degree that a man puts into his theology all that
he is and has and has been, for the sake of becoming the one
he is destined to be, by his own health and pathology. Thus,
for Luther, Voice and Word, which were his own main organs
of adaptation as well as sources of conflict, became also the
major instruments of faith. His praying was not only a confessing of sin but at the same time a recapturing of a stable
love object, God. As he experienced rebirth by prayer, he also
came to embrace a new, enduring mother: the Bible, which
became his model of generosity, flowing over with the milk
of grace.

Being identified with Christ, finding Christ within himself,
a new sonship became possible for Luther which allowed him
to see Christ's life in God's face. "The Passion is all that man
can know of God: his conflicts, duly faced, are all that he can
know of himself." In trying to tackle the crucial issues of
each identity crisis as it came, Luther not only solved some of

6. Paul W. Pruyser, "Some Trends in the Psychology of Religion," *Journal
of Religion* 40 (1960):113–29.

his personal problems but also attempted a solution of the theological problem of his time by putting a "new emphasis on man in *inner* conflict and his salvation through introspective perfection." He saw that nature is always divided and that reality can be probed only through paradoxes. "Luther's formulation of a God known to individual man only through the symbolism of the Son's Passion redefined the individual's existence in a direction later pursued in both Kierkegaard's existentialism and Freud's psychoanalysis—methods which lead the individual systematically to his own borders, including the border of his religious ecstasies."[7]

But until rather late in his life Luther's statements about God still contained echoes of his only partially solved personal problem of self-hate and intolerance of disobedience; he would have to live with a God who was neither pure wrath nor pure compassion. "God is given the attribute of *ira misericordiae*—a wrath which is really compassion. With this concept, Luther was at last able to forgive God for being a Father, and grant Him justification."[8]

Attempts to sum up Luther in capsule statements, be it as twice-born man or as typical sufferer from fear, or to contain him in an anal-erotic formula, are doomed to failure. This is not only because Luther was too great to be thus summarized but because he was human, that is, complex and contradictory enough to strain any typology. Only good clinical case-study writing, aided by a comprehensive psychological theory, can avoid such pitfalls; it is sensitive to the inner contrasts as well as the inner consistencies and continuities. Erikson's book proves the point.

Although Erikson's book bears the subtitle "A Study in Psychoanalysis and History," this work is rich enough to suggest many alternative subtitles, among which "A Study in the Psychology of Religion" is a very viable one. Lovers and students of this field will find it vastly enriched by Erikson's articulate application of psychoanalytic concepts. They will

7. Erikson, *Young Man Luther*, pp. 213–14.
8. Ibid., p. 222.

now find that the psychology of religion, with Erikson's chapter added, has come a long way, and that it is a specialty of which to be proud; they will also find that psychoanalytic theory has come a long way, and that it is a tool of which to be envious.

5. Faith and Identity

William Meissner, S.J., M.D.

The tangled web of influences which link the efforts of psychoanalytic inquiry to the perennial objects of theological speculation has no more profoundly perplexing or significant area of
interaction than that of the psychological determinants of the
experience of faith. It is not without significance, then, that
the most telling area of Luther's impact on the religious experience of the Christian world was precisely in the area of
faith. Luther's own religious odyssey, tortured and tormented
as it seems to have been, can be envisioned as an intensely
conflicted and problematic search for the essence of a true
faith. His *justificatio per solam fidem* was in one sense a resolution of that inner torment and conflict, even as it served as a
dialectical challenge, a battle cry, a call to arms in a conflict
that tore the unbroken warp and woof of Europe from top to
bottom. In some sense the divisiveness and torment of the
Reformation can be seen as an externalization of Luther's own
inner conflict—even though the conflict became an external
force of its own right and gathered unto itself forces which
Luther could not have foreseen and could even less have con-
trolled.

The real impact of Luther's greatness, then, lies in the fact
that what could be externalized of his own inner turmoil became the turmoil not only of history, but also internally reflected in the religious consciousness and experience of count-
less millions—not only of his time and culture, but of other
times and other cultures. Erikson does great justice, in fact, to
this aspect of the problem.

But our present concern is somewhat more narrow and specific. We want to examine Luther's quest for faith from the

vantage point of the interplay between psychoanalytic determinants and the more theologically relevant influence of grace.
Within a Christian perspective, faith is subsumed within a
larger theological context that is provided by the salvific action
of the divine will. Faith is thus prompted, elicited, sustained
and fulfilled through the action of grace. Faith thus somehow
expresses the action of divine purposes within the human soul.

Our purpose is to try to examine this intimate intertwining
of divine and human action—not from the point of view of its
theological specifications, but rather from the point of view of
the dynamic significance that it may have within the human
soul. From this point of view Luther's struggle with his own
conscience, his tormented searching for religious truth and
solidarity, his seeking after a salvific experience that would
quell the inner doubts and anguish that tormented his soul
must be seen as taking place under the influence of divine
grace.

Psychologically speaking, it remains a moot point whether
Luther's struggle ever achieved any satisfactory resolution or
not. Erikson does not, and cannot, satisfy us on this point.
Neither does Luther himself. If the case can be made, as Erikson's effort suggests, that a part of Luther's accomplishment
was to achieve a sense of identity that provided sufficient meaning and purposefulness to quell, at least in part, the inner
doubts, conflicts, insecurities, and depressions, the question
nonetheless remains open as to whether he found under grace
those rudiments of inner conviction and abiding trust which
might have provided him a peace beyond all understanding.

Our first task is to trace some of the parameters of Luther's
titanic struggle. We can best do this by following in Erikson's
footsteps, since he has successfully elucidated some of the
major dimensions of Luther's highly conflicted young life. Our
examination of this data will be highly selective, therefore,
and will strike a slightly different note than that stressed in
Erikson's treatment.

Erikson remarks on the sense of criminality—or abiding

unconscious guilt—that seemed to be a consistent element in Luther's inner life. He comments, "Luther all his life felt like some sort of criminal, and had to keep on justifying himself even after his revelation of the universal justification through faith had led him to strength, peace, and leadership."[1] In some measure, of course, such an inner experience of guilt is prompted by the reverse logic which dictates that the severity of punishment should somehow be proportioned to the severity of the crime. Thus the innocence of the child falls victim to the incomprehensible and uncomprehending absolutism of adult consciences that are unable to distinguish between big sins and little sins. Thus little sins are punished with the severity that might be due to major crimes out of an abiding parental preoccupation that, if little sins are not nipped in the bud and crushed with the full weight of parental wrath, they will grow to be heinous crimes. Erikson's comment is to the point: "Criminals are thus often made; since the world treats such small matters as a sure sign of potential criminality, the children may feel confirmed in one of those negative identity fragments which under adverse circumstances can become the predominant identity element."[2] Thus young Martin felt the sting and the lash of the primitive wrath of his father's troubled conscience. But, psychologically speaking, we are well aware that the potential criminality that old Hans had to repress with such rigor was in fact a criminality within himself—a sense of evilness and sinfulness that had to be crushed within, even as it had to be beaten out of his little son. And, if Erikson is correct in judging that the resolution of Luther's crisis of faith brought him strength and leadership, it remains questionable whether it brought him real peace. If old Hans had beaten the sinfulness out of his son, he had also beaten in an inner sense of evil that was not so easily discharged.

Along with a sense of sinfulness there seemed to be a readiness for judgment that haunted Luther at every step.

Kierkegaard once said that Luther always spoke and acted as

1. Erik Erikson, *Young Man Luther* (New York: Norton, 1962), p. 68.
2. Ibid.

if lightning were about to strike behind him the next moment.
He was referring, of course, to the mysterious thunderstorm
considered the revelatory cause of Luther's decision to become
a monk. Yet an excessive expectation of catastrophe, an all-
too-anxious wish to be ready for the judgment, was part of
Martin's world long before that thunderstorm, and it may
have made that storm what it became.[3]

Luther's steps were dogged by the constant fear of death, the
expectation of the sudden catastrophe—like the abiding, if
sometimes unconscious, expectation of the miner in his
father's mines (if not of his father himself) of an unforeseen
disaster to come thundering down upon his head.

Luther lived in the shadow of death. His premonitions of
it cast their dark shadow throughout the whole of his career.
As Erikson comments,

> The counterpart of this waiting, however, is often a fear of an
> early death which would keep the vengeance from ripening
> into leadership; yet the young man often shows signs of preco-
> cious aging, of a melancholy wish for an early end, as if the
> anticipation of prospective deeds tired him. . . . A young
> genius has an implicit life plan to complete; caught by death
> before his time, he would be only a pathetic human frag-
> ment.[4]

So young Martin grew to manhood with a burdened sense of
accountability, a sense of impending judgment which felt itself called to render a total account of life even before it was
lived. He was haunted by a trepidation, an anxiety that prevented, or at least postponed, his own seizing of an identity
before he had passed the test of acceptability of everything
that had gone before.

He was raised in a context of belief—or, more accurately,
of superstitious credulity—which was haunted by demons,
devils, sorcerers, and witches. Such a superstitious matrix provides the locus of the externalization of one's own unconscious
impulses and malicious thoughts. As Erikson says,

> In all magic thinking, the unknown and the unconscious meet

3. Ibid., p. 59.
4. Ibid., p. 83.

at a common frontier: murderous, adulterous, or avaricious wishes, or sudden moods of melancholy or friskiness are all forced upon me by evil-wishing neighbors. Sexual fantasies, too, can best be treated as extraterritorial. Even sexual events, such as an all-too-vivid dream, or a neighbor in one's bed, can be blamed on the devil's sneaky habit of lying underneath sleeping men, or on top of sleeping women: *unter oder oblegen* in Luther's words; *succubus et incubus* in those of theology.[5]

Luther's spiritual world, then, was peopled with malicious forces and spirits whose evil purposes placed him in constant jeopardy or moral catastrophe and danger. It was a spiritualized world in which devils and potential disasters lurked at every turn. The potential for projection in such a magically spiritualized world of experience was very large indeed. Nor does it subtract from the vividness of young Martin's own experience that this was the common clay of spiritual reality in the world in which he lived. It did not diminish the intensity of his own inner guilt and his sense of precariousness and fragility.

Nonetheless, as Erikson suggests, these are not mere superstitions or primitive obsessions. They were also a form of collective mastery of the unknown, which provided a source of shared security in a world full of dangers. They gave the unfamiliar and the unknown a local habitation and a name. Thus if young Martin was haunted by such dangers and insecurities, he was not the only one so haunted. It may be that such shared and commonly experienced projections provide an important starting point for the alleviation of otherwise unmanageable and unmasterable anxieties. We can also note that such relief is offered not simply in communal terms, but serves to alleviate inner intrapsychic dangers and insecurities as well.

To put this overweening sense of criminality, sinfulness, accountability and fragile susceptibility to dangers from the forces of the world and the machinations of the devil into proper perspective, we must remind ourselves of the roots of

5. Ibid., p. 60.

this inner turmoil in the significant internalizations which the young Luther acquired from his parents. Erikson focuses this issue in the following terms:

> Only a boy with a precocious, sensitive, and intense con-
> science could *care* about pleasing his father as much as Martin
> did, or would subject himself to a scrupulous and relentless
> form of self-criticism instead of balancing the outer pressure
> with inventive deviousness and defiance. Martin's reactions
> to his father's pressure are the beginnings of Luther's preoc-
> cupation with matters of individual conscience, a preoccupa-
> tion which went far beyond the requirements of religion as
> then practiced and formulated. Martin took unto himself the
> ideological structure of his parents' consciences: he incorpor-
> ated his father's suspicious severity, his mother's fear of
> sorcery, and their mutual concern about catastrophes to be
> avoided and high goals to be met. Later he rebelled: first
> against his father, to join the monastery; then against the
> Church, to found his own church—at which point, he suc-
> cumbed to many of his father's original values. We can only
> surmise to what extent this outcome was prepared for in
> childhood by a cumulative rebelliousness and by an ever-so-
> clandestine hate (for our conscience, like the medieval god,
> knows everything and registers and counts everything).[6]

Thus Luther took within himself the aggressive and deeply punitive aspects of his father's conscience, even as he took in the more helpless and more victimized aspects identifiable in his mother. He thus carried within him both the brutal perse-cutor and the susceptible and fragile suffering victim. As Erick-son comments, "The double role of the mother as one of the powerless victims of the father's brutality and also as one of his dutiful assistants in meting out punishment to the children may well account for a peculiar split in the mother image. The mother was perhaps cruel only because she had to be, but the father because he wanted to be."[7] We are poignantly reminded of another tortured son who suffered like persecution at the hands of a rigidly and powerfully sadistic father and a power-lessly abetting mother—I refer to the famous case of Daniel

6. Ibid., pp. 73–74.
7. Ibid., p. 70.

Paul Schreber who was to be immortalized by Freud's study.[8]
Schreber's experience of "soul-murder"—whose kinship with
young Martin's beaten submission is worthy of note and further exploration—laid the basis for those pathogenic introjects which formed the substance of his paranoid psychosis. So
Luther's introjection of the brutal aggressor/persecutor in his
father and the passive victim/abettor of the father's will in
his mother provided the inner stuff of his own fragmented
and burdened conscience.

We can remind ourselves that Luther not only saw himself
as the helpless victim of powerful authority figures—replace-
ments for the brutal and punitive figure of the father of his
childhood—but also that he identified with that punitive
power which sought ways to express itself against the submission of the powerless and the helpless. Thus when the Peasants'
Revolt looked to him as their leader, he repulsed them, saying, "No insurrection is ever right no matter what the cause."
Then, as Erikson notes,

> The peasants, as it were, quoted Martin back to Luther. He
> advised compromise, and he, Hans' son, found that he was
> being disobeyed and ignored. He could forgive neither the
> peasants for this, nor later the Jews, whom he had hoped to
> convert with the help of the Scriptures where the Church
> had failed to do so. In 1525 he wrote his pamphlet *Against
> the Robbing and Murdering Hordes of Peasants,* suggesting
> both public and secret massacres in words which could adorn
> the gates of the police headquarters and concentration camps
> of our time. He promised rewards in heaven to those who
> risked their lives in subduing insurrection. One sentence indi-
> cates the full cycle taken by this once beaten-down and then
> disobedient son: "A rebel is not worth answering with argu-
> ments, for he does not accept them. The answer for such
> mouths is a fist that brings blood in the nose."

And Erikson adds, "Do we hear Hans beating the residue of
a stubborn peasant out of his son?"[9]

8. Sigmund Freud, "Psychoanalytic Notes on an Autobiographic Account of
a Case of Paranoia (*dementia paranoides*)," *The Standard Edition of the
Complete Psychological Works of Sigmund Freud* (London: Hogarth Press),
vol. 12, pp. 1–82.
9. *Young Man Luther,* pp. 235–36.

Martin's identification with the aggressive and brutal father seems to be reasonably well established, since we know from his frequent outbursts in later life that he had his father's temper in him. Old Hans must have thought that he had beaten it out of little Martin. In fact the older Luther showed his greatest temper in beating the temper out of his children. The psychological mechanisms for the instilling of hatred and a willful violence in children are clearly delineated. The brutalizing impulses of the parent are introjected by the child and become a part of his own inner world. They thus become the stuff out of which subsequent projections are elaborated. Erikson touches on this aspect in the following words:

> Here, I think, is the origin of Martin's doubt that the father, when he punishes you, is really guided by love and justice rather than by arbitrariness and malice. This early doubt later was projected on the Father in heaven with such violence that Martin's monastic teachers could not help noticing it. "God does not hate you, you hate him," one of them said; and it was clear that Martin, searching so desperately for his own justification, was also seeking a formula of eternal justice which would justify God as a judge.[10]

Thus the forbidding presence of old Hans and the anticipation of his punishment permeated the Luther family and served to intensify the ambivalence in the relationship between father and son. Young Martin was overwhelmed with a pervasive dread and fear of his father, which left him with a heavy burden of guilt and feeling of inadequacy, along with a longing admiration of the father and a wish for closeness and acceptance that was to remain unsatisfied. As Erikson notes, "Where rebellion and deviousness are thus successfully undercut, and where, on the other hand, the father's alcoholic, sexual, and cruel self-indulgence obviously break through his moral mask, a child can only develop a precocious conscience, a precocious self-steering and eventually an obsessive mixture of obedience and rebelliousness."[11]

10. Ibid., p. 58.
11. Ibid., p. 123.

Thus the brutalizing and primitively punitive figure of old Hans became the prototype in young Martin's mind of the jealous and vengeful God whose loving care of his children was lost in the clouds of destructive malice, unforgiving judgment, and punitive retribution. The face of God to whom Luther looked for that profoundly meaningful experience of faith and trust became in fact the face of old Hans, a harsh, punitive, and brutally remorseless god. It led Luther, again and again, to repudiate God in tormented rebellion and to repudiate himself in a malignant and obsessive melancholy. His later focus on figures such as the pope and the devil became obsessive and paranoid, but it seems clear that these figures represent a transference from the pervasive influence of old Hans against whom Luther had rebelled with violent defiance, even as previously he had submitted himself with self-effacing and compliant obedience. It is thus not without significance that the form of Luther's defiance was to express itself in terms of anal vulgarity and obsessive and willful stubbornness.

It was in the context of this inner struggle between Luther's needs to defy and comply that the struggle took place over what Erikson has called "negative identity." The quest for total and final values could only be satisfied by the attainment of values that were completely foreign to everything that had been held up to him as desirable and suitable. Martin was inexorably caught up in this struggle between passive compliance and stubborn resistance. His compliance to his father's wishes on one level was met by the impulsive repudiation of the father's secular aspirations by Martin's embracing— prompted by the perils of the thunderstorm—of traditional monasticism. But the rebellion was not quelled even then. His compliance and fulfillment of the expectations of his religious superiors had once again to be challenged by the rebellious impulses of the crusading reformer. Erikson describes this phenomenon in the following terms:

We will call all self-images, even those of a highly idealistic nature, which are diametrically opposed to the dominant values of an individual's upbringing, parts of a *negative identity*— meaning an identity which he has been warned *not* to become, which he can become only with a divided heart, but which he nevertheless finds himself compelled to become, protesting his wholeheartedness.[12]

Or, as Erikson identifies negative identity elsewhere, it is "an identity perversely based on all those identifications and roles which, at critical stages of development, had been presented to the individual as most undesirable or dangerous, and yet as most real."[13] The inner tension seeks desperately its resolution since it finds the diffusion of identity attendant upon such states of unresolved inner ambivalence intolerable. As Erikson notes, ". . . many a late adolescent, if faced with continuing diffusion, would rather be nobody or somebody bad, or indeed, dead—and this totally, and by free choice—than be not-quite-somebody."[14]

Thus the young Luther found within himself an inner compulsion to embrace that willful stubbornness and rebelliousness that old Hans had worked so hard and so vehemently to suppress. It is important, however, to note once again that in the crystallization of this form of negative identity, the young Luther was in fact entering the course of an identification with the recalcitrant, rebellious, and provocative aspects which old Hans had successfully beaten down in himself, so that his external face was one of civility and compliant observance, while he left room for its unbridled expression in the violence he unleashed toward his own family.

But there was a further step to the shaping of Luther's own identity. Erikson describes it in these terms:

To these we must add the period of the completion of identity development at adolescence, which results in a massive glorification of some of the individual's constituent elements, and repudiation of others. In the life of a man like Luther (and in

12. Ibid., p. 102.
13. Erik H. Erikson, *Identity and the Life Cycle* (New York: International Universities Press, 1959), p. 131.
14. Ibid., p. 132.

lesser ways in all lives), another screen is strongly suggested: the beginning of an artificial identity, the moment when life suddenly becomes biography. In many ways life began for Luther all over again when the world grabbed eagerly at his ninety-five theses, and forced him into the role of rebel, reformer, and spiritual dictator. Everything before that then became memorable only insofar as it helped him to rationalize his disobediences. Maybe this motivation is behind most attempts at historifying the past.[15]

Consequently, if we can take the vignette of Luther's hammering the ninety-five theses to the Wittenberg cathedral door as somehow symbolic, we can take it not only as an act of rebellion which resolved the inner tensions and conflict within Luther's own troubled soul and conscience, but also as a challenge and a stimulus to which the troubled soul of Christian Europe responded. It was the pull of the trigger, the touch of the match, which ignited the deeply conflicted forces in the troubled consciences of millions, such that the partial resolution of Luther's own identity crisis became a catalyst for the conscience of Europe and planted the seeds of religious rebellion which came into fruition in the form of a powerful religious movement. The reverberations of those hammer blows on the cathedral door in 1517 were to send shock waves through the whole of western Europe, and the reverberations were not to be quieted for centuries, not until millions had lost their lives in the blood bath of religious wars and persecution.

So it was that Luther's inner struggle resonated with the inner conflicts, doubts, and suppressed hostilities and ambivalences of many. The seeds of rebellion had lain fallow for centuries. The inner unity that had held Catholic Europe together had become weakened by the wearing away of inner stresses and strains. The church had become excessively secularized. It had felt the influence of new wealth and a new flood of influences born of the Renaissance. The papacy had become embroiled in Italian and European politics, and when Luther visited Rome in his earlier monkish days he was treated to a

15. *Young Man Luther*, p. 54.

shocking spectacle of deviousness, hauteur, display, and corruption.

But closer to home he launched his attack against a practice
that had become odious in the eyes of good Germans and was
associated with the exploitation by and effrontery of the
Italian representatives of the pope, who must have seemed to
the provincial Germans of Luther's time as agents of a foreign
power. The money raised from the sale of indulgences was
destined for the enrichment of the papacy. Certainly the German princes who rallied to Luther's cause stood to gain considerably, not merely financially by stemming the flow of
German money to the papacy, but also by the confiscation of
wealthy monastic properties and churches. For them the embracing of Luther's cause served not only the ends of German
patriotism, but also provided an opportunity for defying the
power of the emperor and the pope.

Despite the many influences which ripened the brew—historical, economic, social and cultural—Luther was still the
catalyst. His defiance and flamboyant, even sometimes violent,
rhetoric fanned the flames and helped to focus the latent rebellious attitudes which until then had lain dormant in the German
soul. His dramatic and defiant stance at Worms in 1521 became the watchword and the battle cry of the Reformation:
"Hier stehe ich. Ich kann nicht anders. Gott hilf mir. Amen."
In essence he provided an ideology which served to resolve
the ambivalence of his own tortured conscience and took hold
of the frustrated desires and fears of his contemporaries. As
Erikson puts it:

> Ideological leaders, so it seems, are subject to excessive fears
> which they can master only by reshaping the thoughts of their
> contemporaries; while those contemporaries are always glad
> to have their thoughts shaped by those who so desperately
> care to do so. Born leaders seem to fear only more consciously
> what in some form everybody fears in the depths of his inner
> life; and they convincingly claim to have an answer.[16]

Thus ideology emerges as a powerfully constructive force in

16. Ibid., p. 110.

the sustaining of identity. Erikson defines it as "an unconscious tendency underlying religious and scientific as well as political thought: the tendency at a given time to make facts amenable to ideas, and ideas to facts, in order to create a world image convincing enough to support the collective and the individual sense of identity."[17] Thus it is through the forming of an ideology—a system of beliefs and values—that the group achieves an identity which it properly assumes as its own, and achieves the coherence and solidarity of membership that insures its persistence and effectiveness as a group. Without such an ideology the group is nothing and it has no inner life.

It is only in terms of such an ideology that members can attach themselves to the group with a sense of commitment and fidelity which provides an abiding sense of membership and belonging, and a sharing in the objectives and purposes for which the group exists. This is particularly true of religious ideologies, since they touch upon and preserve those purposes which involve the most profound levels of human existence. Thus the commitment and fidelity to an ideology provides one of the strongest supports and foundations for the emerging sense of identity in adolescence as well as its sustaining and preservation in later stages of life.

But the blessings of ideology are not unmixed. Erikson's comments deserve to be quoted here also:

> Ideologies seem to provide meaningful combinations of the oldest and the newest in a group's ideals. They thus channel the forceful earnestness, the sincere asceticism, and the eager indignation of youth toward that social frontier where the struggle between conservatism and radicalism is most alive. On that frontier, fanatic ideologists do their busy work and psychopathic leaders their dirty work; but there also, true leaders create significant solidarity. All ideologies ask for, as the prize for the promised possession of a future, uncompromising commitment to some absolute hierarchy of values and some rigid principles of conduct: . . . it is in the totalism and exclusiveness of some ideologies that the superego is apt to regain its territory from identity: for when established identi-

17. Ibid., p. 22.

ties become outworn or unfinished ones threaten to remain
incomplete, special crises compel men to wage holy wars, by
the cruelest means, against those who seem to question or
threaten their unsafe ideological bases.[18]

Thus if we are to judge by Luther's own continuing struggles
with the enemies he proposed for himself—by his vituperative
and vindictive tirades cast in terms of the most outrageous
vulgarities and obscenities, and the paranoid cast of his struggles which continued to the end of his life with the pope, the
devil, and the Church of Rome—the ideology that he created
and its theological rationalization did not serve to quell the
inner doubts and uncertainties, the conflictual torments which
seemed to gnaw away at the foundations of his sense of truth-
fulness and purposefulness and seemed to provide a shifting
sand on which the foundations of his own inner sense of
identity rested.

In a larger sense the same seems to be at issue in the subsequent history not only of Lutheranism, but of Protestantism
and its persistent antagonist, Catholicism. We can ask ourselves if we do not and cannot recognize in these vicious and
violent struggles that marked the course of the subsequent
centuries the erosion and the demise of ideology. Further, we
must ask ourselves why it is that the power of ideology is so
constrained and so undermined. Why is it that religious
ideologies, conceived in inspiration and buttressed by the tradition of centuries, seem unable to sustain the solidity and
inner power of a maturely grasped and purposefully sustained
identity in its adherents? Must we recognize that ideology is
not enough? May we not, in fact, be faced by the stark realization that ideologies themselves are born of inner conflict and
ambivalence and ultimately bear the mark of their origins?

The problematic to which these considerations lead us is
this: in Martin's tormented quest for true faith did he in fact
achieve Luther's ideology with regard to the inner satisfaction
of faith? It becomes immediately evident that faith and ideol-

18. *Identity and the Life Cycle*, p. 158.

ogy are not necessarily correlatives. But how do they differ? What does it mean to achieve an ideology without faith? Or to have faith without an ideology? The adherence to an ideology calls for a rudimentary commitment, a credulity and credence which makes such adherence possible. But this need not yet be faith. The faith, which we seek for ourselves, and which was the object of Martin's quest, is a spiritual faith which in some sense derives from and expresses the deepest dimensions of trusting adherence in a human soul. It is also a dimension of human religious experience which expresses profoundly the sustaining and curative influence of divine grace. We must seek to know this faith better than we do.

I will take as my keynote some illuminating comments recently provided by Lynch on the question of the images by which we conceive of an experience of faith. He writes:

> The first is an imaging of faith as the most primary, the most elemental force in human nature; it is a force which *precedes* what we ordinarily call knowledge and all forms of specific knowing; this force is uneducated and needs education; it is educated by knowledge of every kind, by people of every degree, by irony but not by every irony; last of all it is formed and educated by Christ. . . . It is in this powerful, turbulent, primal form that we must first image faith, . . . but the first understanding of it . . . is that of a primal and broad force of belief, promise, and fidelity which—by its presence or absence, by its operation or collapse, by its goodness or fury, by its fidelities or treacheries—shapes (or misshapes) the welfare, shall I say the very existence, of men and women in life and society.[19]

We must first inquire whence comes this elemental force in terms of its psychological roots and derivatives.

In his study of faith, Martin Buber[20] remarks that although there are many contents of faith, we really only know faith in two basic forms, one form from the fact that I trust someone else without necessarily being able to offer adequate reasons for that trust, and the other from the fact that I can acknowl-

19. W. F. Lynch, S.J., *Images of Faith: An Exploration of the Ironic Imagination* (Notre Dame: University of Notre Dame Press, 1973), pp. 9–10.
20. Martin Buber, *Two Types of Faith* (New York: Harper and Row, 1961).

edge something to be true, also without being able to provide sufficient reason. Consequently faith is not a matter of inadequate intelligence, but derives essentially from the relationship to a trusted person or thing acknowledged as true. The believing consequently is not a matter of mere rationality, but it engages one's whole being; it is more than rationality and more than feeling. Buber continues, "The relationship of trust depends on a state of contact, a contact of my entire being with the one in whom I trust, the relationship of acknowledging depends upon an act of acceptance, an acceptance by my entire being of that which I acknowledge to be true."[21]

The process of faith cannot be adequately conceived without embracing both trust and acknowledgement. Thus the intellectualistic emphasis in Christian theology is elaborated in the context of living trust in the revealing God. If that faith, which was born in the patriarchal migrations of the desert, took shape in the tradition of guidance and covenant and expressed itself as perseverance and trust both in that guidance and the promises of that covenant, the later doctrinal emphasis on intellectual acknowledgement cannot abstract itself from the psychological roots that vitalize all faith. As Buber comments, "When anybody trusts someone he of course also believes what the other says."[22]

The influence of trust touches the deepest structures of the human mind. The capacity for trust is an expression of one's whole self; it engages one's total being. But as Buber has observed, the realization of faith does not take place in a single decision made at a single moment which is then decisive for the existence of the decider; rather it takes place in a person's whole life, in the totality of one's relationships, not only to God but also to one's world and to oneself. Faith is not, therefore, an isolated act standing apart from the context of the believer's life cycle. It is indeed a process that has a history and a genesis and thus represents the fundamental disposition of human existence.

21. Ibid., p. 8.
22. Ibid., p. 35.

In probing the relevancies of basic trust, Erikson has cast a powerful illumination on the intertwining of faith and trust. He observes:

> The psychological observer must ask whether or not in any area under observation religion and tradition are living psychological forces creating the kind of faith or conviction which permeates a parent's personality and thus reinforces the child's basic trust . . . in the world's trustworthiness. . . . All religions have in common the periodical childlike surrender to a Provider or providers who can dispense earthly fortune as well as spiritual health; the demonstration of one's smallness and dependence through the medium of reduced posture and humble gesture; the admission in prayer and song of misdeeds, of misthoughts, and of evil intention; the admission of inner division and the consequent appeal for inner unification by divine guidance; the need for clearer self-delineation and self-restriction; and finally the insight that individual trust must become a common faith, individual mistrust a commonly formulated evil, while the individual's need for restoration must become part of the ritual practice of many, and must become a sign of the trustworthiness of the community.[23]

Thus it seems that the capacity for trust is an implicit dimension of faith. It represents a receptivity, an openness, a willingness to accept and integrate God's presence and his Word. Faith then involves a basic trust in God, a sense of confidence in his love and saving power, and in addition a sense of confidence in one's self and one's capacity to make the commitment of self which is called for, to bridge the chasm between the security and self-reliance of reason and the absurdity and other-reliance of faith.

The basic sense of trust—the essential ingredient of other-reliance—is initiated from the first moments of infantile experience. In its taking shape, there is also a laying-down and a forming of the rudiments of faith. Lynch describes this process of faithful coming-to-being in the following terms:

> Perhaps we can say that it comes into force (which is better than saying that it comes into being) as soon as promises begin to be made to it. These promises need not always be

23. *Identity and the Life Cycle*, pp. 64–65.

spoken. I have said that most of the fundamental forms of faith are carved without words into the very structures of nature. The womb of the mother is a promise to the child. From earliest childhood faith becomes an increasingly active dialogue with promise. It is almost a dance of gestures between the mother and the child, a dance of offer, response, increasing complexity, testing, verification, misplacements, anticipations, overdemands, joys, cries, screams, withdrawals, renewals. There are so many steady, verified promises that there is a law of God: Honor thy father and thy mother. They are the makers and executors of promise.[24]

The same words can be said, parenthetically and analogously, of the process of psychotherapy which hopes to bring faith and trust and promise where they have never flourished or have been destroyed.

We can say more than simply that faith rests upon such fundamental trust, for it is precisely in faith that trust finds its unique expression. Erikson remarks, "The ratio and relation of basic trust to basic mistrust established during early infancy determines much of the individual's capacity for simple faith. . . ."[25] Man's capacity to turn to God a trusting face depends upon the basic disposition of trust. One's openness to God in faith, one's confidence in God in faith, one's trusting in the trustworthiness of God in faith, the confidence of one's own trustworthiness before God in faith, and the basic trust of one's own sense of judgment and self-commitment in the faithful leap into the darkness of the absurd, all these are impossible without an adequate foundation in basic trust.

It is in these terms that Erikson places the inner struggle that Martin Luther engaged in and out of which he wrought his greatest religious and theological accomplishment. Erikson observes:

> His basic contribution was a living reformulation of faith. This marks him as a theologian of the first order; it also indicates his struggle with the ontogenetically earliest and most basic problems of life. He saw as his life's work a new delineation of faith and will, of religion and law: for it is clear

24. Lynch, *Images of Faith*, p. 125.
25. *Young Man Luther*, p. 255.

that organized religiosity, in circumstances where the faith in a world order is monopolized by religion, is the institution which tries to give dogmatic permanence to a reaffirmation of that basic trust—and a renewed victory over that basic mistrust—with which each human being emerges from early infancy. In this way organized religion cements the faith which will support future generations.[26]

However solidified and recapitulated, true faith in order to remain, psychologically speaking, an elemental force in religious experience must not lose contact with its motivating infantile determinants. Thus its trusting is a reaching back to those decisive moments of childhood trust. That reaching back is equivalently an unconscious regressive moment within the vitality of faith. But it is not merely a return, whether conscious or unconscious; it is a recapitulation, a reorganization, a reintegration, a synthetic process within the ego that summarizes and reasserts basic trust.

But more than a reassertion, it is a creative expression of something beyond trust and far more significant. The regressive return to trust carries within it the seeds of its own capacity to transcend itself. There is something similar to what Kierkegaard expressed in terms of the infinite resignation—man resigns all finite goods in order to find them again in virtue of faith. He must in a sense resign the imperfection and finitude of basic trust in order to reach beyond it and thereby recapture more profoundly and more meaningfully true faith. Erikson has touched upon this creative potentiality of faith in the following terms:

> But must we call it regression if man thus seeks again the earliest encounters of his trustful past in his efforts to reach a hoped-for and eternal future? Or do religions partake of man's ability, even as he regresses, to recover creatively? At their creative best, religions retrace our earliest inner experiences, giving tangible form to vague evils, and reaching back to the earliest individual sources of trust; at the same time, they keep alive the common symbols of integrity distilled by the generations. If this is partial regression, it is a regression

26. Ibid., p. 257.

which, in retracing firmly established pathways, returns to the present amplified and clarified.[27]

A further essential in the notion of faith is its relation to fidelity. Faith involves an element of perdurance, constancy, the security of stable persistence, the assurance of God's continued faithfulness to his promises, a confidence in the finality and eternity of what one believes—in short, fidelity. There is a correspondence and a mutual reciprocity between the stability of belief and God's faithfulness on the one hand, and the psychological dimension of fidelity on the other. The commitment of faith consequently is not a commitment of transient and momentary assent. It is rather a trusting commitment of one's total being in an absolute perduring relationship to God.

To Erikson's mind fidelity represents a peculiar ego-quality which bespeaks "the ability to sustain loyalties freely pledged in spite of the inevitable contradictions of value systems."[28] Fidelity is thus a major component of the sense of emerging identity which shapes itself typically during adolescence and receives its inspiration from confirming ideology. Thus both identity and fidelity are necessary but not sufficient components of ethical strength.

Faith is not the only source or receptacle of fidelity. But it stands forth as the most important and prototypical one, inasmuch as its scope and intention of constancy and meaning extend beyond all other ideologies that can lay claim to human fidelity.

Consequently it must be said that all faith has a psychological capacity to sustain the individual sense of identity. But beyond these dynamic and identity-sustaining dimensions, there lies a risk. The commitment to ideology tends to be exclusive, even as ideologies themselves tend to be intolerant of each other. The danger, of course, is overcommitment. The history of religious faith carries a fecund record of such over-

27. Ibid., p. 264.
28. Erik H. Erikson, *Insight and Responsibility* (New York: Norton, 1964), p. 125.

commitments. In fact, such overcommitment or overidentification really distorts the significance of the ideology that made commitment a necessity to begin with, and served to provide it with its strength and purpose.

The outcome is not merely a distortion of ideology as such, but it provides the basis for a fault in identity as well. To look at it from another perspective, it remains true that a fault in identity can also underlie overcommitment. The implicit incapacity of the ego provides a channel for the expression of deneutralized aggressive and libidinal drives, legitimized in a sense by a distorted and perverted ideology. The issue becomes a blend of sadism, sanctimoniousness, and hypermoralism against which true religious faith must wage an endless and unremitting struggle. Lynch's comments are to the point:

> It is the mark of an elite group to claim that it alone knows the meaning of words, it alone has the true faith, it alone is on the inside of things. If there are many forms of irony—many forms of language in which words say more than they seem or say the opposite of their seeming—this is the special irony of the elite, to declare that they alone are on the inside of words and things. This kind of irony is often used to create a sense of identity; it marks people off from the everyday run of people. . . . It is clear that it is divisive. It does not *pass through* a lesser or the lower or the literal way; it is cabalistic and secret. It does not give any real power to the lower to move into the higher meaning. It does not want to move through the lower, but to transcend it. Secretly, therefore, it has no use for the human and is never really funny.[29]

Such a distorted and excessive sense of exclusiveness, then, is quite inconsistent with true faith, just as it is ultimately inconsistent with true identity. In a sense, we must admit that the essence of faith comes to lie beyond fidelity, although it is impossible, in psychological terms, to translate that essence without putting.it in terms of fidelity, or, as we have seen, in terms of basic trust. Fidelity is, after all, a finite good, which must—if we remain true to Kiekegaard's insight—be resigned if we are to have true faith. But the resignation is a moment

29. Lynch, *Images of Faith*, pp. 98–99.

beyond which absurdity and absolute relation become possible. To be able to pass beyond fidelity thus requires a strength of the ego surpassing mere ideology. And to reach beyond fidelity is paradoxically not to surrender it, but to find it again; but in this refinding it is enriched, more profound and more meaningful in virtue of the faith within which it is subsumed.

A vital question that concerns us here is whether Luther's tormented inner struggle was ever able to reach the level of ideological commitment, or even further, to reach the expanses of true faith. Erikson's treatment of Luther's psychological development would tend to lean in the direction of affirmation —namely, that Luther's religious struggle achieved the level of a confirming ideology which served to crystallize the elements of his tattered and diffused identity and tended to fuse them into a meaningful configuration, which established his self-generated and communally sustained identity as reformer, guide, and spiritual leader.

As we have suggested, the evidence is not conclusive, and there is plenty of evidence to suggest that Luther remained a tormented and troubled soul even till the end. The doubts remain, and there have been many people—particularly religious antagonists—who have not been slow to point them out and to make of them what they will. Nearly a score of years before Erikson's treatment of Luther was written, Erich Fromm provided his own analysis of the sweep of economic, social, and cultural factors which joined themselves to Luther's rebellion to create the onslaught of the Reformation. Fromm picks up the inner contradiction between Luther's inner torment and the self-justifying security of his appeal to faith. He writes:

> Luther's doctrine of faith as an indubitable subjective experience of one's own salvation may at first glance strike one as an extreme contradiction to the intense feeling of doubt which was characteristic for his personality and his teachings up to 1518. Yet, psychologically, this change from doubt to certainty, far from being contradictory, has a causal relation. We must remember what has been said about the nature of this

doubt: it was not the rational doubt which is rooted in the freedom of thinking and which dares to question established views. It was the irrational doubt which springs from the isolation and powerlessness of an individual whose attitude toward the world is one of anxiety and hatred. . . . The compulsive quest for certainty, as we find with Luther, is not the expression of genuine faith, but is rooted in the need to conquer the unbearable doubt. Luther's solution is one which we find present in many individuals today, who do not think in theological terms: namely to find certainty by the elimination of the isolated individual self, by becoming an instrument in the hands of an overwhelmingly strong power outside of the individual. For Luther this power was God and in unqualified submission he sought certainty. But although he thus succeeded in silencing his doubts to some extent, they never really disappeared; up to his last day he had attacks of doubt which he had to conquer by renewed efforts towards submission. Psychologically, faith has two entirely different meanings. It can be the expression of an inner relatedness to mankind and affirmation of life; or it can be a reaction formation against a fundamental feeling of doubt, rooted in the isolation of the individual and his negative attitude toward life. Luther's faith had that compensatory quality.[30]

Consequently the question of Luther's resolution of the inner struggle remains unresolved. Our purpose here, however, is neither to settle that question nor to pass judgment on Luther. Rather our intent is to try to elucidate the role of faith in such a tension-filled and existentially anguished searching and seeking. To better envision the role of faith in this fateful process, I would like to focus at this juncture on the function of faith in the psychic economy.

Faith is a dynamic process that embraces and expresses man's total existence. It implies a reaching back to the basic wishes and impulses that characterize the most primary and basic human experiences. The reaching back is both regressive and recapitulative, but it returns to infantile sources with reorganizing and revitalizing consequences. It finds in them sources

30. Erich Fromm, *Escape from Freedom* (New York: Avon Books, 1965), pp. 96–97.

of power and reconstitutive creativity which derive their motivational impetus from the vital stratum of man's psychic structure.

In addition, faith functions as a derivative from and a dynamic extension of basic capacities that have emerged from the course of individual developmental history. It requires and depends on, as well as enlarges and enriches, the basic sense of trust with which the infant emerges from his earliest developmental experiences in the relationship with his mother. Thus faith builds upon trust, but reciprocally it also builds trust. Insofar as trust is always imperfect, carrying within it the burden of mistrust, so in all belief there is the burden of unbelief, just as in all unbelief there lurk the rudiments of belief. Thus believer and unbeliever are more closely related than either realizes or cares to admit.

True faith further embraces and builds upon man's inner capacity for fidelity. The emergence of faith, therefore, must wait upon the emergence of fidelity and a sense of personal identity. But even as it touches them, it transforms them. Fidelity becomes not merely an adherence to an ideology, but is enlarged and enriched in meaning and purposefulness. Moreover identity itself is profoundly affected, since in faith man finds the true and authentic validity of his existence. Thus faith is a transforming process that touches all parts of the psychic structure and reorganizes them and integrates them into a more mature and effective pattern of functioning.

Faith serves, therefore, an integrative function in the psychic economy. Consequently, true faith is restorative, recuperative, and effectively maturing. We must hasten to add, however, that faith rarely achieves all these functions, or that it achieves them only partially. The impoverishment of faith derives from many causes. As a process, it endures many vicissitudes and rarely if ever survives them unimpaired. One can ask whether all believers really have faith. Kierkegaard was sure that few in fact did. It is perhaps safer and more charitable to say that most believers have some minimal degree of faith, but the fullness of faith is rare; it requires a degree of ego strength and the development of identity that few in fact possess.

I would like to suggest here that the failure of faith is correlative in some degree to the distortion of ideology. In Luther's case, there were both ideological rebellion and adherence to a new and personally more meaningful ideology—particularly in his reassuring notion of justification without works. Consequently the defects in ideological commitment can be a matter of degree, extending from degrees of excessive overcommitment, through degrees of defective undercommitment, to the ranges of ideological rebellion and rejection of commitment.

The psychopathology of rebellion and rejection has its own peculiarities which merit discussion. Certainly it has undeniable pertinence for understanding Luther's psychology. But that psychology cannot be divorced from an understanding of its opposite, namely, excessive compliance and adherence. As Erikson has clearly pointed out, we are able to see both sides of the coin operating in Luther.

What I wish to suggest here is that the distortion of ideology, whether by excess or defect, can result in the formation of a "false self." The notion of false self was introduced by Winnicott in 1965,[31] and carries with it implications that need to be examined in relation to the problem of identity and the formation of identity. An underlying problem is the exclusivity of ideologies and the pressures exerted by ideological groups, which demand relatively unquestioning adherence and compliance in the endorsement of their particular ideologies. Such ideological commitments tend to set themselves off against other ideologies which are decried as heretical, dangerous, evil, and so forth.

The fragile identity, however, which commits itself unreservedly and unquestioningly to such an ideology does so out of a sense of compliance and out of a need to overcome, compensate for, and defend against the pervasive inner sense of fragility, weakness, inadequacy and powerlessness. In such

31. D. W. Winnicott, *The Maturation Process and the Facilitating Environment* (New York: International Universities Press, 1965).

circumstances, the adherence to an ideology does not bind the inner wounds, and it leaves the inner sense of fragmented and fragile identity little better off than before. Nonetheless, there can arise a false sense of identity that builds itself around the false self-configuration that derives its strength and stability out of the compliant adherence to its respective ideology, together with the approval and sustaining acknowledgement given it by the group with which it shares and participates in that ideology and that set of values. One variant of such a false-self organization is that which attaches itself through compliance and commitment to a group ideology, thus stabilizing its fragmented and fragile sense of identity. Another variant, however, corresponds to what Erikson describes as "negative identity"—an identity formed and sustained in the rejection of and rebellion against a proffered ideology. It is a false self rooted in defiance rather than compliance.

Such a formula comes strikingly close to the formulations which Erikson uses to describe the links between ideology and identity in the positive and constructive frame of reference that he intends them. If the differences are subtle, they are nonetheless important. My own feeling would be that one useful way to discriminate and test the difference is that, in the measure to which identity fails or becomes distorted, and the false-self organization takes its place, there is a corresponding need for enemies. In other words the false self is ultimately built on a substructure of defensive introjects, which can only be sustained and defended in terms of correlative projections which see opposing ideologies and commitments in terms of persecutory threats and malicious destructive intentions towards the in-group and the self. If we remind ourselves for a moment of the extent of human prejudice, bigotry, and conflict among nations, races, and classes, we can assure ourselves that the matter in hand is the basic stuff of human experience —and may in fact be universal.

If we undertake to schematize this view of the linkage between identity and faith—with the attendant risks of any sche-

matization, namely, that it may be interpreted as a simplification
—the distortions of ideology, which we have been discussing,
can be linked to the formation of a false identity as a component
of a false-self organization. On the other hand, the mature and
constructive expression of ideology to which Erikson addresses
himself can be linked with the emergence of a sense of personal identity, that conscious sense of individual identity and
striving for continuity of personal character, which involves an
evolving configuration which "gradually integrates constitutional givens, idiosyncratic libidinal needs, favorite capacities,
significant identification, effective defenses, successful sublima-
tions, and consistent roles."[32]

The entrance of faith into this process, however, adds a
new and different dimension. As Luther himself commented, a
man without spirituality becomes his own exterior. The exte-
riority of compliance and adherence is what we have described
in terms of a false-self organization. The entrance of faith,
however, adds a dynamic dimension which leads the process of
identity formation to transcend itself. It is the elemental force
of faith, then, dynamized and motivated by the power of grace,
which elicits and elaborates a spiritual identity. The spiritual
identity builds on and perfects personal identity—*gratia perficit
naturam*.

Faith, then, is only one dimension of that spiritual identity
which emerges under the action of grace, acting through and
with the synthetic capacities of the ego. Its action is thus in
some sense reparative, curative, and supportive of the underlying identity within which it functions and expresses itself.
The exploration of the psychology of faith is thus an exploration into some of the relationships that exist between spiritual
identity, so conceived, and the personal identity upon which
it builds and which, in building, it enriches and transforms.
I have attempted the initial and rudimentary steps of such an

32. Erikson, *Identity and the Life Cycle*, p. 116.
33. William W. Meissner, *Foundations for a Psychology of Grace* (Glenrock,
N.J.: Paulist Press, 1966), and "Notes on the Psychology of Faith," *Journal
of Religion and Health* 8 (1969):47–55.

understanding elsewhere,[33] and at this juncture can only indicate its relevance and centrality.

The basic question, to which this reflection is addressed, is
this: can a true sense of identity—transcending the vicissitudes
of ideology and loyalties partially conceived and exclusively
pledged—be achieved and sustained without the elemental
motivating power of faith, generated and energized by the
persistent influence of grace? Or must we recognize that the
claims of ideology, the pledging of human loyalties and fideli-
ties, can provide only partial resolutions for the fragmentations
and diffusions that afflict the inner divisions of the human
condition?

A further note that must be added to this consideration is
that faith takes place in relation to a community of believers
and in relation to institutionalized religions. These provide a
context of social integration by which the faith of a given
community rejuvenates and replenishes itself from the input
of individual faith. Even if the faith of the community so
enforces the faith of the individual, the relationship is nonetheless precarious. Faith is essentially a dynamic process. The
institution of faith, however, is cast in static, dogmatic formulae
and repetitious ritual and cult. The vitality of the process and
the renewed significance of the objects of faith must be related.

The personal act of belief and what is grasped in the act of
belief are distinguishable but inseparable. *Fides qua* and *fides
quae creditur* form a totality. Belief is always belief in something. The process cannot be cast simply in dogmatic terms,
since its very nature is radical openness. It is always an inten-
tional and existential act. The complexities of the relationship
between faith as act of belief and faith as content of belief
belong to a theology of faith rather than to its psychology, yet
it seems reasonable to insist that the reaffirmation of trust, the
enrichment of fidelity, and the clarification of identity are
somehow stabilized and enriched by a participation in the
shared meaning of communal beliefs.

To bring this reflection to a close, we must remind ourselves that we stand at a most intricate and problematic inter-section of the problems of psychopathology, psychic health and identity formation, and the restorative and transforming action of grace. The elements of faith involve a complex inter-play of these multiple factors. The case of Luther and his profoundly dramatic religious experience provides us with a probing study of the powerful actions of grace stirring within a tormented human soul. We cannot judge the outcome of Luther's struggle, nor can we absolve him of the powerful contaminants of primitive hatred and persecutory anxiety.

Like the unremitting furies, the devils never left Martin alone. They were buried deep within his heart and soul. Psy-chologically speaking, they were embedded within the complex or pathogenic introjects which came from the brutal and primi-tive image of old Hans and the victimized vulnerability of Martin's mother. Around these pathogenic introjects was organized a false self based upon those elements of the repressed parental conscience, which young Martin had interna-lized and had become his own.

I would like to suggest that powerful and graceful forces were unleashed in Martin's soul, drawing him toward a greater freedom, a greater integrity, and more secure and creative autonomy. His first attempts at rebellion came in his religious conversion, but he succeeded in merely substituting one false self for another. For his compliance to the secular tyranny of his father he substituted another which found him in obedien-tial subservience to a more spiritual tyranny. The struggle of submission and defiance had been moved from the external realm into the interior realm of the soul.

The second rebellion exchanged one spiritual ideology for another. It exchanged the ideology of obediential compliance to God's all-powerful will, which required the satisfaction of that perfection-demanding will through continuing good works —an enterprise which Martin felt was beyond his grasp be-cause of the evil contamination that flowed from within (again the pathogenic introjects)—for the security and assurance of an ideology of justification through simple faith. If in each rebellion and at each stage of the struggle Martin was able to win some greater degree of freedom, it seems probable that he was never able to shake himself loose from the inner torments and malignant evils that possessed his heart. And it suggests to us that the power of faith in the greatest souls may not be limited by the constraints of dogmatic rigidities and ideological persuasion.

6. Psychohistory as Religious Narrative: The Demonic Role of Hans Luther in Erikson's Saga of Human Evolution

Roger A. Johnson

When Erikson introduced the notion of psychohistory in *Young Man Luther*, the meaning of that term seemed fairly clear: the utilization of a particular psychological theory—in Erikson's case, his distinctive version of psychoanalytic ego psychology—to interpret selected personalities or events of the past. As such, psychohistory appeared to be a subdiscipline of history, a new methodology available to the historian. The contributions and/or deficiencies of the method would be judged according to the norms of historical scholarship. Only later, with the publication of Erikson's volume on Gandhi, did it become apparent that psychohistory also had a second meaning, namely, a particular psychological view of the development of history as a whole—including the evolutionary antecedents of history, the urgent ethical crises of the present, and hopes for the future. In this latter sense of the term, psychohistory clearly bore more affinity to religious narrative, theology, and the philosophy of history than to the modern discipline of history. Not only a methodological tool for exploring the past, psychohistory also provided a frame of reference for locating the psychosocial evolutionary significance of any particular event of that past. In part, this essay represents an effort to draw a clear distinction between these two quite different uses of the term *psychohistory*, and I will contend that Erikson's *Young Man Luther* needs to be understood as one chapter in his evolving psychohistory of humanity.

In order to develop this argument, I have chosen to focus on the figure of Hans Luther. Several reasons account for this choice. First, Erikson's portrait of Hans is, from a historian's point of view, one of the most problematic portions of the book. Historians reviewing *Young Man Luther* have devoted considerable attention to elucidating the maze of confused translations, dubious sources, and gross errors which cluster so firmly around the figure of Hans. Hans is therefore a convenient focal point for illuminating some of the most apparent historical deficiencies in *Young Man Luther*.[1] Second, Hans is also an enigmatic figure from a psychological point of view. Historian critics of *Young Man Luther* are quick to blame psychological speculation as the root cause for the historical errors of the book. In actual fact, however, Erikson's portrait of Hans is as deviant from his psychological theory as it is from available historical evidence.

For example, psychological ambiguity and complexity is a *sine qua non* in any of Erikson's psychological studies. His developmental theory articulates a careful balance—or ratio— of positive and negative qualities in each stage; and his clinical case studies display an unusual ability to unravel the psychological complexity of a personality. Hans Luther is a notable exception to this rule. His character borders on the purely pathological. He is compulsive in his economic pursuits, simultaneously violent and moralistic in the treatment of his children. And, most significant of all from an Eriksonian perspective, he is devoid of any redeeming virtue or strength.

Such a one-sided view of Hans is not required by available historical data. Martin recounts several incidents about his father that manifest quite different traits and that could have been utilized to form a far richer account than the simple stereotype Erikson presents.[2] In addition, a more complex psychological portrait of Hans would have been more consistent with the mix of strengths and weaknesses characteristic of Martin. As it is, Martin appears on the stage of history as something of a psychological miracle, the product of a second

1. The historical components of this essay presuppose—but do not repeat— the evidence and arguments of the first two essays in this volume (e.g., those by Spitz and Bainton).
2. See Spitz and Bainton, above.

virgin birth. Martin's numerous and notable ego strengths are rooted in his relationship to his mother and his faith in God; from Hans he receives only the unresolved neurotic tendencies that plague him throughout his life and lead to his ultimate decline. Unlike those of other sons, Martin's ego strengths can in no way be understood as continuous with his father or his childhood experience with that father, for in this case the father had nothing to give. Hans was, quite simply, evil—and I use the term *evil* in the technical Eriksonian sense of weakness or absence of strength.

Third, Hans epitomizes a major crisis in Erikson's saga of evolving humanity. Historically, Hans embodies the dark side of Martin's life and ideology and of that reformation which he initiated; ethically, Hans symbolizes the unfinished business of the Reformation, that mixture of economic complacency and proclivity to violence that permeates the present and poses an ultimate threat to the future. To read the story of Hans is not primarily to gain access to the life history of a sixteenth-century peasant turned miner but to gain insight into the dilemmas of the corporate and individual histories of the present. For Hans is a reverse image of Erikson's model of the good; he dramatizes the evil which needs to be overcome if humanity is to take the next step in psychosocial evolution. In brief, Erikson's characterization of Hans is best understood as an ideological construct—a product of psychohistory in the cosmic sense of that term—and not as a result of the application of psychology to a particular portion of the past.

In order to explicate the demonic role of Hans in Erikson's story of human evolution, it will be necessary to leave the context of the sixteenth century and pursue Erikson's study of Gandhi. For Gandhi appears in the next installment of the story; he is the prophet whose nonviolence may be able to heal the fractured legacy of the Reformation. At this point in the essay I will abandon the psychologically informed historical inquiry of the first section and adopt an explicitly religious format. For demonic figures, even if they are psychologically one-sided, belong to the genre of religious narrative. And it is my contention that Erikson also belongs to a tradition of religious narrators that extends back at least to the Jahwist of tenth-century-B.C. Israel.

HANS AS SUPERSTITIOUS MINER AND AMBITIOUS BOURGEOIS

The point of departure for Erikson's portrait of Hans Luther is the limited information available about Hans's social and economic origins and achievements. Born a peasant in Thuringia, he left the family farm in his twenties to make his career as a miner. Shortly after Martin's birth the Luther family moved again to Mansfeld, where Hans lived until his death. Hans also owned shares in the mines he worked and became, as Erikson notes, "a small industrialist and capitalist."[3] Economically, he was sufficiently successful to pay for the cost of an entourage of twenty relatives and neighbors for Martin's ordination, as well as to supply the food for the occasion and a gift of money to the monastery. When he died, he left an estate that included his house in Mansfeld and twelve hundred gulden.[4] Socially, Hans was equally successful in his upward mobility; having arrived in Mansfeld as a migrant miner, he was later elected to the town council, with responsibility for various ecclesiastical and social services of the town. As one reviewer has observed, Hans's concern for social and economic advancement seems to correspond to a "modern secular" paradigm far more closely than to Martin's religious preoccupation with matters of conscience.[5]

To this social profile of Hans, derived from conventional historical data, Erikson adds his psychological insights. At this point, as Erikson repeatedly reminds his readers, the historical evidence about Hans needs to be supplemented by clinical *inferences* derived from the words and deeds of Martin; the

3. Erik Erikson, *Young Man Luther* (New York: Norton, 1958), p. 53.
4. Ibid.
5. Heinrich Bornkamm, "Luther und sein Vater: Bemerkungen zu Erik Erikson, *Young Man Luther*," *Zeitschrift für Theologie und Kirche* 66 (1969): 38–39.

known son, whose verbal precocity disclosed so much about himself, also serves to reveal the unknown father.

But even at this point, in the psychological reconstruction of Hans from Martin's life history, it is important to note that Erikson begins by correlating psychological inferences with known social data. For example, Erikson sketches in a series of character traits common to Hans and Martin that reflect Hans's life in the mines. Both Hans and Martin were suspicious, distrustful of appearances, and on their guard against deception, a necessary trait for the miner who is always tempted to see gold "where there is nothing."[6] Similarly, Martin's "extreme expectation of catastrophe" is also consistent with the character of the son of a miner, accustomed to danger as part of daily work. And finally, Martin's lifelong preoccupation with the devil and his frequent vision of Satan appearing before him in a very concrete form also bear witness to his father's vocation, for miners, even more than peasants, lived in superstitious dread of those spirits of the underworld.[7] In each of these instances, known psychological characteristics of Martin are combined with social traits of a class of miners to form a coherent picture of Hans. As Erikson puts it, "Hans Luder in all his more basic characteristics belonged to the narrow, suspicious, primitive-religious, catastrophe-minded people."[8] While not particularly complimentary, Erikson's portrait of Hans as a miner does seem credible, for the traits described correspond with what is generally known about both Martin and the more primitive qualities of the medieval mind which he shared with his age.

But Hans as a miner is far less interesting to Erikson than Hans as a member of the emerging bourgeois class—and the psychological trait dominant for the bourgeois is ambition: "But most of all Hans Luder was an ambitious man."[9] If the

6. *Young Man Luther*, p. 58.
7. Ibid.
8. Ibid., p. 77.
9. Ibid., p. 54.

reader detects in this line an ominous tone, he is rightly warned that Hans's economic aspirations are to play a pervasive, fateful, and demonic role in Erikson's story of Martin. Erikson begins his narrative with the legend of Martin's "fit in the choir," an incident he locates psychologically in the conflict between Hans's economic ambition and Martin's choice of a religious vocation. Martin had renounced the legal career planned and "supported only with great sacrifice by his ambitious father."[10] Much of Martin's monastic life had been laden with inner conflict, which seemed to confirm his father's suspicion that the thunderstorm call to the monastery was from a demon and not from God; and "his greatest worldly burden was certainly the fact that his father had only most reluctantly, and after much cursing, given his consent . . . to the son's religious career."[11] Erikson concludes his story of Martin in middle age, in a serious depression, and still bearing the burden of Hans's economic ambitions: "In view of Luther's relation to his father, it makes sense that his deepest clinical despair emerged when he had become so much of what his father had wanted him to be: influential, economically secure, a kind of superlawyer, and a father of a son named Hans."[12]

In between the tormented fit in the choir and the despair of middle age, Erikson sketches a series of vignettes which portray the destructive impact of Hans's economic ambition on his son Martin. For example, in Martin's early childhood, Hans played the role of "a jealously ambitious father who tried to make him [Martin] precociously independent from women, and sober and reliable in his work."[13] "Hans Luder was a 'jealous god,' one who probably interfered early with the mother's attempt to teach her children how to be before he taught them how to strive."[14] Traversing the crisis of the oedipal period is a difficult enough task for any little boy; in

10. Ibid., p. 24.
11. Ibid., p. 26.
12. Ibid., p. 243.
13. Ibid., pp. 255–56.
14. Ibid., p. 123.

Martin's case it became an almost impossible hurdle and a titanic struggle. Hans's "challenging injunction against the little boy's bond with his mother" combined with his "prohibitory presence [pervading] the family milieu" created "an ideal breeding ground for the most pervasive form of the oedipal complex."[15]

If the oedipal crisis was difficult for Martin, complicated by the father's driving ambition, adolescence was even worse. For at this point Hans sought, through his son's career, fulfillment of his own ambitious needs. The school of law at Erfurt was one of the best, and "Hans Luder's fondest dream was that Martin should graduate from it."[16] About the same time, Hans also began to plan for his son's "early and prosperous marriage."[17] Poor Martin! From weaning through adolescence, and on to middle age, he suffered consistently under the yoke of his father's tyrannical ambition.

Erikson's story of the fateful role of Hans's ambition in Martin's life depends on one piece of solid historical information: the conflict between father and son precipitated by Martin's decision to enter a monastery. Hans originally refused to give his son permission to join the Augustinian order. Erikson interprets this refusal as consistent with Hans's precociously secular and bourgeois mentality. Consistent with the emerging "capitalistic trend in Germany . . . he was not going to be cheated out of his dearest investment."[18] Only after the death of two of Martin's brothers did he grudgingly give his consent. Later, in the festivities after Martin's first mass, he let the assembled company of monks and scholars know what his true feelings were. He admonished them to recall the scriptural command to honor thy father and mother, and he questioned Martin's call to monastic life in the thunderstorm experience.

While there is no reason to doubt the facticity of this father-

15. Ibid.
16. Ibid., p. 84.
17. Ibid., p. 91.
18. Ibid., p. 95.

son conflict, there is also no reason to interpret the incident as revelatory of Hans's excessive and compulsive ambition. Indeed, if the incident is understood within the framework of medieval society, such an interpretation seems quite implausible. Hans was not the only medieval parent who felt angry, disappointed, and betrayed by a son's decision to join a religious order. In a social structure in which healthy sons' prosperous future careers represented the closest equivalent to our social security system, a parent who experienced no sense of loss and disappointment when deprived of that security by monastic vows would seem abnormal. Erikson himself notes that such father-son conflicts were "a typical event in Martin's day" and belonged to the sociological context of the medieval world.[19] Indeed, the trauma of Hans and Martin concerning the decision to enter the monastery seems quite normal if compared with, for example, the struggle of Thomas Aquinas and his family. In the case of Thomas, it was reported that the family actually arranged to have the son kidnapped and secluded with a prostitute, and generally employed every ruse available to entice him to abandon his monastic decision.[20] Other elements in Erikson's portrait of ambitious Hans, apart from his own modest achievements and his angry response to Martin's religious decision, lack any independent historical evidence and are solely derived from psychological reconstruction.

But if we turn from historical evidence to psychological theory, the case for economic Hans is hardly improved. Two observations may highlight the incongruity of Erikson's version of Hans with his own psychological theory. First, the ambition which Erikson finds in Hans Luther is in no sense benign, nor is it even ambiguous. In Erikson's theory of psychosocial development he described a variety of ego strengths and virtues which might be associated wtih ambition, such as industry, initiative, and competence. It is important to note that Erikson

19. Ibid., pp. 96–97.
20. S. Baring-Gould, *The Lives of the Saints* (Edinburgh: John Grant, 1914), vol. 3, p. 124.

never employs these categories—or any positive terms—in describing the ambition of Hans Luther. In his case, ambition is only a compulsive driving force which comes to dominate his relation with Martin—the oldest son, both beneficiary and victim of all his father's hopes and dreams.[21]

Second, while Erikson dismisses the psychological significance of work for Hans Luther under the rubric of compulsive ambition, he has deliberately chosen to make the theme of work central in his case study of Martin. Early in the book he announces that psychoanalysis has long neglected the role of work in therapy: "Decades of case histories have omitted the work histories of the patients or have treated their occupation as a seemingly irrelevant area of life . . ."[22] In correcting this error, Erikson proceeded in his study of Luther to highlight consistently the psychological significance of work.[23] Thus it is precisely through the means of his work that Martin wins a resolution of his identity crisis.[24] In another context, Erikson observes the extraordinary psychological resiliency manifest in Martin's work life. Even his most serious depressive episodes hardly slowed the production of the manuscripts and new translations.[25] In each of his works, whether theological treatise or sermon, Martin remained a disciplined craftsman, responsible to the intellectual norms of his age, and did not use his work simply as an expression for his own subjectivity.[26] While emphasizing the qualities of discipline and craftsmanship, Erikson also noted that Martin came alive, affectively and intellectually, precisely through his work.[27] And finally, Erikson remains appreciative of Luther's distinction between works and work—the distinction between the holy busywork of

21. *Young Man Luther*, p. 66.
22. Ibid., p. 17.
23. "Only later . . . he had to establish his own pattern of work—which, in spite of his complaints, he did magnificently" (Ibid., p. 161).
24. In relation to the young Luther, Erikson speaks of ". . . the curative as well as the creative role of work . . ."
25. Ibid., p. 232.
26. Ibid., p. 200.
27. Ibid., p. 220.

obsessive rituals and the craftsman who means what he says and does in his work.[28] In all of these ways, Erikson calls attention to the extraordinarily creative role of work in the psychology of Martin Luther. And yet, as the psychological progenitor of Martin, old Hans appears to represent the most simple stereotype of the bourgeois mentality.

In summary, Erikson's psychological theory does not require —or support—the story of economic Hans. On the contrary, a more balanced psychological account of Hans would have been more consistent with Erikson's general style of clinical case studies and more appropriate to illuminating the particular role of work in the life history of Martin. In order to account for the creation of ambitious Hans, who embodied so thoroughly the most destructive psychological traits of the bourgeois mind, factors other than psychological theory and historical evidence will have to be examined.

THE MORALISTIC BRUTALITY OF HANS

Erikson's treatment of Hans as a suspicious miner and ambitious bourgeois was supported by some historical evidence, however ambiguous or tangential. In describing Hans as brutal, however, we should note that Erikson has no historical evidence for his case; more seriously, perhaps, the one piece of evidence which he does cite is distorted in a very strange and peculiar way which is not at all consistent with Erikson's more careful use of historical materials. While there is no evidence for Hans's cruelty, the impact of Hans's uncontrolled violence on his son is absolutely vital to Erikson's account of both Martin's theology and his unresolved personal neurosis.

Erikson's portrait of Hans depends upon a dichotomy between external behavior and inner feeling. While Hans Luther appeared in his public life with neighbors and fellow workers as a respectable, law-abiding citizen, his inner life was determined by "a feeling close to murder."[29] This inner rage, which Hans dared not express in his "disciplined public identity," he

28. Ibid., pp. 210, 219–20.
29. Ibid., p. 66.

could and would "let loose against his family."[30] He physically beat his children—including Martin—and not simply as a punishment for specific offenses in the manner of that age, but more, because of his own compulsion to beat physically out of his children what he had never mastered within himself.[31] Martin's mother, consistent with the customary household arrangements of that time, played a double role in these violent episodes; she was herself "one of the powerless victims of the father's brutality and one of his dutiful assistants in meting out punishment to the children."[32] Besides having a violent temper, Hans was also an alcoholic, and excessive drinking frequently set off the "cruel self-indulgence" of his anger that was often "murderous."[33] To make matters worse, Hans's orgies of intrafamily violence were perpetrated in the name of righteousness and justice; his brutality was moralistic. He justified his outbursts of violence as being for the good of the children.[34] Indeed, Hans's violent temper dominated so much of the Luther household that it even spilled over to the economic scene; Erikson describes it as "the father's driving economic ambition, which was threatened by something (maybe even murder) done in the past, and a feeling close to murder which he always carried inside."[35]

This, then, is Erikson's account of Hans's unbridled aggression. Erikson wishes to leave no doubt in the reader's mind that Hans was a mean man. He describes his behavior and character in terms such as "violent harshness," "alcoholic impulsiveness," "questionable use of brute superiority," "viciousness," and "brutal."[36] As best I can determine, there is no historical evidence to support this view of Hans, and much

30. Ibid.
31. Ibid.
32. Ibid., p. 70.
33. Ibid., pp. 65, 123. Note that Erikson also characterizes Adolf Hitler's father as having "an inclination toward . . . alcohol and brutality—that is, at home, where he could afford it" (Ibid., p. 105).
34. Hans "showed the greatest temper in his attempts to drive temper out of his children" (Ibid., p. 58; cf. p. 66).
35. Ibid., p. 66.
36. Ibid., pp. 66, 67, 70.

to contradict it.[37] For the purposes of this essay I wish to examine only two issues: (1) the question of historical evidence, especially the murder charge which Erikson assigns to Hans; and (2) the psychological plausibility of brutal Hans as the father of Martin.

The one piece of historical evidence that Erikson cites to confirm his view of Hans's violent disposition is a purported murder charge. In recounting the story of the charge, Erikson first notes that "Little Hans," who was Martin's uncle and the younger brother of "Big Hans," moved to Mansfeld during the time of Martin's early schooling. He apparently moved to Mansfeld to flee the authorities from another jurisdiction; he had a very black court record; and his arrival in town was colored by some deep scandal, perhaps murder.[38] In fact, we know from other sources that the core of the story recounted by Erikson is that "Little Hans" was supposed to have killed —or been charged with killing—a shepherd before he arrived in Mansfeld.[39] What is intriguing about Erikson's account is that, by the end of this paragraph, he has displaced the murder charge from "Little Hans" to "Big Hans," who "was, in fact, supposed to have killed a shepherd before coming to Mansfeld."[40] An error of such magnitude, and occurring within a single paragraph, clearly is not consistent with Erikson's use of historical evidence for his characterization of Hans. But this only raises the question, Why does Erikson need to create a murdering Hans? Why is this role so indispensable to his story of Martin?

Freudian psychological theory could provide one answer to this question. There is no doubt that Martin, throughout the span of his life, exhibited a bewildering array of aggressive disorders. Erikson describes the neurosis of the early monastic years as obsessive-compulsive; Martin's aggression was here

37. For a detailed consideration of the historical issues involved in Erikson's view of Hans's brutality see the essays of Spitz and Bainton above; see also Bornkamm, "Luther und sein Vater."

38. *Young Man Luther*, p. 57.

39. See Spitz, pp. 72–73 above.

40. *Young Man Luther*, p. 57.

directed at himself: fasting, long hours of prayer and intro-spection, and self-flagellation were some of the means he em-ployed to satisfy the devouring beast within himself.[41] And this same aggression, manifest later as the problem of the negative conscience, constituted the core of Luther's theological concern: "How do I find a gracious God? How does my anguished con-science find peace and forgiveness?" Later Martin's unresolved aggression was projected onto a host of enemies—the pope and papists, sacramentarians and enthusiasts, Jews and revolu-tionaries—who were perceived not simply as opponents, but most often as embodiments of that one real and persistent enemy, the devil himself. Still later, aggression was internalized again, in the manic-depressive episodes of 1527. And so the story goes. Martin Luther was clearly a neurotic personality, at the end as well as at the beginning of his career, and the core of his neurosis was bound up with an aggressive instinctuality which repeatedly flared up in ways destructive to himself and to others. From the standpoint of orthodox Freudian theory, such a case history would appear to suggest—or perhaps even require—a father who had himself failed to master and inte-grate his own aggression. At least, this is one explanation for the creation of aggressive Hans.

But if we do follow this psychoanalytic line of inquiry and examine from a clinical point of view the character of Hans which Erikson has created, we find quickly that the character creates more problems than he solves. For example, in his description of Hans's aggression, Erikson totally lacks the kind of balance characteristic of his ordinary case studies. Hans has no tender side to balance his harshness; he is never reliable or just, as a parent, to balance the capriciousness of his harsh discipline. He is, in plain language, an evil man and nothing else.

Erikson clearly documents the psychological legacy which Martin received from his mother: his capacity for recovering basic trust, both in himself and in others; his integration of libidinal energies expressed in his enjoyment of sensuality,

41. Ibid., pp. 156, 174.

nature, and sexual intimacy; his simple hedonism; and his love of music.[42] Erikson also goes on to describe and appreciate Martin's tenderness, his generosity, and his capacity to care for others.[43] These qualities also represent his psychological bond with his mother. But from his father Martin received nothing—nothing except the driving need to rebel against that father (at home, in Rome, or in heaven) whose capricious brutality masqueraded as justice. Martin was sufficiently autonomous to follow resolutely his course of action, regardless of the consequences, and Erikson generally regards the sense of autonomy as rooted in paternal relationships.[44]

But this is not true in the case of Martin. Martin also enjoyed a rich and varied mixture of relationships with his students, peers, and superiors; but these male relations reflect nothing of his own childhood relationship to his father. Martin was a loving husband, who obviously enjoyed a marriage that did not begin until late in his life—but this also disclosed nothing of his psychological legacy from his father.[45] Psychologically there emerges the picture of Martin who embodied a wide range of ego strengths, some more paternal, some more maternal in origins; however, only his mother was a source of psychological strength, as he could claim for his father only the demonic figure of Hans, who never shared his affections with his son or supported his son's emerging autonomy.

At the core of Erikson's account of cruel Hans is the charge of child brutality. Hans physically beat Martin, not occasionally but frequently, not for the sake of disciplining the child but to satisfy his own inner needs. Contemporary studies of child brutality suggest that the pattern tends to be repetitive: parents who were beaten in childhood are most likely, in turn, to beat their own children. In the case of Martin, we have ample testimony from numerous boarders who lived in his household—jotting down each word he spoke and each deed he did—that

42. Ibid., pp. 72–73, 250, 255, 257–58.
43. Ibid., p. 250.
44. Ibid., pp. 124, 236.
45. Ibid., p. 237.

Martin was a devoted father who loved and enjoyed his children.[46] Such adult behavior hardly seems consistent with that of a child of a brutal father.

However, Erikson is not only a psychologist and historian; he is also an ethicist, a religionist, or—in a modified use of his term—an ideologist. He is telling a story of the psychosocial, moral, and spiritual evolution of humanity, a story whose past —like the past of all religious stories—is informed directly by the perceived crises of the present. If, therefore, we turn from the sixteenth century to the present, the historical distortions and psychological inconsistencies of Hans may make more sense; for it is my contention that the character of Hans is finally determined by his role in a cosmic drama of good and evil.

HANS AS A THERAPEUTIC CONSTRUCT

Erikson does not view the Reformation as a mere incident of the past, but as an event continuing into the present, "something we have neither completely lived down nor successfully outlived. Such is the material of psychoanalysis."[47] Nor is the impact of the Reformation confined to a remnant of believing Protestants or those Western nations most influenced by Protestant traditions. Even postrevolutionary Catholic Mexico— where Erikson wrote his Luther book—belongs within the orbit of the Reformation. For "the Reformation is continuing in many lands, in the form of manifold revolutions, and in the personalities of protestants of varied vocations."[48]

From this perspective, Erikson's illumination of the ambiguities in the life and theology of Martin Luther has more than historical significance. He is not only reconstructing the life history of Luther, but also redefining the salient characteristics of an ideological movement which he perceives as operative in present societies. In this role, he is extending to the sphere of society at large something of the therapeutic model of psycho-

46. Erikson acknowledges that Martin's love of children and music leads one to "assume some early happiness in his own childhood" (Ibid.).
47. Ibid., p. 10; he says also, "Luther was the herald of the age which was in the making and is—or was—still our age" (p. 224).
48. Ibid., p. 266.

analysis.[49] Just as a therapist seeks to aid his client in recognizing strengths and weaknesses from his individual past, so does Erikson identify for his readers the resources and liabilities of those traditions which inform our collective past.

Luther's positive legacy for succeeding generations is clear. His theology supported the emergence of personalities freed from excessive and unrealistic burdens of guilt and nourished by a sense of trust, so basic to human development.[50] But the liabilities of the Reformation are equally apparent: the creation of a bourgeois class of managerial males, ethically and spiritually complacent and trapped by their compliant religiosity into an alliance with the dominant political-economic order; and fresh outbursts of violence, manifest in a brutality of language, deeds, and even art. As a social movement, the Reformation is the offspring of both Martin's strengths and Hans's liabilities, and the ghost of that stubborn German peasant persists in haunting our contemporary social landscapes, even in as unlikely a place as modern Mexico.[51]

Erikson reserves his strongest indictments of Luther for that period of middle age when "the belatedly manifest identification with his father . . . began to determine much of Luther's life."[52] This was the period when Luther himself married and became the father of a son named Hans. It was also the time when Luther "abnegated much of his postadolescent identity."[53] The man who had spoken so passionately for the freedom of the Christian now became the spokesman for the authority of the ruling princes. Even the law of Moses, "honor thy father and mother"—used by Hans so tellingly against Martin's monastic decision—was now appropriated by Martin as a religious

49. Erikson describes his Luther study—"relating historical forces to the basic functions and stages of the mind"—as a first step toward "a psychoanalytic critique of society" (Ibid., p. 21).

50. In Erikson's words, Luther "formulated for himself and for all of mankind a new kind of ethical and psychological awareness; . . . at the end, this awareness, too, was marred by a return of the demons, whoever they may have been" (Ibid., p. 48).

51. Ibid., pp. 266–67.

52. Ibid., p. 237.

53. Ibid., p. 238.

demand for obedience to political authorities.[54] And the critic
of all religious works left as his social legacy "a way of life in
which a man's daily works, including his occupation, became
the center of his behavioral orientation, and were rigorously
regimented by the church-state."[55]

In Erikson's version of the story, the economic ambition
of old Hans emerged as dominant in the later theology of his
son: "Martin became the metaphysical jurist of his father's
class."[56] The robust conscience, for which the young Luther
struggled so valiantly, was replaced by a "petty bourgeois
optimism" nourished by a "religiosity compliant to the needs
of progress in the new, the mercantile, line of endeavor."[57]
"The metaphysical misalliance between economic self-interest
and church affiliation so prominent in the Western world,"
which has its origins in the later writings of Martin, is ultimately rooted in the aspirations of old Hans.[58] In the end, it
was Hans's vision of his son's future which finally triumphed
in the West.

As a result, it makes a good deal of sense to read Erikson's
story of Hans and Martin not in its medieval context, but as a
dramatic representation of our own social situation. For the
economically ambitious Hans and the religiously rebellious
Martin enact a father-son struggle characteristic of the managerial class dominant in this society. Hans relates to his son
predominately—if not exclusively—as an extension of his own
unlimited ambition, while Martin chooses the downward mobility of a religious vocation as the most logical path of rebellion against a thoroughly secular and materialistic father.[59]
While such a scenario may not be convincing to historians
concerned with the actualities of the medieval world, it is

54. Ibid.
55. Ibid., p. 239.
56. Ibid.
57. Ibid.
58. Ibid.
59. "Only if we remember that his father wanted him to be politically ambitious in a new, a secular sense, rather than spiritually good, can we understand that Martin was choosing a negative identity when he decided to become
a monk" (Ibid., p. 129).

precisely the kind of drama that enables a psychohistorian to perform a therapeutic function in the present social context. The driven Hans, whose ambition compelled him to interfere in the normal developmental process of his son at every stage, may be a gross distortion of the real Hans—or any medieval peasant turned miner—but he is certainly a father figure familiar to many therapists.[60] It is therefore not surprising that Hans's ambition lacks any redeeming virtue or psychological balance. For Erikson does not intend to portray Hans as a balanced personality. Rather, Hans appears on the stage of history as an unmitigated villain, a scapegoat who bears in himself the burden of the compulsions, drives, and excessive ambition of the economic man of today.

NONVIOLENT GANDHI AND BRUTAL HANS

Hans, though, is not only the prototype for the neurotically ambitious and ethically impotent bourgeois; he is also Erikson's model of moralistic brutality, and the link between brutality and morality becomes increasingly prominent in Erikson's writings of the late sixties. As a result, the concluding portion of this essay will proceed through a long and complex detour: Freud's theory of aggression and his concept of instinct; the animal studies of Konrad Lorenz; Gandhi's practice of militant nonviolence; the growing gap between traditional systems of morality and the technology of nuclear delivery; and the destructive consequences of moralistic patterns of child raising. The glue which binds together this mix of history, theory and ethics is the unresolved problem of human aggression, that failure of ethical imagination and psychological insight which Hans Luther embodied so thoroughly.

In developing Erikson's view of human aggression, I will utilize a paradigm borrowed from classical theology: creation, fall, sin, apocalyptic dread, and prophetic deed. In part, I have chosen this paradigm for heuristic reasons; the narrative form,

---

60. Erikson describes present child-raising patterns as hurrying children "from one good moment to better ones, to climb, improve, advance, progress" (Ibid., p. 69).

ethical focus, and dialectical balance of classical theology seem ideally suited to make explicit the distinctive thrust of Erikson's vision of human nature. In addition, the utilization of this format also discloses the strong affinity of Erikson with traditional religious narratives. For the theologian, it suggests that Erikson's psychosocial schema may prove so attractive as a dialogical partner precisely because Erikson, covertly if not explicitly, is already operating within a quasi-theological framework. For the historian, Erikson's role as a constructive ideologist, articulating the meaning of history as a whole, may suggest that Erikson's brand of psychohistory has as much affinity with patterns of classical philosophy and theology as with more typical models of scientific history.

Erikson's saga of the human drama begins, like Genesis, in the beginning; for Erikson, this is the evolutionary origin of history. As he writes, "historical considerations lead back into man's prehistory and evolution."[61] For his guide in this journey backwards in time, Erikson draws primarily upon the ethological studies of Konrad Lorenz. In particular, Lorenz provides Erikson with data on animal behavior essential to his critique and revision of Freud.

In theological language, Lorenz confirmed Erikson's perception of the essential goodness of the created order of nature. The tendency of humanity to indulge in violent behavior—"characterized by irrational rage, wild riots, and systemic extermination"—may not be attributed to animal instincts inherited from man's evolutionay origins.[62] Freud was incorrect in claiming that the craving to torture and kill other members of the human species was rooted in the continuity of man's instinctive life with wild beasts.[63] This distorted view of the character of animal instincts was a product of Freud's uncritical acceptance of popularized Darwinism and not based on actual observations. Erikson reminds his readers that beasts of prey, as perceived through telescopic lenses, do not display any sign

61. Erik H. Erikson, "Psychosocial Identity," *International Encyclopedia of the Social Sciences* (New York: Macmillan, 1968), vol. 7, p. 62.
62. Erik H. Erikson, *Gandhi's Truth* (New York: Norton, 1969), p. 429.
63. Ibid., pp. 424, 429.

of anger or rage in the process of killing other species for food; they are simply "doing their job."[64] And while intra-species aggressive behavior is a characteristic of many kinds of fish and animals, that aggression is securely balanced by a variety of pacifying rituals, symbolic displays and boundaries of attack which minimize destructive consequences. Erikson frequently cites Lorenz's example of the antler tournament of the *Damstag* as an example of "instinctive pacific behavior."[65] While the antler weapons of each animal could easily gouge the opponent to death, in actual fact both animals are instinctively drawn to lock horns and engage in a wrestling contest which has a victor but no victim. For Erikson, as for Lorenz, the animal kingdom is characterized by an indefinite number of analogous pacifying rituals; and all of these pacifying rituals are instinctive. Man alone in the animal kingdom—with the possible exception of rats under very specific conditions—tends to engage in mass annihilation of his own species.[66]

In order to make conceptually explicit the resulting revision of Freudian theory, Erikson proposes two different terms to replace Freud's ambiguous concept of instinct. On the one hand, Erikson defines *instinctive* as "an inborn pattern of adaptive competence."[67] The goodness of humanity's natural endowment from evolution is thus built into the definition of the term. On the other hand, he defines *instinctual* as "a quantity of drive or energy in search of satisfaction whether adaptive or not."[68] So, when Freud spoke of man's "instinctive" craving for pleasure manifest in cruelty and violence, he should have spoken instead of an "instinctual" craving.

While the instincts which constitute the evolutionary legacy of the human animal never lose their power or goodness, they also are not sufficient in themselves to engender human be-

64. Ibid., p. 425.

65. Ibid.

66. Ibid.

67. Erik Erikson, "Psychoanalysis and Ongoing History: Problems of Identity, Hatred and Nonviolence," *The American Journal of Psychiatry* 122 (1965): 245.

68. Ibid.

havior; they "are never and cannot ever be in themselves adaptive or consummative (or, in brief, 'natural'), but are always governed by the complexity of individualization and cultural form."[69] The gates of the garden of Eden are sealed off as firmly in Erikson's saga as in the biblical version. Man, in Erikson's model, is a biocultural-existential animal; cultural forms combined with inherited fragments of instincts are actualized only in and through individuated processes. Man's instinctive legacy may be a necessary ingredient of human goodness, but it is never sufficient. As Erikson loves to quote Lorenz, drives are also driven, and in the case of the human animal, instinctual energies available for utilization in a variety of human tasks are far more prominent than the fixed behavioral patterns of instincts.

This freedom from fixed, instinctive patterns is the biological basis for the adaptability of the human animal. Unlike animal predecessors, whose survival depended upon the continuity of their environment, the human animal can adapt itself to a wide array of changing environments. As Erikson notes, human childhood is "characterized by a minimum of instinctive patterns and a maximum of free instinctual energy available for investment in a growing variety of basic psychosocial encounters."[70]

But while freedom from fixed instinctive behavioral patterns is the glory of the human animal, it also constitutes the necessary condition for his misery. For it is precisely the unbounded energies, available for "a growing variety of psychosocial encounters," that set off such a bewildering array of instinctual disorders. While Erikson shows no great fondness for the biblical notion of a primeval fall, his version of the human story does require a doctrine of original sin which is as pervasive and fateful as that biblical notion.[71] For the

69. Ibid.
70. Ibid.
71. Erikson regards the theological notion of original sin as inseparably bound up with moralistic judgments. Hence, while he grants that the notion may be descriptively necessary, it is too potentially destructive to be embraced (*Gandhi's Truth*, p. 249).

evolutionary antecedents of history include not only the goodness of instinctive patterns, but also those instinctual energies
which let loose such destructive orgies between and within the
human animals.

> But alas . . . man's instinctual forces are never completely
> bound and contained in adaptive or reasonable patterns; they
> are repressed, displaced, perverted and often return from re-
> pression to arouse human anxiety and rage. We can thus never
> go back to nature, but neither can we hope for a utopian cul-
> ture not somehow forfeited to its past as rooted in the child-
> hood of all individuals and the history of groups.[72]

In Erikson, as in classical theology, there is always a dialectical tension between the goodness of inherited instincts
and the corruption of instinctual disorders which taint all individual and collective pasts. As a result, moral ambiguity is a
universal condition of the human animal. No religion, morality, or ideology can presume to promise deliverance from
the paradoxical conditions of historical existence. Just as there
is no return for humanity to a state of pure nature, so there is
no utopian transcendence of history which could obliterate
"man's florid and paradoxical drive equipment."[73]

The disorder of human instinctuality does not lend itself to
rational explanation in Erikson any more than in classical
theology. Instinctual energies, considered in and of themselves,
are potentially as good as inherited instinctive patterns. Evil
arises from the fact that these energies are not "bound and
contained . . ."[74] In Erikson's version of sin, he speaks of
man's "wayward instinctuality," and for Erikson, as for Augustine, it is the waywardness of instinctuality—rather than instinctual energy itself—which is constitutive of the misery of
the human animal.[75]

The "instinctual aberration" of the human animal appears
most clearly, for Erikson as well as for classical theology, in

72. Erikson, "Psychoanalysis and Ongoing History," p. 246.
73. Ibid., p. 245.
74. Ibid.
75. Erik H. Erikson, "On the Nature of Psychohistorical Evidence: In Search
of Gandhi," *Daedalus* (1968):712.

the ambiguous function of morality.[76] Like Lorenz, Erikson regards the social restraints of morality as originally intending to serve the same function in human society as the pacifying rituals of the animal kingdom, namely, to limit the destructive consequences of aggression. In actual fact, however, the evolution of the species and the life history of individuals both disclose morality to serve also its opposite function: to legitimize violence.[77] Like St. Paul, Erikson regards the *results* of moral law—in contrast with the *intention*—as always "paradoxical and maladaptive," and he views with alarm the growing tendency of the human animal to abuse, exploit, and massacre other persons in the name of some higher righteousness.[78]

"Brutal righteousness" thus appears to Erikson not only as the salient characteristic of Hans, but also as "an overwhelming propensity of human nature."[79] In part, this prevalent perversion of morality is a product of those religious ideologies which divide the human personality into the dual role of "cruel judge" and "helpless sinner."[80] In this dichotomy, man finds "the license to view and treat others as if they are no better than the worst in himself."[81] "For there is, as we now know, a clear connection between the murderousness with which righteous man attacks his enemy and the cruelty with which moralistic man views himself. Too long, in fact, has man excused his cruelty to others with the claim that he does not spare himself."[82]

If moralistic religious ideologies are waning, their secular offspring continue to thrive as moralistic patterns of child raising. Erikson, who began his work as a child analyst, repeatedly returns to the experience of the violated child—both the child who is physically beaten by his parents and the child

---

76. Erikson, *Gandhi's Truth*, p. 391.

77. Ibid., p. 428.

78. "Psychoanalysis and Ongoing History," p. 245.

79. *Gandhi's Truth*, p. 390. "Cruel righteousness" is also, for Erikson, a predominant characteristic of Protestantism (*Young Man Luther*, p. 234).

80. *Gandhi's Truth*, p. 248.

81. Ibid.

82. Ibid., p. 234.

who learns at a very early age to hate some part of himself—for understanding the sources of human violence. "It is in daily life and especially in the life of children that the human propensity for violence is founded; and we now suspect that much of that excess of violence which distinguishes man from animals is created in him by those child training methods which set one part of himself against another."[83] If humanity wishes to mitigate the social transmission of violence from one generation to another, it will be necessary for a new breed of parental figures—unlike Hans and his successors—to devise patterns of child care which respect the wholeness and the integrity of the young. "For this cure it is essential . . . that the moral adult, so easily given to moral vindictiveness, should learn to educate without violence, that is, with a recognition of the inviolacy of the counterplayer even if, and especially when, that counterplayer is a child."[84]

Because Erikson regards morality as so dangerous, he will not accept the Freudian model of instinct and inhibition as an adequate conceptual account of "good" behavior. In many ways, Freud regarded himself as a modern-day version of a prophet of the law, a new Moses, albeit one who translated psychologically some functions of moral law from unconscious and involuntary processes of the superego to ego processes. Erikson, in contrast, would have to ally himself with those prophets of covenant who despaired of the sufficiency of any system of instinctual restraint and sought a cure for the human condition in new and larger patterns of mutuality. Lorenz is thus incorrect when he attempts to explain the pacifying rituals of animals in terms of the Freudian model of instinct and inhibition.

> The very use of the word "ritual" to describe the behavior of the stag seems to characterize the described scene as something that does not fit the simple model of naked and then inhibited aggression. Obviously, the ritualization already demands a preselection of partners of nearly equal strength,

83. Ibid.
84. Ibid., p. 248; cf. *Young Man Luther*, pp. 69, 70, 267.

endowed with the same readiness for the clock-like display of a whole set of scheduled and reciprocal reactions of which the final turning away is only the conclusion, and a capacity to assume either one of the terminal roles convincingly and effectively. Much of animal aggression is already thus ritualized.[85]

As will soon become apparent, the failure—or success—of the human regulation of instinctual energies depends, for Erikson, not primarily upon effective psychological mechanisms of inhibition, but rather upon social processes of covenant making —not only the covenants of mutual love and care but also the covenants of opponents locked in conflict and struggle.

Erikson's distinction between a morality of inhibition and an ethic of mutality has its counterpart, at the international level, in his contrast between a system of diplomatic "avoidances (prevention, deterrence, containment)" on the one hand, and the face-to-face combat characteristic of ancient war on the other.[86] While Erikson is no great friend of warfare, he is willing to grant that wars in past ages may have served adaptive values.[87] He describes the martial style of two primitive New Guinea tribes—portrayed in the film *Dead Birds*—as analogous to the pacifying rituals of animals.

> But with all such martial obsession, there is no attempt at annihilation, suppression, or enslavement; and while shouted contempt is part of the bragging display, these tribes must have maintained, for decades or centuries, a *convention of warfare,* in which the enemy can be trusted to abide by a certain ritualization which sacrifices to the martial ethos only a minimum number of individuals on either side.[88]

In the conflict of these primitives, the humanity of the enemy was clearly manifest in the act of battle. The physical presence of the opponents, combined with the highly stylized conventions of warfare, served to regulate the instinctuality of each so as to mitigate destructive consequences. Erikson de-

85. Erikson, "Psychoanalysis and Ongoing History," p. 244.
86. Ibid., p. 245.
87. *Gandhi's Truth*, p. 430.
88. Ibid., p. 429.

scribes this kind of warfare as "a cultural arrangement some-where between the instinctual and the instinctive."[89]

The practice of war in modernity stands in stark contrast to the battle of these two primitive tribes. Modern technology has created a situation in which neither opponent has the opportunity to confront his counterpart. The bombardier flying at an altitude of thirty thousand feet or the missile technician removed from his target by thousands of miles is not permitted to recognize a shared humanity in the face of his opponent. "Both attacker and attacked are removed from encounters such as the higher animals seem to have achieved, namely, op-portunities to confront each other not only as dangerous but also as pacific opponents within one species."[90]

Even the language of modern warfare conceals the humanity of the enemy by reporting only body counts. In addition, the same technology which deprived the modern warrior of a social context to regulate his instinctual aberrations also equipped him with an extraordinarily increased capacity for destruction. The combination of these two circumstances has created a situation "of utmost danger to the survival of the species," and Erikson's writings of the late sixties frequently sound the note of apocalyptic doom.[91] The gap between an increasing technological capacity for destruction and the regu-lation of an aggressive instinctuality has brought modern man into a situation of historical crisis. Either he finds a new ethic, more adequate than the moralisms of the past, or he faces the prospect of mass annihilation. "The super brakes built into the super weaponry"—the whole system of diplomatic avoid-ances and balance of powers—is "in the long run," not ade-quate to bridge the "deep and nightmarish gap . . . between man's technological and his humanist imagination."[92]

Into the midst of this historical crisis steps the prophet Gandhi—or, more accurately, Erikson's story of Gandhi. For

89. Ibid.
90. Erikson, "Psychoanalysis and Ongoing History," p. 245.
91. "Psychosocial Identity," p. 62.
92. *Gandhi's Truth*, p. 51; "Psychoanalysis and Ongoing History," p. 245.

in Erikson's version of "psychosocial evolution," Gandhi is the prophet who enacts a genuine alternative to a future of mass destruction, the prophet who extends into sociopolitical arenas the strengths of the therapeutic tradition from Luther through Freud while healing the liabilities of that same tradition, and finally, the prophet who recapitulates in himself the prehistory of humanity, manifesting both adaptive instinctive patterns and the healing of instinctual aberrations. If this appears to be a large task for a single individual to bear, we need to remember that Gandhi, in Erikson's saga, is not an ordinary man but a *homo religiosus*, one of those rare agents of the historical drama who—through a confrontation with their own nothingness and the psychosocial crises of their day—extend the process of psychosocial evolution. Like Luther before him, Gandhi performs a role analogous to that of the prophet of traditional religious narratives. The meaning of the life and deeds of such a prophet may not be confined to his own time and space, but extends backwards into the unknown past and forwards to an unknown future while intersecting with the most urgent ethical crises of the present.

While Gandhi's role in a 1918 workers' strike in Ahmedabad, India, is the focus of Erikson's study, Gandhi's significance in psychosocial evolution appears in relation to a post-Hiroshima international context. Early in the book Erikson tells his readers that he has traveled directly from a disarmament conference in America to Ahmedabad, and the link between the threat of nuclear war and the figure of Gandhi is as direct as the itinerary of Erikson's journey.[93] Throughout the book, Erikson insists that Gandhi's significance cannot be confined to "the issues of industrial peace in Ahmedabad," but must be understood in relation to "a future which will pit man's naked humanity against the cold power of super machineries."[94]

In relation to the perils of international conflict, Erikson depicts Gandhi's role in a manner analogous to older theological accounts of Jesus. Sometimes Gandhi is presented as a moral

93. *Gandhi's Truth*, p. 51.
94. Ibid., p. 12.

influence on world history, a figure who continues to confront humanity with the one genuine alternative to a future of mass annihilation. Thus, Gandhi's conduct in the 1918 Ahmedabad strike continues to "confront the world . . . with a choice" long after the Russian Revolution and the League of Nations— events contemporaneous with that strike—have disappeared from the moral horizon.[95] Sometimes Gandhi's willingness to sacrifice himself for the cause of peace appears as the exemplar of right human conduct. And there is an *imitatio Gandhi*, like the older *imitatio Christi*, which Erikson documents in the willingness of contemporary American youth to risk their bodies in confrontation with "the cold and mechanized gadgetry of the modern state."[96] Finally, Gandhi is also a kind of *Christus Victor* figure whose triumph over evil in the human spirit has created a new situation. Gandhi has established in his time and place the feasibility of a basic nonviolent attitude which, even "in an electronic and nuclear age, nevertheless remains a human alternative."[97] In *Christus Victor* language, later generations are free to engage in the "mopping up operations"—in this case, the utilization of new technology to communicate a benign intention to the enemy—precisely because Gandhi has established this possibility as a real alternative for all humanity.[98]

Like other prophets, Gandhi not only spoke to a future but out of a past; and for Erikson, that past includes both a Hindu tradition focused on ahimsa and a Western tradition represented by Luther. The link between Luther and Gandhi is, of course, Freud: "Freud is both a successor to Luther and a contemporary to Gandhi."[99] In this context, the terms *successor* and *contemporary* are to be understood both chronologically and ideologically.

In *Young Man Luther,* Erikson articulated a series of simi-

95. Ibid., p. 391.
96. Ibid., p. 198.
97. Ibid., p. 431.
98. Ibid.
99. Ibid., p. 99.

larities between Luther and Freud. Both men utilized their personal neuroses in the service of a breakthrough to a new form of human awareness. Both men "did the dirty work of their generation" by focusing on the problem of conscience, and both men shared a paradoxical model of human existence which Luther expressed in theological language and Freud in psychoanalytic conceptuality.[100] Central to this view of human life is the relative freedom of the ego from the destructive tyranny of both conscience and desire—a freedom which includes a continuing awareness of the claims of both these other psychic agencies.[101]

While Freud's concern for ego dominance has its "late medieval precursor" in Luther, Gandhi's style of historical intervention has its parallel in the practice of Freudian therapy.[102] In his "personal word" to Mahatmaji, Erikson itemizes the similarities between satyagraha and psychoanalytic therapy. Both presuppose the equality of the participants in the transaction. Freud rejected hypnosis or authoritative suggestion because such methods prevented the patient's conscious acceptance of the truth about himself. Freudian therapy depends upon actualizing the strengths of the patient as an ally in the therapeutic venture, just as Gandhi did with his opponents. Freudian therapy presupposes the power of truth to break down barriers of resistance, again as Gandhi did. There is a strong passive component in psychoanalytic treatment, as in satyagraha. Both assume that only the exclusion of all violence, or the threat of violence, from the transaction will enable a genuine resolution to emerge. And the Freudian therapist regards a patient's accusations not as occasions for retaliation, but as a necessary part of the therapeutic process. "Thus . . . we are somehow joined in a universal 'therapeutics,' committed to the Hippocratic principle that one can test truth (or the healing power inherent in a sick situation) only by action which avoids harm—or better, by action which maximizes

100. *Young Man Luther*, p. 9.
101. Ibid., pp. 216–18.
102. Ibid., p. 9.

mutuality and minimizes the violence caused by unilateral coercion or threat."[103]

Independently of each other, Freud and Gandhi won an exactly parallel method for healing man's proclivity to violence. As a result, Gandhi and Freud are joined in a parity not true of the relation between Freud and Luther. Erikson is explicit in stating that he did not decide to study Gandhi's life only to apply what he learned from Freud.[104] At the conclusion of the book, he notes with some surprise that he rediscovered psychoanalysis in the process of studying Gandhi and in Gandhi's terms of truth, self-suffering, and nonviolence.[105] For Erikson, Gandhi demonstrated a method for resolving conflicts in the social and political arena so as to maximize the strength of both parties to the dispute, just as Freud discovered a way of healing psychic conflicts so as to enhance the strength of the total personality. In this way, Gandhi completes a Western tradition of healing that extends from Luther to Freud, both of whom refused—in different ways—to extend their insights or methods into the domain of politics. And the conjunction between Freud's psychological therapy and Gandhi's sociopolitical therapy is "more than a vague analogy; it is a correspondence in method and a convergence in human values which may well be of historical, if not evolutionary, significance."[106]

While Gandhi extended the insights of Luther and Freud into the arena of politics and society, he also corrected the untamed aggression which played so prominent a role in Luther's life and the history of the West. The most relevant point of contrast here is not Martin or young Gandhi, but Hans Luther and Kaba, Gandhi's father. Like Hans, Kaba also had the reputation of being short-tempered and prone to engage in physical violence. However, in sharp contrast with Hans, Kaba "never laid hands on this boy."[107] Erikson recounts

103. Erikson, *Gandhi's Truth*, p. 247.
104. "On the Nature of Psychohistorical Evidence," p. 712.
105. *Gandhi's Truth*, p. 439.
106. Ibid., p. 245.
107. Ibid., p. 123.

a story from Gandhi's autobiography, describing a youthful theft of a bit of gold and his confession of this wrong to his father. Gandhi feared a thrashing for his theft, but the father neither struck him nor took the punishment upon himself by striking his own forehead in the manner of the Indian custom. Instead Kaba wept, and young Gandhi experienced his father's tears as cleansing him from his wrong. Later, as a reformer, Gandhi looked back upon this childhood incident as a religious experience of ahimsa. Kaba's response expressed something more than a father's love; it was pure ahimsa, an all-embracing power that could transform everything it touched.[108] Perhaps only the son of such a father could complete and correct the religious movement initiated by Hans's son.

But prophetic deeds arise not only from the legacy of historical traditions but also from a prehistorical past of the race. Jesus, in Paul's theology, is the new Adam, and Erikson's Gandhi, in a somewhat different way, is also a second Adam. For Gandhi, through his sociocultural invention of satyagraha, wins anew for humanity the possibility of a ritualized resolution of conflicts in a manner that is strictly analogous to the pacifying rituals of animals or more primitive forms of human life. To be sure, in Erikson's schema, there is no direct recovery of the lost innocence of the old Adam. Not only is this true because man depends upon cultural forms to structure his unbound energies, but also because the instinctual complexity of the human animal needs first to be "cured"—a healing process which requires a combination of "insight, imagination, and conviction."[109] And Gandhi's technique is specifically designed to permit the recovery in his opponent of the "latent capacity to trust and to love."[110] Only through such a therapeutic intervention are the "pacific propensities" of the human animal liberated from that "instinctual and technical excess" which is its peculiar perversity.[111]

108. Ibid., p. 124.
109. Ibid., p. 428.
110. Ibid., p. 437.
111. Erikson, "Psychoanalysis and Ongoing History," p. 248.

But the possibility for such healing presupposes a recovery of a more original instinctive legacy: to mix conceptualities, the original adaptive competence of Adam. Gandhi only recreates under the conditions and complexities of history behavioral patterns from the archaic past. To make this explicit, Erikson articulates a point-by-point comparison of Gandhi's satyagraha technique with Lorenz's description of animal behavior. Like the *Damstags*, Gandhi engages his opponent at close range; he confronts him at the outset of a struggle, clearly specifying his intention and the grievance at issue. Throughout the struggle he keeps his opponent informed of each new move in order to maximize his capacity for response. Similarly, Gandhi himself improvises a series of responses to each new move of the opponent, and the whole scene resembles something like the scheduled and reciprocal antics of two parading stags. And just as these stags respect the vulnerability of their opponent's exposed side, so Gandhi refuses to take advantage of any temporary weakness in his opponent. Nor does he allow himself or any of his followers to inflict injury on the opponent, either through property damage, attack on the person's good name, or moralistic condemnation. Instead, Gandhi appeals to the best instincts of his opponent, interpreting the issue as a result of misunderstanding and not malice.

While Gandhi's battles were strenuous and the consequences serious, he conducted the affairs in a spirit of "Franciscan gaiety" which was sufficiently contagious to create the mood of a joyous dance rather than a solemn struggle. And the guiding rule of the dance was that none of the partners could leave until the music stopped. Gandhi initiated his first fast in response to the deterioration of the workers' morale; they appeared ready to give up the struggle before the conflict was resolved. From both sides, Gandhi insisted upon a respect for the convenant of their struggle, as well as a recognition of the real relationships of interdependency which joined workers and owners in a larger humanity. In summary, Erikson concludes that "Gandhi, in his immense intuition for historical actuality and his capacity to assume leadership in 'truth in action,' may have created a ritualization through which men, equipped with both realism and spiritual strength, can face each other with a mutual confidence analogous to the instinctive safety built into the animals' pacific rituals."[112]

At this point our journey through Erikson's saga, from the origins of humanity to Gandhi, has come full circle. In Gandhi there is both a healing of instinctual aberration and a reconstitution in sociocultural forms of humanity's latent capacity for pacifying rituals. Gandhi's satyagraha may not be reduced to naturally given instinctive patterns—but his religious actualization does presuppose a more primordial instinctive legacy. In postulating this relationship of religion and nature, Erikson's phylogeny is consistent with his ontogeny: the religious faith of the adult also presupposes—but may not be reduced to—the developmentally prior basic trust of the infant. To summarize this relationship in a theological formula we could say, in the language of Thomas Aquinas, that grace heals and completes, but does not violate, nature. Erikson concludes his discussion of the relation between animal behavior and Gandhi in a somewhat similar manner: "Only faith gives back to man the dignity of nature."[113]

SOME UNFINISHED MATTERS

Meanwhile, back in the sixteenth century, Hans and Martin remained locked in battle. Shall we conclude that this father-son conflict, enacted in the social forms of the medieval world, resembles the contest of the two stags, with both parties bound to each other in a relationship of mutual respect and interdependency, refusing to cause irreparable harm to the other? Or, must we conclude that these two stubborn Teutonic opponents are driven by irrational rage and the need to inflict a pain devoid of redeeming purpose?

I doubt that we know enough about the specificities of these two opponents to give a clear answer. But what we do know, from the town records of Mansfeld and the letters of Martin,

112. *Gandhi's Truth*, p. 433.
113. Ibid., p. 435.

is sufficient to reject Erikson's caricature of Hans. We do know that Hans expressed tender feelings, not only to Martin but also to friends and neighbors. We know that when he did drink he became somewhat gay, prone to silliness and song, but quite the opposite of Martin's nephew, who was reprimanded as a surly drunk. We also know that no murder charge was ever filed against "Big Hans," and that even "Little Hans" could not have fled to Mansfeld to escape murder charges in Thuringia, for both towns were under the same legal jurisdiction. We know from Martin's one account of the specified one thrashing he received from his father that Hans took the initiative to win back his son's affection, and was anxious until the two were reconciled.[114] And we know that Martin was highly critical of any physical punishment for children, at school or at home, in a manner quite untypical for that age, and that he enjoyed a loving relationship with his own children.[115] Martin appears to have been as gentle in his private life as he was verbally abusive of opponents in his public life. But while all these tidbits of historical evidence may be sufficient to dismiss Erikson's portrait of Hans as historically unreliable, they are hardly adequate, in my judgment, to construct a historically and psychologically credible alternative. In some matters of history—as well as metaphysics—agnosticism remains the most appropriate response.

As for psychohistory, I hope I have not created the impression that Erikson's version of this new discipline is "nothing but" religious narrative. Erikson's psychohistory is also, though never *only*, an application of psychoanalytic insights to figures and events of the past. Hopefully this aspect of Erikson's contribution has been discussed sufficiently in recent literature to be taken for granted.[116] My purpose in this essay

114. See Spitz, p. 71 above.

115. Erikson, *Young Man Luther*, pp. 78, 237.

116. For a collection of essays on this subject see Bruce Mazlish, ed., *Psychoanalysis and History* (Englewood Cliffs, N.J.: Prentice-Hall, 1963). For a bibliographical survey see Robert M. Crunden, "Freud, Erikson and the Historian," *The Canadian Review of American Studies* 4, no. 1 (Spring 1973): 48–64. See also Cushing Strout, "Ego Psychology and the Historian," *History and Theory* 7, no. 4 (1968):291–97, and Frank E. Manuel, "The Use and Abuse of Psychology in History," *Daedalus* (1971):187–213.

has been to correct what I regard as an oversimplified reading of Erikson's psychohistory by highlighting its specific religious characteristics. Because *Young Man Luther* occupies such a privileged position in the development of this fledgling discipline, it may appear as if Erikson's religious and ethical passions are intrinsic components of the discipline itself. Such a confusion would have unfortunate consequences for psychohistory as a historical discipline. It is axiomatic that religious narratives do distort the past to an unusual degree for the sake of the present. The several stories of the people of Israel in the Hebrew Scriptures, the differing gospel accounts of Jesus, and the many sutras which tell the story of Gautama Buddha share in common an extraordinary freedom to alter the past for the sake of communicating faith, hope, or some other virtue deemed vital for a perceived crisis of the author's present. Considered in itself, there is no reason why psychohistory should not be informed by that intellectual skepticism which is such a prominent quality of the reliable historian, but its confusion with religion is not likely to further this end.

As for Erikson's contribution to the field of religious studies, this is a subject which requires more clarification than could be provided in this essay. So far, much of the theological discussion of Erikson has regarded him as a psychologist with religious sympathies whose developmental theory may be useful to illumine a religious understanding of human life.[117] The theological schema in Erikson's thought has not been explicated as a theme for inquiry in its own right. But Erikson is a lay theologian as well as a lay historian; he has appropriated with his Western cultural heritage a whole array of religious motifs and incorporated them into his own eclectic synthesis. The religious dimensions of his intellectual venture, like the historical ones, also merit critical attention. Only the most obvious points of similarity could be noted here. Buried beneath, I suspect, is a far richer mix of issues waiting to be explored.

---

117. Don Browning, *Generative Man: Psychoanalytic Perspectives* (Philadelphia: Westminster, 1973).

7. Bonhoeffer in the Context of Erikson's Luther Study

Clifford J. Green

In Erikson's reading, Martin Luther not only weathered an acute identity crisis as a gifted young man and produced a creative religious-psychological synthesis, but by so doing he also opened up new possibilities of identity and "ideology," of psyche and society, for his contemporaries and for following generations. Consequently he has held a special place of affection in the lives of his followers, not only for the legacy of theology and church he bequeathed but also as a living, personal presence. Although few theologians have held such a position in Christian history—a position usually reserved for saints and martyrs—our own century perhaps has a similar phenomenon in Dietrich Bonhoeffer. He too has exerted a personal magnetism on modern Christians seeking to weld faith and identity. In the thirty years since his death at the hands of the Nazis in 1945, his charisma has had two poles: his seminal articulation of a style of faith affirming autonomy, freedom, mutuality, responsible action and ego strength (his "religionless Christianity," in striking contrast to the religiosity Freud dissected); and his courageous political action as a member of the German resistance movement, a commitment which cost him his life.

Two intrinsic connections link Bonhoeffer to Erikson's Luther study. First, there is an autobiographical dimension to Bonhoeffer's theology which invites an exploration similar to Erikson's study of Luther. If Bonhoeffer suffered an identity crisis in his early twenties, how does his existential problem compare to Luther's, how did he resolve it, and how does this resolution inform the pattern of his theology? To what extent

162

was the problem of Bonhoeffer's personal life history sufficiently typical for modern people that his own resolution could
provide a paradigm for others?

Second, Bonhoeffer as a German Protestant was informed
by the Lutheran theological tradition. No proponent of Lutheran traditionalism, even in a repristinated form, Bonhoeffer
was clearly influenced by basic Lutheran themes and theological
style. Yet his work amounts to a transformation of Luther's
legacy, particularly at two crucial points, soteriology and social
ethics. The theological category of soteriology corresponds to
the psychological category of identity in Erikson's schema,
while social ethics (broadly understood) corresponds to Erikson's category of ideology. In discussing soteriology and social
ethics, therefore, it is the intersection of the theologian's faith
and thought with his psychosocial experience that is the subject matter.

These two links set the agenda for this essay, which can be
formulated broadly in Erikson's phrase, "life history and the
historical moment." My concern is with the distinctive psychosocial dynamics which inform theology and ethics in different
historical eras, in this case the twentieth-century theologian
and activist Bonhoeffer compared with Luther, the late medieval monk-turned-reformer.

Two cautions must be entered here. In no sense does this
essay aspire to parallel Erikson's study of Luther even in minia-
ture. Apart from limits of space and psychological competence,
there are also limits imposed by the fact that some biographical
data are not yet available. Yet while some tentativeness is
enjoined, enough has been published, I believe, that one can
be reasonably confident about the following sketch of Bonhoeffer in its main outlines. But—and this is my second caution
—it would be unforgivably ironic to psychologize Bonhoeffer
and neutralize his passion for the social and ethical character
of human life. The type of person Philip Rieff has called "psychological man" would be anathema to Bonhoeffer. Near the
end of his life he said: "I know less than ever about myself,
and I'm no longer attaching any importance to it. I've had

more than enough psychology, and I'm less and less inclined
to analyse the state of my soul. . . . There is something more
at stake than self-knowledge."[1]

There is something more at stake, indeed, as documented by
Bonhoeffer's death at the hands of the Nazi tyrants he had
opposed. And Erikson, as demonstrated by his Gandhi study
in the context of his psycho*social* method, would hardly
approve the subjective and asocial reductionism of a person
such as Bonhoeffer. If this exploration of the autobiographical
dimension of Bonhoeffer's thought helps illumine his hard-won,
mature faith, his breakthrough from the constrictions of traditional Lutheran ethics, and his own ethical thought and action,
then the integrity of his life will be respected.

My purpose, then, is twofold: to explore theology and autobiography in Bonhoeffer, and to compare theology and ethics
in Luther and Bonhoeffer in relation to their respective psychosocial infrastructures. The first half of this essay concentrates
in some detail on Bonhoeffer's earlier life and writings, particularly several passages on the soteriological problem written
between 1927 and 1932. These have received much less attention than his famous *Letters* and his role in the resistance
movement, yet are indispensable for understanding his better-
known writings and actions. The fulcrum here is a late adolescent identity crisis and a turning "from the phraseological to
the real," as he later called it, in 1932. While this resembles
Erikson's approach to Luther, Bonhoeffer did not achieve in
one step what Luther accomplished with his insight of justification by faith. Bonhoeffer's *Nachfolge* (*The Cost of Discipleship*) embodies the "great liberation" of 1932, but also
expresses unresolved theological and personal conflicts. The
latter half of the essay, then, briefly considers Bonhoeffer's
Letters as fulfilling the 1932 experience and expressing new
insights about Christian faith and also about himself, based on
experiences in the church struggle and the resistance move-

1. Dietrich Bonhoeffer, *Letters and Papers from Prison*, enlarged ed. (New
York: Macmillan, 1972), p. 162; cf. pp. 347–48. In a number of instances
below I have altered the published translations of Bonhoeffer's works.

ment and with his own family. Then, finally, the comparison of the theology and ethics of Luther and Bonhoeffer discloses the intrinsic connection between the thought and the life histories of the two theologians, the distinctness of their respective positions, and Bonhoeffer's challenge to the Lutheran tradition.

Dietrich, born in 1906, was one of eight children. He had a twin sister, one younger sister, and two older sisters who came between him and his three brothers, who were five to seven years older than he. His father was a professor of psychiatry at Berlin and a scientifically oriented agnostic, as was the eldest son, the brilliant physicist Karl-Friedrich. Walter, the next son, was killed in World War I when Dietrich was twelve, a traumatic experience for his mother. Klaus, the third brother, was a lawyer. The family expected and nurtured impressive personal strengths in its members, whose common solidarity was matched by their individual independence. Dietrich was a brilliant student, completing his doctorate at the age of twenty-one. He excelled in music, surpassing at an early age his elder brothers in this art. He was successful in track sports and tennis and loved chess and bridge, competitive games of intense, intellectual concentration. He brought to these games a will to win, and expected the same of his partners. His father expected his children to think and speak precisely, and showed his pleasure when they did so; he gave them ample freedom to make decisions about their own lives, and when Dietrich chose theology his father did not voice for a decade his own doubts about the choice. (Contrast Hans Luther's opposition to his son entering the monastery, and his attack on Martin at his ordination.) In later life Dietrich wrote that "astringency in the relationship between father and son is a sign of great strength and inner security."[2] His mother was a stimulating, energetic, strong-willed and independent woman,

2. In a letter of January 22, 1944, in Eberhard Bethge, *Dietrich Bonhoeffer* (Munich: Chr. Kaiser, 1970), p. 38 (hereafter cited as Kaiser ed.); English translation *Dietrich Bonhoeffer* (New York: Harper & Row, 1970), p. 6 (hereafter cited as Harper ed.).

who gave her children an excellent start in their educations by teaching them herself, being critical of the state schools. It was she who provided the religious education for her children, though independently of the church. Enjoying all the advantages of Berlin culture early in the century, the Bonhoeffers belonged to the intellectual and social elite. In all, the family could have been designed to produce the strong, autonomous personalities which Bonhoeffer celebrated in his prison letters.

Dietrich was fourteen when he made his decision to become a theologian. His biographer points out that while there were precedents among ancestors and relatives, Dietrich's "isolation in the grouping of brothers and sisters is far more likely to have nourished the desire to accomplish something himself which all of them had not achieved."[3] His brothers responded with disdain, saying he was taking the path of least resistance; compared with the distinguished professions of his father and themselves in psychiatry, physics, and law, they argued, he had chosen a miserable petit-bourgeois institution. The theologian-to-be responded with defiance: "Well, I will reform that church!" There is a revealing 1932 memoir in which Bonhoeffer speaks of his "theatrical fantasies" about death during his boyhood: he is on his deathbed, dying "a fine devout death," and speaking to his surrounding family words he had secretly rehearsed many times. "He would have liked them all to see and understand that to a believer in God dying was not hard, but was a glorious thing."[4] His youthful decision to become a theologian expressed strong competition with the scientific-agnostic elder brothers and father, and, as we shall see, a good deal of ambition and vanity.

By the time he was twenty-six he had indeed accomplished something for himself. His doctorate and *Habilitation* were well behind him, his outstanding intellectual gifts were highly regarded by senior colleagues in Berlin where his teaching at the university was attracting considerable student attention, and he commanded positions of leadership in the ecumenical

3. Bethge, *Dietrich Bonhoeffer* (Kaiser ed.), p. 62.
4. Ibid. (Harper ed.), p. 24.

movement. He had lived up to the high standards of achievement the family expected and had impressively established his
own independence.

His early theology, however, pointed to urgent problems as
well as to the foundations for his later thought. This theology
is best understood as a theology of sociality, a theme he pro-
grammatically announced in his dissertation[5] and one that
remained, with modifications, throughout his whole theological
development. A concentration on the person's relations with
others and his responsibility for corporate, human communities, and a preoccupation with Christ who is *socially* present
to free and shape authentic social life, pervade his thinking.
Within this theology of sociality, his theological anthropology
is articulated in a clear and consistent set of categories, and
the anthropology includes a specific soteriological-psychological
problem.

A striking phenomenon in Bonhoeffer's early writings delin-
eates this soteriological problem and reveals its autobiographical
dimension. In at least seven passages written between 1927
and 1932, Bonhoeffer states the problem, often using identical
phrases and metaphors. These passages are the more striking,
first, because he does not consciously highlight or systematically
relate the passages to each other, and, second, because they
recur in quite diverse discussions ranging from an exegesis of
Genesis 3 to a critique of German idealism. I will quote three
examples which repeat and elaborate themes already found in
his two dissertations.[6]

The first example is chosen from his inaugural lecture in

5. Dietrich Bonhoeffer, *Sanctorum Communio* (London: Collins, 1963), p. 13.
Cf. Clifford Green, *Bonhoeffer: The Sociality of Christ and Humanity* (Mis-
soula, Montana: Scholars Press, 1975).

6. See Bonhoeffer, *Sanctorum Communio* (completed in 1927), pp. 71–72, and
Act and Being (New York: Harper & Row, 1962), pp. 156–59. See also the
deathbed fantasy mentioned above (Bethge, *Dietrich Bonhoeffer* [Harper ed.],
pp. 24–25) and his adolescent attraction to Michelangelo's statue "The Victor"
(Green, *Bonhoeffer*, pp. 212–13). The seven passages mentioned above, including those not quoted here, appear in the latter volume on pp. 150–57,
where several other related passages are also indicated.

1930, "The Question of Man in Contemporary Philosophy and Theology." Describing the condition of sin, Bonhoeffer writes:

> Man . . . finds himself in a mankind which has fallen away from God because it wanted to be like him, and now stands under his judgment. He sees himself condemned as an individual and as everyman. . . . The spirit of sin has torn him away from the Spirit of God and from his neighbor. Now his spirit circles continually around itself. Now he is lord of the world, but only of just that world which his ego [*Ich*] interprets for itself; he is lord in his self-enclosed, violated world. He sees his fellow man as a thing, and God as the one who satisfies his religious needs. Now he seeks to establish himself eternally in this world; he does not wish to die, but he wants to justify himself and live eternally. But in searching for this . . . man begins to feel a frightful loneliness. He becomes anxious about his lordship over a dead world, and in his angst he breaks the fearful silence of his loneliness; he breaks loose from himself, encounters himself in order to take the place of the missing other, and indicts himself. That is conscience. But since he is accuser, defendant and judge all in one, the call of conscience proves itself to be nothing other than the ultimate grasp of the ego for itself. . . . And its call fades away in the silent, dominated world of the ego.[7]

A virtually identical statement is found in *Creation and Fall*, dating from lectures of the winter semester of 1932–33. Fallen Adam

> is *sicut deus*. He gets his own way. He is himself creator, source of life, and origin of the knowledge of good and evil. He is alone, he lives out of his own self, he no longer needs any other person. He is lord of his world, but now of course the lonely lord and despot of the mute, violated, silenced dead world of his ego [*toten Ichwelt*].
>
> But as man *sicut deus* he really cannot live . . . without God, without the other person or without the other creatures. In conscience and remorse he always seeks to feign the presence and the reality of another in his life. He accuses and torments himself; and he glorifies himself—all in order to

7. *Gesammelte Schriften*, ed. Eberhard Bethge (Munich: Kaiser, 1966), vol. 3, pp. 81–82.

escape, through lying, from the dreadful loneliness of an echo-less solitude.[8]

The next passage is of a different genre, but makes the same points and uses familiar imagery. The memoir, written in 1932 when Bonhoeffer was twenty-six, recalls an occasion in high school when the teacher asked him about his future, and he announced with "conflicting feelings of vanity and humility" that he was going to study theology. It then continues as fantasy:

Now they all knew, he had told them. Now he was faced with the riddle of his life. Now he stood solemnly before God and his class. Now he was the *center of attention.* Did he appear as he had wished, his features serious and resolute? . . . The moment swelled to pleasure, the classroom expanded to the infinite. There he stood in the *center of the world as the herald and teacher of his knowledge and ideals*; now they must all hear him in silence, and the approval of the Eternal rested on his words and his head. But again he was ashamed of himself. He well knew his contemptible vanity.

How often he had sought to master it. But it always crept back again, and it spoilt the pleasure of this moment. Oh, how well he knew himself at the age of seventeen. He knew all about himself and his weaknesses. And he also knew that he knew himself well. And through the corner of that piece of self-knowledge his deep vanity again forced an entry into the house of his soul and made him afraid.

It had made an incomparable impression on him when he had read in Schiller that man need only mortify a few small weaknesses in order *to be like the gods.* Since then he had been on the look-out. Here, it flashed through his mind, *he would come forth from the battle a hero.*

[Seeing "the curious, mistrustful, bored, disappointed, mocking eyes of his class-mates," he questions himself.] Don't they trust him? Don't they believe the sincerity of his commitment? Do they know something about him of which he is unaware?

Why are you all looking at me like that? . . . Scream at me that I am a vain, mendacious man *who does not believe what*

8. Dietrich Bonhoeffer, *Creation and Fall: Temptation* (New York: Macmillan, 1967), p. 90.

he says! But don't remain so considerately silent as if you understood me! . . .

There is the crowd. *He stands in the center and speaks;* he speaks fervently, enthusiastically. He does himself proudly. *A leaden stillness hangs over the crowd, a dreadful silent mockery.* No, that cannot be. He is not the man they take him for. He means it really seriously. They have no right to disdain me. You do an injustice—all of you. He prays.

God, say yourself if I am serious about you. Destroy me this very moment if I lie. Or punish them all; they are my enemies, your enemies. They do not believe me. I know myself that I am not good. But I know it myself—as you do, God! *I do not need the others. I, I, I will conquer.* Do you see how I am winning? Do you see how they are retreating, how they are confounded? *I am with you! I am strong. God, I am on your side!*

Do you hear me? Or don't you hear? To whom am I speaking? To myself? To you? To these others here?

Who is speaking? My faith? My vanity?

God, I will study theology. Yes, I have said so. They all heard it. There is no turning back. I will.[9]

In this passage we have candid autobiography, almost totally lacking any conscious theological analysis, and yet remarkably congruent with the themes in the preceding theological passages. Considered in light of other theological and autobiograhical texts, it demonstrates beyond doubt the extent to which Bonhoeffer's urgent, personal concerns were reflected in his theological writings. The problem Bonhoeffer is addressing theologically and personally can now be explored by identifying the main themes of these texts.

Bonhoeffer himself uses the broad term *egocentricity* to describe the problem which concerns him. Fallen Adam is "extremely egocentric";[10] he has replaced the self-giving and love of the created, "primal community" with demanding and self-seeking [*Selbstsucht*].[11] Fallen man inhabits a "world of egocentricity";[12] he "refers everything to himself, puts himself

9. Bethge, *Dietrich Bonhoeffer* (Harper ed.), pp. 25–26 (Kaiser ed. pp. 65–66) (italics mine).
10. *Sanctorum Communio*, pp. 81–82, 107, 110.
11. Ibid., pp. 71 ff.
12. *Gesammelte Schriften*, vol. 3, p. 126.

in the center of the world, does violence to reality, makes himself God, and God and the other man his creatures."[13] He experiences "total self-introversion [*gänzlichen In-sich-selbst-gekehrt-Seins*], the self-confinement and isolation of the very loneliest solitude with its tormenting desolation and sterility."[14]

Translated psychologically, "egocentricity" means narcissism, to which Bonhoeffer also points by regularly using Luther's phrase, *cor curvum in se*. Yet narcissism can take many forms, and if Luther's self-preoccupation focused on the demands of the superego, Bonhoeffer's seems to focus on *disordered ego functions*.

The distinctiveness of Bonhoeffer's concern emerges by keeping Luther in mind while analyzing the four predominant themes in the passages on the soteriological problem of "egocentricity." The person Bonhoeffer describes as "fallen Adam," "man in sin," is, first, a godlike, Promethean figure, heroic and conquering, a "creator and lord"—in short, a man of impressive *power*. His credo is, "God is man himself,"[15] and he means to overcome his few small weaknesses to emerge as God's self-appointed champion and victorious defender. He is endowed with many personal gifts through which he has won success. Particularly prominent are his *intellectual powers*: by his autonomous thought he rules a "self-interpreted world," grounding reality and truth in himself and asserting himself over others by his knowledge, ideals and impressive speech. Intellectual achievement glorifies the self: "the thought and philosophy of man in sin is self-glorifying"; moral self-knowledge also serves self-assertion and self-justification.

Bonhoeffer does not treat the problem of "egocentricity" as simply an internal, subjective concern of the individual; one's thinking and experience are intrinsically social. So his soteriological passages stress, secondly, the way the egocentric self *dominates others*. He rules over other persons as "things," and regards even God as a "religious object." Demanding re-

13. Ibid., p. 101.
14. *Act and Being*, p. 28.
15. *Gesammelte Schriften*, vol. 3, p. 120.

places giving, and competition excludes mutuality. His "self-interpreted world" is a "self-dominated world," an "over-powered and misinterpreted world."[16] "I do not need the others," he dreams, "I, I, I will conquer." "The ego stands in the center of the world, which is created, ruled, overpowered by the ego."[17]

Thirdly, *human relationships are violated*; others are dominated and true community is destroyed. Other people are not genuine "others" to be acknowledged, respected and loved in their own right, but things to be used; the "limits" which other persons present to the self are not respected but subordinated to the self. Power, not mutual love, characterizes the self-other relationships. So this powerful, egocentric man lives in "bleak isolation," in the "cold silence of his eternal solitude,"[18] in isolated self-sufficiency.

The fourth theme is *conscience*. Typically, as in most of the quoted passages, conscience is aroused in the false solitude of egocentricity. Negatively, it accuses the self for violating genuine social life with others; positively, conscience summons the "better self" who would relate freely to others in love and community. Yet conscience itself is a prisoner of the narcissistic circle, according to these passages. It is "the confirmation and *justification* of his autocratic solitude,"[19] "the ultimate grasp of the I for itself." Consequently, conscience is not depicted as the source of a transforming personal crisis; rather, it "sounds without echo in the self-dominated and self-interpreted world,"[20] and "its call fades away in the silent, dominated world of the ego." Can these statements be taken at face value? The autobiographical memoir seems to show a deep unresolved conflict of conscience: is he really sincere in his commitment to be a theologian, or is he self-serving and self-deceived? Who is speaking—faith or vanity? In this confession the claim of con-

16. Ibid., p. 123.
17. Ibid., p. 119 (Bonhoeffer's English).
18. Cf. *Act and Being*, pp. 156–59.
19. Ibid., p. 158 (italics mine).
20. Ibid.

science appears more effectual than in the theological statements. Nevertheless, we should note that Bonhoeffer apparently
did not suffer the paralyzing attacks of negative superego which
so tormented Luther. "Despite all my abandonment," Bonhoeffer later wrote, "I was very pleased with myself."[21] This
helps explain a pointed departure, found in his first book and
repeated elsewhere, from the classical Lutheran view of conscience: "Conscience can just as well be the ultimate prop of
man's self-justification as the place where Christ strikes home
at man through the law."[22]

Bonhoeffer's life situation during the time of these writings
sheds additional light on his concern and brings us to his first
step toward a resolution. In the years leading up to 1932 he
experienced considerable personal conflict. Then in his early
twenties, it is safe to say that he was in the midst of a fairly
acute identity crisis. The schoolroom memoir is ample evidence. It focuses on his vocation, which we know involved a
deep, competitive drive both to excel like the other men of
the family and at the same time to secure an identity quite
distinct from them. And, while religion was not a contentious
issue in the family, we observe that he followed not the
agnosticism of his father but the religion of his mother. In
his career as an academic theologian in the university he perhaps felt he could have the best of both worlds. But his first
couple of years in the university were restless and searching.
The memoir says he was faced with the *riddle of his life*. He
candidly acknowledges the conflict between the humility appropriate to his professed faith and his own vanity, pride and
posturing; between serving Christ and promoting his own
ambition through theology. Even more, he suspects that his
classmates realize the contradiction: "Didn't they believe the
sincerity of his commitment? . . . Scream at me that I am a
vain, mendacious man who does not mean what he says." And
finally he asks himself: "Who is speaking? My faith, or my
vanity?"

21. Bethge, *Dietrich Bonhoeffer* (Harper ed.), p. 155 (Kaiser ed. p. 249).
22. *Sanctorum Communio*, p. 72.

During these few years Bonhoeffer was gripped by the early novels of Georges Bernanos, *Sous le soleil de Satan* and *L'Imposture*, which appeared in German in 1927 and 1929. Bethge describes the impact as follows:

> He was disconcerted to find again here his most personal problems: the priest and saint as the chosen target of the tempter, the man who can scarcely endure the alternating assaults of *desperatio* and *superbia* . . .
>
> The renegade priest is the intellectual sceptic whose "wilful thought is the best weapon against grace"; he writes theological books, "treacherous, wilful work, scintillating, unfruitful books with a tainted heart, masterpieces!"
>
> Bonhoeffer's encounter with these early works of Bernanos is the most revealing personal sign we know of in this period. The question of his life commitment was more burning than ever. The discovery of Bernanos so disturbed him that he did something he very seldom ventured, namely tried to interest his father in what he was reading.[23]

Several years after this, Bonhoeffer repeatedly recommended Bernanos's later book, *The Diary of a Country Priest*, to his seminarians, commenting, "When [these] priests speak . . . , their words carry weight. The reason is that they are not the products of some sort of verbalized reflection or observation but quite simply of daily, personal intercourse with the crucified Jesus Christ. These are the depths from which a word must come if it is to carry weight."[24] Quite some time had to elapse from the conflict and crisis depicted in the schoolroom memoir, however, before he was able to offer this advice.

In the interim Bonhoeffer experienced "a great liberation," in which the years of personal struggle and conflict culminated; we can be fairly confident in dating this breakthrough in the summer of 1932.[25] Near the end of his life he described it as a movement "from the phraseological to the real,"[26] an apt phrase in light of the problem that Bernanos's priest mirrored

23. *Dietrich Bonhoeffer* (Harper ed.), pp. 103–4.
24. Ibid., p. 471.
25. Green, *Bonhoeffer*, pp. 171 ff.
26. *Letters and Papers from Prison*, p. 275; cf. Green, *Bonhoeffer*, pp. 145 ff.

to him. Closer to the experience, the most explicit account of this "conversion" comes from a letter he wrote to a girlfriend on January 27, 1936 (the text itself proves that he is speaking of an experience prior to 1933):

> I plunged into work [teaching, pastoral work, ecumenical activities] in a very unchristian way. An . . . ambition that many noticed in me made my life difficult. . . .
>
> Then came something else, something that up to this day has changed my life and turned it sharply round. For the first time I came to the Bible. Previous to that I had often preached and seen a great deal of the church, . . . but I had not yet become a Christian. . . .
>
> I know that to that time I had made the cause of Jesus Christ into an opportunity for my own advancement. . . . I had never, or hardly ever, prayed. Despite all my abandonment I was very pleased with myself. The Bible, especially the Sermon on the Mount, liberated me from that. Since then everything has been different. I have felt this plainly, and so have other people about me. It was a great liberation. It became clear to me that the life of a servant of Jesus Christ must belong to the church and step by step it became clearer to what extent this must be so.
>
> Then came the crisis of 1933. That confirmed me in it. Also I now found others who shared that aim with me. All that matters to me now is the renewal of the church and the pastorate. . . .
>
> Christian pacifism, which I had recently combatted passionately, . . . suddenly became self-evident to me.
>
> My calling is clear to me. What God will make of it I do not know. . . . But it is a fine thing, to have this calling.[27]

A year earlier he had written to his brother, the agnostic physicist Karl-Friedrich, about the same experience. Noting that his brother might think him "somewhat fanatical" and might prefer him to be "more reasonable," he writes that he is very happy to feel that he is on the right track for the first time in his life. He is now taking the Sermon on the Mount seriously; his life now means something totally different than when he began with "theology . . . [as] a more academic affair." Stating that

27. Bethge, *Dietrich Bonhoeffer* (Harper ed.), pp. 154–55 (Kaiser ed. pp. 248–49).

his new-found biblical faith also seems to him the only source of power capable of resisting and overthrowing Hitler and all his works, he concludes, "I still cannot really think you genuinely believe all these ideas are so completely crazy. There are things for which an uncompromising stand is worthwhile. And it seems to me that peace and social justice, or Christ himself, are such things."[28] Bonhoeffer still feels a need, it appears, to explain and even justify himself to his eldest brother; but he also seems to have a degree of independence and self-assurance which he surely lacked when the older brothers mocked him about his adolescent decision to become a theologian.

A third letter about the same experience was written to his brother-in-law, who saw himself in the religious tradition of Harnack and Naumann. Bonhoeffer again mentions the Bible as a source of new-found security, and as a protection against his greatest temptation: "I am afraid of running into a divine counterpart [*göttlichen Doppelgänger*] of myself." "You cannot imagine," he concludes, "how glad one is to find one's way back to these elemental things after wandering on a lot of theological side-tracks."[29]

We can now attempt a summary of the personal problem with which Bonhoeffer wrestled in his younger life and which he expressed in his earlier theology, and we can examine his effort to resolve it in the years from 1932 to 1937. A very talented and conspicuously successful young man, he was driven by an elemental ambition and competitiveness to prove himself equal, if not superior, in the eyes of his older brothers and father. The arena he chose for this contest was "theology [as an] . . . academic affair." The psychic weapons were those nurtured and prized by the family, especially intellectual ego functions; ego skills were mobilized in service of the narcissistic self. Success followed his efforts and reinforced his ambition and vanity. The autonomous thought of his intellect ruled over a

28. Ibid., p. 155 (Kaiser ed. p. 249).
29. Ibid., pp. 155–56 (Kaiser ed. p. 250).

self-interpreted world. By his academic achievements he had become, as it were, a godlike figure; he is the champion of God, who, in the schoolroom memoir, he assures of his victorious support. God is, in fact, his own *Doppelgänger.*

Yet victory brings bitter rewards. He experiences a profound isolation, for in this world of the powerful narcissist other persons are only things. Conscience articulates the inner division, for he feels that "he does not believe what he says." In Erikson's terms, his behavior is at odds with his ideology, his theology of sociality which spoke so impressively of human community and mutual love. And his vocational commitment, thrown down like a gauntlet in adolescence, is a contradiction: the professed minister of Christ has made the cause of Jesus an opportunity for self-advancement. His words and deeds and work are all phraseological; they are not integrated with his psychic reality, but contradict it. How did Bonhoeffer try to deal with this identity crisis? What changes appear in his theology after the "great liberation" of 1932?

"The Bible, especially the Sermon on the Mount, liberated me from that. . . . It became clear to me that the life of a servant of Jesus Christ must belong to the church." After completing the 1932–33 academic year, Bonhoeffer left the university for the church. He was first pastor of the German congregations in London, and then directed the Confessing Church's seminary at Finkenwalde until he became involved in the resistance movement after war broke out. If the writings considered above concentrate on the psychic dimension of Bonhoeffer's liberating experience, we must also underline the *sociopolitical* aspect of that breakthrough, given the prominence of resistance to Hitler and Nazism in his life after 1933. "Then came the crisis of 1933. That confirmed me in it." Both psychic and social factors, then, informed Bonhoeffer's move from academic theology in the university to pastoral work in the church.

What of "the Bible, especially the Sermon on the Mount"? (This is hardly the normal place for a Lutheran to resolve an existential crisis of faith!) In November, 1932, Bonhoeffer gave an address to the Berlin Student Christian Movement entitled "Christus und der Friede."[30] He spoke of the whole-hearted love to God and man required of the disciples of Jesus. Jesus Christ is the one "absolute authority" above all earthly authorities, and discipleship is *following*, simple obedience to the commandment of Christ—the Sermon on the Mount speaks unambiguously to the single-minded reader. To understand law and gospel as divorcing obedience from grace is "cheap grace." In short, the *authority* of Christ and *obedience* to his *command*, particularly as given in the Sermon on the Mount, is the essence of discipleship.

We have here, of course, the basic theological ideas of *Nachfolge*, which was written during the next few years and published in 1937. Its readers then—and it had considerable impact—heard it as a stringent and uncompromising call to "costly grace" from a leading theologian of the Confessing Church in the midst of the struggle with Hitler. And so it was. But they did not know that it was also existentially rooted in the theologian's own personal life. Like Bonhoeffer's earlier writings, *Nachfolge* too is pervaded by an autobiographical dimension. The most obvious clue is the prominence of the Sermon on the Mount (about two-thirds of the book is devoted to it and related passages), which Bonhoeffer had singled out in his letters as clarifying his "calling." Indeed, his design was that part one of his book, on the Sermon, and part two, on the Pauline corpus, should be shown in complete harmony with each other. This deliberate departure from the Lutheran tradition is a direct consequence of the Sermon's importance to Bonhoeffer himself. There he heard the authoritative word which spoke to his condition. Not Luther's message that grace alone justifies the man enmeshed in guilt, futile works, self-hatred and hatred of God, but the command that the successful, self-satisfied, willful, autonomous man must abandon his own ambitions and single-mindedly follow Christ—that is what

30. Ibid., pp. 158–59; Green, *Bonhoeffer*, p. 178. The text is printed in *Die Mündige Welt*, ed. Jørgen Glenthøj (Munich: Kaiser, 1969), vol. 5, pp. 69–71.

Bonhoeffer heard in the Sermon. *"Only he who believes is obedient* and *only he who is obedient believes."*[31]

The autobiographical dimension of *Nachfolge* is quite evident in Bonhoeffer's account of becoming a disciple. The book is replete with criticism of "the slavery of a self-chosen way."[32] Genuine discipleship is not a career for an ambitious man. There may indeed be in the church men who, with their intellectual ability or prophetic insight, seek not Christ but power and fame, and they may be quite untroubled by the contradiction in their lives; in fact, Bonhoeffer stresses, their contradiction against God is seen precisely "the more convincing and proud their apparent success."[33] Perhaps the most effective way to avoid the call to obedient discipleship is this: treat Christianity as a matter of ideas, principles, abstract questions —in other words, as a "phraseological" and "academic" intellectual enterprise.

Obedience, a concrete change in life and behavior, was the way Bonhoeffer moved from the phraseological to the real. This was his answer to the ambitious autonomy of the egocentric self glorifying in its own powers and successes. In this context I think we can understand both the content and the tone of his *Nachfolge*. Christ is above all the *authority* who commands and demands *obedience* from his followers. The disciple must make a total break from his former life, and this involves the complete surrender, mortification, and renunciation of his own will. By so doing he is freed from himself, drawn out of isolation, and united with the community of Christian brothers—just as Bonhoeffer was at Finkenwalde, in the community he named, significantly, the *Bruderhaus*. To be sure, Bonhoeffer also speaks of the grace and love of Christ, of the disciple being justified by faith, and of the joy, confidence and freedom of the disciple. But these are set within the context of the commanding Christ who *overpowers* the strong

31. Dietrich Bonhoeffer, *The Cost of Discipleship*, rev. ed. (New York: Macmillan, 1966), p. 69 (italics original).
32. Ibid., p. 52.
33. Ibid., p. 338.

self-will of the autonomous man and draws the isolated, narcissistic self into community with the Christian brothers.

At many points Bonhoeffer's exegesis reveals the influence of projection.[34] Particularly revealing is his treatment of the rich young man of Matthew 19:16–22, who wants to hold an intellectual "discussion" with the "good master," thus avoiding obedience to the unconditional, binding divine order. Most interesting is Bonhoeffer's knowledge of the young man's motivations, about which the text is quite silent. He has kept the commandments, but this is not enough for him; he wants to do "something extraordinary and unique." This ambitious desire is the height of obstinate defiance of Jesus, the young man's "final effort to retain his autonomy." Jesus calls this man to die to "his own will."[35] Bonhoeffer is drawing heavily on his own experience here, thus verifying his own dictum: "Understanding cannot be separated from the existence in which it has been won."[36]

Especially intriguing is Bonhoeffer's portrait of Luther, both in its lines and its spaces.[37] "Luther taught that man cannot stand before God even in his most pious efforts, because everything he did was basically self-seeking." We may take this as a reference to Luther's diagnosis of the *cor curvum in se* and his repudiation of justification by works. But Bonhoeffer becomes more specific. "The knowledge of grace was for him the final, radical break [*Bruch*] with his besetting sin. . . . Laying hold of forgiveness was the final, radical refusal of a self-willed life." If this already begins to sound like somebody else we know, Bonhoeffer spells out that Luther's problem is essentially the egotism of a willful, ambitious man. Entering the monastery was only an apparent renunciation; really it was "the ultimate, spiritual self-assertion of the religious man."

Luther's problem, Bonhoeffer implies, was not that monastic works did not bring him salvation, but rather that monasticism

34. See Green, *Bonhoeffer*, pp. 187 ff.
35. *The Cost of Discipleship*, p. 99.
36. Ibid., p. 55.
37. Ibid., pp. 50 ff.; Green, *Bonhoeffer*, pp. 190 ff.

was a form of elitist self-assertion by willful men. Accordingly, grace was for Luther "liberation from the slavery of a self-chosen way." The lines, then, sketch a Luther like a knight storming the gates of heaven. What of the spaces? Bonhoeffer tells us nothing of Luther's desperate guilt and angst. Where is the Luther who said repeatedly that a mere rustling leaf could strike terror into the human heart? And did Luther say that his problem was egocentric ambitiousness? The historical Luther desperately wanted to serve and love God; he understood his problem rather as hatred of the God whose demands he felt to be insatiable, and as guilt because of that hatred. Because his portrait of Luther is a thinly veiled picture of himself, Bonhoeffer can contend that the reformer "did not reject the fact that in the monastery heavy demands had been made, but only that obedience to the command of Jesus was understood as the achievement of the individual."[38] Ironically, one only has to consult the writings of his own Luther teacher, Karl Holl, to recognize Bonhoeffer's own urgent, personal concerns projected into this modern portrait of "Luther."[39]

How did Bonhoeffer himself evaluate the book as a whole? At the age of thirty-eight, seven years after writing *Nachfolge*, he looked back on it as the end of a necessary stage. Writing from prison, and then in a new personal and theological position, he related the book to a conversation with Jean Lasserre at Union Seminary in 1931.

> We were asking ourselves quite simply what we wanted to do with our lives. He said he would like to become a saint. . . . At the time I was quite impressed, but I disagreed with him and said, in effect, that I should like to learn to have faith. For a long time I didn't realize the depth of the contrast. I thought I could *acquire faith by trying to live a holy life,* or something like it. I suppose I wrote *The Cost of Discipleship* as the end of that path. *Today I can see the dangers of that book, though I still stand by what I wrote.*
>
> I discovered later . . . that it is only by living completely in this world that one learns to have faith. *One must abandon*

38. *The Cost of Discipleship*, p. 297.
39. Cf. Green, *Bonhoeffer*, pp. 191 ff.

> *any attempt to make something of oneself,* whether it be a
> saint, or a converted sinner, or a churchman. . . .[40]

The personal liberation which informed *Nachfolge,* and which
obliged him to stand by what he wrote, nevertheless still had
something forced and unnatural about it. Bonhoeffer was still
trying "to make something of himself," though, to be sure, it
was now something rather different from that of the first decade
after he chose theology as a career. We should not downplay
the genuineness of his hard-won commitment and faith, nor
the dedication of his service to the Confessing Church. He had
gained considerable freedom from his ambition and egocentricity. But we cannot overlook the problems which remain
unresolved in *Nachfolge.*

Chief among these is a strained effort to renounce personal
autonomy and a forced attempt to suppress his own powers.[41]
Bonhoeffer is overreacting against his own recent past. Because
his personal powers had been mobilized in a self-serving and
narcissistic way, he now teaches that they should be completely
renounced. When all is said and done, the Christ of *Nachfolge*
is an overwhelming power of absolute authority who demands
total submission to his commands. The power of Christ is set
over against the power of the self. Bonhoeffer has not yet distinguished—theologically or personally—between the narcissistic use of personal powers which dominates others and the
mature affirmation of human strengths in community with
others and in responsible service. He is still caught up, it seems,
in an inner struggle, probably at a quite unconscious level. (As
signs of continuing conflict, note the amount of violent language
in *Nachfolge,* the vacillation between authoritarian power and
theologia crucis in its Christology, and the anthropological
ambivalence of aggressive power and complete submission.)

It should be stressed that Bonhoeffer's actual behavior in the
1930s was hardly subdued or submissive. (Similarly, we cannot take the soteriological passages of the early theology as a
full description of all his behavior and actual relationships to

40. *Letters and Papers from Prison,* p. 369 (italics mine).
41. Cf. Green, *Bonhoeffer,* pp. 193 ff.

other people, since he highlights there only the *problematic* aspects of his experience.[42]) He threw himself with a vengeance into the battle against Hitler—and that may be personally significant as well as ecclesiastically and politically meaningful. He mobilized the German congregations in England for the Confessing Church, was active in ecumenical affairs in the cause of peace, was vigorously involved in German church politics and creatively directed the Finkenwalde seminary; in all of this he conspicuously employed, in the service of Christ and the church, those strengths of mind and will he so notably possessed. Nevertheless, he later looked back on the *Nachfolge* period as a necessary stage which he had transcended.

We come now to the celebrated *Letters and Papers from Prison.* I take it as self-evident that Bonhoeffer enters a new stage of theological development with his letter of April 30, 1944, to Eberhard Bethge, from Tegel prison. Here we find the well-known celebration of the "adulthood" (*Mündigkeit*) and "autonomy" of modern people, his critique of "religion," and his proposal for a "nonreligious Christianity."[43] It is also obvious, from his undisguised excitement and enthusiasm, that these ideas are quite important for him personally.

Without diminishing the wider cultural and historical pertinence of the prison theology, we must attend to the more immediate human context in which it emerged. Which nonreligious people, characterized by autonomy and maturity, did Bonhoeffer particularly have in mind as he wrote? From 1940 until his imprisonment in April, 1943, he devoted his efforts to the resistance movement, his seminary having been closed by the gestapo. Not only was the whole Bonhoeffer family united in opposition to Hitler from the beginning, but above all, since the outbreak of war, Dietrich worked in close partnership with his brothers and their friends, united in a comrade-

42. Ibid., p. 224.
43. Ibid., ch. 6; Johnson, Wallwork, et al., *Critical Issues in Modern Religion* (Englewood Cliffs, N.J.: Prentice-Hall, 1973), ch. 9.

ship he had never shared with them before. (In this partnership planning Hitler's overthrow, Dietrich used his ecumenical contacts to carry information on the resistance movement to the Allies, helped write memoranda on reorganizing Germany after a coup, and offered ethical counsel on the ambiguous experience of conspiracy.)

Bethge reviews the stages of Bonhoeffer's life as follows. In face of the predominantly scientific attitude in the family and the disdain of his elder brothers for the church, Bonhoeffer found it "more worthwhile to become a theologian than a parson and to deal in that way with other people's philosophies and agnosticism." Then, after 1932, he found in the church a new circle of brothers in the Finkenwalde *Bruderhaus,* whom he later left to join a different circle of fellow workers.

> He again joined his own brothers in their political efforts and found himself among comrades who knew little of his Finkenwalde associates. . . . The enthusiastically rediscovered church [expressed in *Nachfolge* and the Confessing Church] turned out to be sterile in its conception, and liberal brothers and friends turned out to do the necessary Christian deeds. This situation had to be penetrated and theologically verbalized in a way that expressed the true character of Christ and the true character of those worldly, secularized men. It was to serve *this* purpose that Bonhoeffer set out to rewrite his theology under the rubric of "nonreligious interpretation of the Gospel in a world come of age."[44]

Bonhoeffer's new relationship with his brothers and secular colleagues, then, was the the immediate social setting for his new theology. In them he saw the qualities he summed up as *"Autonomie"* and *"Mündigkeit"*; he now also saw and unreservedly affirmed these same qualities in himself. When he wrote to his godson about the family tradition the child had entered, Bonhoeffer was also speaking about his own family and himself.

> The urban culture of the bourgeois tradition embodied in the home of your mother's parents has created in its bearers the

44. Eberhard Bethge, "Turning Points in Bonhoeffer's Life and Thought," *Union Seminary Quarterly Review* 23, no. 1 (Fall 1967):9, 12–13, 19.

> proud consciousness of a calling to high public responsibility,
> to intellectual achievement and leadership, and the deep-
> rooted sense of obligation to be guardians of a great historical
> legacy and cultural tradition; it will give you, even before
> you realize it, a way of thinking and acting which you can
> never lose without being untrue to yourself.[45]

Bonhoeffer was not untrue to himself; in the *Letters* he found
the way to be a Christian without trying to deny his deepest
feelings about his true self.

The concept of *Mündigkeit* is the one quite new ingredient
in the *Letters*. Bonhoeffer is describing a new psychic posture
which, historically, gained particular impetus in the Renaissance and the Enlightenment. In essence it means that people
who have "come of age" have much more knowledge and
power than their ancient and medieval forebears, which they
exercise in an autonomous way to shape their lives. This
applies, Bonhoeffer believed, in the various sciences and also
in human affairs generally. Examples would include the whole
range of technologies used to control nature, and the attitude
of analysis and planning used to organize society and our personal lives. Psychologically, Bonhoeffer is talking about ego
functions which people use with a considerable freedom and
confidence to affirm and shape their lives and to take responsibility for their world. He is adamant in opposing Christian
apologists, and secular philosophers and psychotherapists,
whom he suspects of undermining these personal strengths.
His critique of religion is the corollary of his affirmation of
autonomy and adulthood, and his "nonreligious Christianity"
is designed precisely to give Christian shape and content to
the psychic posture of *Mündigkeit* and autonomy.

I think it is safe to claim that in his prison letters Bonhoeffer
is rehabilitating for himself just those personal strengths which
he sought to suppress in the *Nachfolge* period, and which he
had found so problematic in his late adolescence. What were
the autobiographical foundations of this new self-affirmation?
Bonhoeffer's "becoming a Christian" in 1932 gave him con-

45. *Letters and Papers from Prison*, pp. 294–95.

siderable freedom from that ambitious, competitive, and isolating "egocentricity" which had driven him in adolescence. But he was still trying "to make something of himself" in the *Nachfolge* period, and trying to contain himself by severe teachings about submission to Christ, renunciation of autonomy, and denial of self. In the resistance movement he put his life on the line and, I believe, thereby won true freedom over narcissism; he was then also free to affirm himself and his own strengths, overcoming the self-violation he advocated earlier. (His decision in New York in the summer of 1939 not to stay in isolated safety—a decision involving a deep, existential struggle—was a watershed in this development.[46]) He was also free, significantly, to become engaged, a venture in intimacy he had never made before. Furthermore, and essential to this personal growth, he was also bound together in the resistance movement with his brothers, from whom he had earlier found it necessary to distance himself. In them, their associates, and himself he found the free and responsible use of human strengths in the service of others. An important distinction between *power,* as personally and corporately destructive, and the *strength* of healthy, adult psyches, is made implicitly in the *Letters.* In this context Bonhoeffer was now free to affirm unreservedly those strengths which he and his family so conspicuously possessed. After he had been in prison for a year he knew that, with his life literally at stake, he was finally free from the long struggle with himself—and also free to be himself. Then it was that the new theology began to burst forth.

It is notable that the shorthand christological formula which recurs in the *Letters* describes Jesus as "the man for others"; and from this paradigm Christian existence and the life of the church is epitomized as "being-there-for-others." The overpowering Christ of *Nachfolge* has gone, and in his place is the crucified Jesus who enlists human strengths in the free and responsible service of others.

As indicated above, the chief theological categories corres-

46. Bethge, *Dietrich Bonhoeffer* (Harper ed.), pp. 552 ff.

ponding to Erikson's psychosocial rubric are soteriology and social ethics. In theology there is usually an intimate relation between the soteriology and ethics of a given position, just as in Erikson there is a mutual interaction between identity (psyche) and ideology (society). This is certainly the case in the theologies of Luther and Bonhoeffer, and in this part of the essay I will briefly compare Bonhoeffer to Luther with reference to the psychosocial dynamics of their theology and ethics.

The soteriological problem in Luther, theologically and personally, centers on the guilty conscience. Theologically, conscience apart from faith is the internal seat of the accusing law. In the 1545 preface to his Latin writings Luther described his early predicament in vivid terms.

> Though I lived as a monk without reproach, I felt that I was a sinner before God with an extremely disturbed conscience. I could not believe that he was placated by my satisfaction. I did not love, yes, I hated the righteous God who punishes sinners, and secretly . . . I was angry with God, and said, "As if, indeed, it is not enough, that miserable sinners, eternally lost through original sin, are crushed by every kind of calamity by the law of the decalogue, without having God add pain to pain by the gospel and also by the gospel threatening us with his righteousness and wrath!" Thus I raged with a fierce and troubled conscience.[47]

Guilty conscience, works to placate the righteous God, hatred of God who demanded satisfaction by works, and full circle back to self-accusation and guilt—that was Luther's treadmill. Erikson, indeed, defined Luther's historical contribution as dealing with this negative conscience. "Luther accepted for his life work the unconquered frontier of tragic conscience, defined as it was by his personal needs and his superlative gifts."[48] Psychologically, the conscience which is decisive in Luther's soteriology is *negative superego*. His own account describes his angry and aggressive feelings toward himself and toward the

47. *Luther's Works*, ed. and trans. Lewis W. Spitz (Philadelphia: Muhlenberg Press, 1960), vol. 34, p. 336–37.
48. Erik H. Erikson, *Young Man Luther* (New York: Norton, 1962), p. 195.

exacting divine authority whose demands he so scrupulously fulfilled in penitential works. Though he "lived as a monk without reproach," he was burdened with guilt and "raged with a fierce and troubled conscience."

His resolution of this soteriological problem was justification by faith: *sola gratia, sola fide.* Given the nature of the problem, the resolution involved a strict distinction of *law* and *gospel*: law must be expelled from conscience, so that it is the seat of Christ alone.

> The law in a Christian ought not to pass his bounds, but ought to have dominion only over the flesh, which is in subjection unto it. . . . When it is thus, the law is kept within his bounds. But if it shall presume to creep into thy conscience, and there seek to reign, see thou play the cunning logician, and make the true division. Give no more unto the law than belongeth unto it, but say thou: O law, thou wouldest climb up into the kingdom of my conscience, and there reign and reprove it of sin, and wouldest take from me the joy of my heart, which I have by faith in Christ, and drive me to desperation, that I might be without all hope and utterly perish. This thou doest besides thine office: keep thyself within thy bounds, and exercise thy power upon my flesh, but touch not my conscience; for I am baptized, and by the gospel am called to the . . . kingdom of Christ, wherein my conscience is at rest, where no law is, but altogether forgiveness of sins, peace, quietness, joy, health and everlasting life. Trouble me not in these matters, for I will not suffer thee, so intolerable a tyrant and cruel tormentor, to reign in my conscience, for it is the seat and temple of Christ the Son of God, who is the king of righteousness and peace, and my most sweet saviour and mediator: he shall keep my conscience joyful and quiet in the sound and pure doctrine of the gospel, and in the knowledge of this passive and heavenly righteousness.[49]

Justification by faith is trust in God's sheer, forgiving grace, his merciful acceptance of man without preconditions and works. Luther is freed from the prison of penitential piety; his conscience is no more ruled by guilty accusation (law) but by

49. Martin Luther, *A Commentary on St. Paul's Epistle to the Galatians*, ed. Philip S. Watson (London: James Clarke & Co., 1953), p. 28.

the gospel, and so he is freed from his hatred of the "active righteousness" demanded by the God of that piety. Luther can now love God, accept himself, and serve his neighbor in "the freedom of a Christian man."

This theological-psychological resolution is intimately related to Luther's social thought: the law-gospel distinction and the two kingdoms doctrine are clearly connected, though it is difficult to give an adequate yet brief statement of this relation. But it is obvious, especially if we compare Luther to a theologian like Anselm, that the reformer is engaged in a major reconstruction of the personal dynamics of the Christian life. The justified Lutheran conscience is not the medieval Catholic conscience (nor, incidentally, is it identical with the Calvinist conscience—a point to which Erikson should give more careful attention). While the law in its theological function remains related to conscience (*secundus usus legis*), conscience for the Christian is solely the seat of Christ's grace, love and forgiveness. The Christian "plays the cunning logician," keeping law within its bounds and confining it to "the flesh" and the outer world.

Accordingly, the law, which now (contrary to the Calvinists) has no positive function in conscience, has to be strongly affirmed in its civil form in society (*primus usus legis*). From the heavenly kingdom of Christ, Luther's *Galatians* passage continues, the Christian "come[s] forth into another kingdom." As a minister, a parent, a magistrate, or a servant, the Christian gladly works well in his vocation, submitting to the magistrates and their laws. And he must submit to these laws even "though they be severe, sharp and cruel, . . . because he knoweth that this is the will of God, and that this obedience pleaseth him."[50]

While the heart of the Christian is motivated by the grace of Christ to love and serve others freely, the Christian conscience for Luther is no longer the inner coercive sanction supporting social order. This is the function of society with its offices and institutions. Civil government is God's "left

50. Ibid.

hand," equipped with authority and force to contain evil and compel obedience. If conscience is the inner seat of Christ's mercy and love, external authority and force are necessary to restrain the sinful deeds of men and keep civil order. The essential function of the state is to contain evil as justly as possible. When this happens the church can minister to the troubled heart. The church preaches the saving Word of the gospel, and through the gospel the "proper work" of God's "right hand" is done.

Luther's two kingdoms doctrine is also, of course, dealing with a practical problem, the confusion of civil and spiritual authority. But it is not just an ad hoc measure. It expresses the very heart of Luther's theology, his soteriology, found in the law-gospel dynamics. There is an intrinsic theological-psychological logic which connects Luther's soteriology and his social ethics; hence law-gospel and two kingdoms form the constitutive structure of all Luther's thought.

Luther's theology, then, was rooted in the religious-cultural situation of the late medieval penitential piety. His soteriology deals concretely with the psychological problems of the negative superego; and his social ethics are profoundly shaped by the reconstruction of the medieval Catholic conscience expressed in his doctrine of justification. Briefly put, the coercion which grace expels from the conscience of the believer is reinforced in the civil realm and articulated in a basically conservative, authoritarian social ethic—as Erikson has tellingly noted.[51]

Bonhoeffer was a son of the twentieth century. Compared with Luther we find in him a different theological-ethical and psychosocial gestalt. In the soteriological passages examined above, Bonhoeffer is troubled about dominance, not guilt; power, not self-doubt; success, not defeat; vanity and self-congratulation, not despair; narcissistic isolation, not heavenly disapproval; Promethean posing as God's self-appointed champion, not hatred and fear of the demanding heavenly Father. Particularly striking are his statements about conscience as an

51. *Young Man Luther*, pp. 238, 256.

instrument of self-justification, in explicit contrast to Luther, for whom conscience was the effective accusation of the law which drove one to despair and paved the way for the gospel. I have suggested that psychologically we can identify Bonhoeffer's concern as a disorder of ego functions, the mobilizing of ego skills in service of the narcissistic self, in distinction from Luther's theological-psychological preoccupation with the negative superego.

If the psychic infrastructure of Bonhoeffer's thought has a different focus from Luther's, so too does the pattern and dynamic of his theology as a whole. Bonhoeffer's personal and theological concern was intrinsically *social*, and that in two inseparable aspects: with the interpersonal relations of individuals, and especially with the *corporate* being of the person and his responsible action for his communities. For him the individual person is essentially social, and his theology is most comprehensively understood as a theology of sociality. In this light, the autobiographical problem of narcissism, or "egocentricity," embodies the crucial soteriological problem, for narcissism contradicts being-with-and-for-others both individually and collectively. In contrast to Bonhoeffer's essentially social paradigm—a paradigm heavily informed by the experience and model of his family as a community—Luther's is primarily individual. To be sure, many social-religious factors contribute to Luther's guilt-justification paradigm, as many social consequences flow from it; but the paradigm itself is primarily intrapsychic.

This positive shape and intrinsic problematic of Bonhoeffer's theology illumines his distinctness from the pattern and dynamic of Luther's thought. Negatively, and unlike that of his traditional Lutheran contemporaries, it is clear that Bonhoeffer's thinking is not constituted by the law/gospel-two kingdoms pattern of Luther, despite the more or less revisionist attempts of some Lutherans to read him as if it were. Naturally, Bonhoeffer appropriated some basic motifs from Luther; the distinctive *theologia crucis* of his *Letters*, justification by faith, the being of Christ as *pro-me* and *pro-nobis*, the Christian as *simul justus et peccator* are examples. And at times he can even use Luther's distinctions of law and gospel, and the two kingdoms. But these motifs are transposed into a new context and transformed by being made to speak to new questions, such as those of the Christian response to the Nazi totalitarian state, and the decay of "religion" in a secular society. In some cases the transpositions are patently forced, as in the Luther portrait of *Nachfolge*, while in others they conflict with newer ideas, as in the treatment of conscience in *Act and Being*.[52]

More specifically, we can document many significant instances of Bonhoeffer's departure from typical Lutheran positions. On the side of social ethics he is constantly trying to break out of the theoretical and practical constrictions of the two kingdoms doctrine. One striking departure is his adoption of pacifism in the early 1930s, a direct consequence of the impact of the Sermon on the Mount, which we know had deep autobiographical roots. Later in the 1930s came the change from pacifism to his resistance movement activities and his part in the conspiracy to assassinate Hitler—again, hardly a typical Lutheran venture! This was not just an ad hoc response to an extreme political situation. Already in his lectures of the winter of 1933 he sharply criticized Gogarten's *Politische Ethik* (1932) as teaching a church-state doctrine preoccupied with the church's condemning of sin and supporting the state's containment of evil. This, Bonhoeffer objects, is a restatement of Christian conservatism which probably agrees with Lutheran teaching but not with the New Testament. The latter knows the ambiguity of the state, seeing its capacity not only to restrain evil but also to take the form of evil itself and perpetrate the greatest wickedness. So the church must continually call the state into question, remembering that "in no case is the church there only to prop up the state." Anticipating a theme of *Nachfolge*, Bonhoeffer continues that the church knows the

---

52. Cf. the appendix, "Note on 'Conscience' in *Akt und Sein*," in my doctoral dissertation, "The Sociality of Christ and Humanity: Dietrich Bonhoeffer's Early Theology, 1927–1933," Union Theological Seminary, New York, 1971; this is not included in the published version cited in note 5 above.

"better righteousness" of God's kingdom; this "establishes a relative, revolutionary Christian right" of the new to oppose an existing order in a radical way. Bonhoeffer wants to affirm and relativize the claims of both order and revolution in the name of the God who is Lord of the state and "who alone can create order and revolution."[53]

Another departure from the two kingdoms doctrine is his experiment with the idea of *"Erhaltungsordnungen,"* which relativizes the autonomy of the state (and other social institutions), making it accountable to Christ. There are no "orders of creation" embodying an autonomous, divine *raison d'être*; Christ is the criterion of the relative validity of any "order of preservation," and the source of a command to overthrow a given order.[54] The command of Christ "can demand the most radical destruction precisely for the sake of the One who builds up."[55] This experiment, while hardly a radical innovation, was certainly consistent with Bonhoeffer's position in opposition to Hitler; he continued this line of thinking with the concept of social orders as "mandates" in his *Ethics.*[56]

Similarly, Bonhoeffer's relentless concern with the concrete command cannot be contained within two-kingdoms thinking. Rather than requiring, in principle, submission to civil authorities, "though they be severe, sharp and cruel," as Luther said, Bonhoeffer requires the church to speak a concrete command as a corporate act at appropriate times; it must be proclaimed as clearly and definitively as the forgiveness of sins. To do so is to commit the church to specific political positions on issues such as war and socialism.[57]

Other examples could be given. But plenty of evidence could be adduced to show that, despite his freedom from many conventional and reactionary Lutheran social attitudes, Bon-

53. Bethge, *Dietrich Bonhoeffer* (2d Kaiser ed.), pp. 1082 ff.
54. *Gesammelte Schriften* 1, pp. 149 ff.; English trans. *No Rusty Swords*, ed. E. H. Robertson (New York: Harper & Row, 1965), pp. 165 ff.
55. Ibid.
56. (New York: Macmillan, 1965), pp. 207 ff., 286 ff., 329, 344 ff., 358.
57. See, for example, *Gesammelte Schriften* 1, pp. 145 ff. (*No Rusty Swords,* p. 163).

hoeffer's social ethics remained fairly conservative and elitist. Nevertheless, the examples given here document his originality compared with Luther and show that a different theological and psychosocial paradigm informed his thinking. In his social ethics it is not the containment of evil compensating for the remission of superego demands which is formative; rather, the freeing of persons and corporate communities for cohumanity and ethical proexistence is his overriding concern, and this presupposes a different psychic gestalt from Luther's.

The side of soteriology can be treated more briefly. We have already seen that the psychological problematic for Bonhoeffer is not negative superego but disordered ego functions of the narcissistic self. (Incidentally, Bonhoeffer's relative freedom from accusing conscience—at least compared with Luther— surely helps explain his participation in the resistance movement and the conspiracy against Hitler: such rejection of entrenched authority—and even demonic authority was not lightly trespassed by those reluctant conspirators—and deliberate shouldering of guilt could hardly be adopted by one prone to severe superego attacks.[58]) We have also noted that the accusations of conscience do not have a decisive role in the drama of salvation, nor are they a structural necessity in the dynamics of the life of faith: for Bonhoeffer, conscience was not the effectual inner voice of God's law, and conscience could even be co-opted in the service of narcissistic self-assertion. Consequently, *Nachfolge* presents as the source of genuine faith the commanding and overpowering Christ of the Sermon on the Mount, not Luther's unconditionally accepting and graciously consoling "Pauline" Christ; and in effect it replaces the law-gospel distinction with a *welding together* of gospel and law: "*Only he who believes is obedient* and *only he who is obedient believes.*"

The *Letters* transcend the christological and anthropological problems of *Nachfolge* in affirming the psychic strengths in-

58. See discussion on "civil courage" (*Letters and Papers from Prison*, p. 6), and the qualified but affirmative statement on the previous page about one "who values the necessary deed more highly than the purity of his own conscience and reputation."

volved in *Autonomie* and *Mündigkeit*. But the Christ whose being is "being-there-for-others" is no mere sanctifier of a new psychic development in secular culture; he is the presence of a transforming and humanizing transcendence. Bonhoeffer was acutely aware of the destructive and oppressive way that the legendary "modern man" has used his newly-won powers. His own experience helped him see that the crucial problems of our time are more related to what people do with their powers than how they will deal with a guilty conscience; indeed, an amorality and lack of guilt about heinous crimes against humanity is probably more conspicuous today than a sense of God's imminent wrath hanging like a sword over the heads of guilty sinners. Accordingly, Christ who is present in the fabric of social existence—most specifically, in a newly-formed church community—embodies a critical and liberating transcendence. The crucified Christ indicts destructive power and oppression; the resurrected Christ frees and liberates mankind into a life of *pro*humanity. This brings to fruition Bonhoeffer's earliest christological theme: Jesus as the reality and paradigm of the new humanity. In this Christology Jesus is not presented in the form of authority and power, but much more as a brother—"the first born among many brothers" (and sisters!), a phrase Bonhoeffer could easily borrow from Paul.[59]

Bonhoeffer's final christological metaphor, Jesus "the man for others," is rich in its very simplicity. It articulates a hard-won and liberating faith which redeems narcissism, and it distills the communal, antiindividualistic spirit of his theology. The latter enabled him to begin overcoming the liabilities of traditional Lutheran social ethics: excessive deference by the Christian to the authority of the state; preference for established order and resistance to fundamental social change; the inability of the church properly to understand the political dimensions of salvation and its unwillingness to take political action as a corporate body; a dualistic anthropology of "inner" and "outer," tied to a preoccupation with individual conscience and individualistic ethics. Along with his significant break-

59. Rom. 8:29.

through on this complex of problems, Bonhoeffer remained
fairly conservative in his social attitudes and largely limited by
the perspective of his own class.[60] Yet he prepared the way for
others by breaking up hard and long-trodden ground.

To Bonhoeffer as well as Luther applies the reformer's saying, *"Vivendo, immo moriendo et damnando fit theologus, non
intelligendo, legendo aut speculando."*[61] Each man had his own
distinct psychological complexion, and for each the questions
of faith, identity, and ethics were posed in different forms
characteristic of their historical moments. Given the difference
of Bonhoeffer's personal, church, and political concerns, and
his own passion and creativity, it was impossible for him to
encounter these issues in secondhand categories and in a conceptuality simply taken over from Luther. In minting a new
theology for himself and his church, Bonhoeffer broke out of the
Lutheran ethic which proved such a liability to Christians and
others in the years in which he lived and died, the most tragic
years of Germany's history. His theology and ethics, enacted in
his life, can be seen as a costly and faithful struggle with the
question Erikson poses, post-Luther and post-Freud, that of
"whether collective man will create a world worth being whole
for."[62]

60. But see "The View from Below," *Letters and Papers from Prison*, p. 17.
61. *D. Martin Luthers Werke. Kritische Gesamtausgabe* (Weimar: Hermann
Bohlaus Nachfolger, 1883–), vol. 5, p. 163; cited in Bethge, *Dietrich Bonhoeffer* (Harper ed.), p. 792, and Erikson, *Young Man Luther*, p. 251: "Living, dying, and being condemned make a theologian, not understanding, reading, or speculation."
62. *Young Man Luther*, p. 253.

Bibliography:
Reviews of Erikson's *Young Man Luther*

Anonymous. Review of *Young Man Luther* and Robert J. Lifton's *Thought Reform and the Psychology of Totalism. Daedalus* 92, no. 1 (Winter 1963):178–87.

Bainton, Roland H. "Luther: A Psychiatric Portrait." *Yale Review* (Spring 1959):405–10; also in *Studies on the Reformation* (Boston: Beacon Press, 1963), pp. 86–92.

————. "Luther und sein Vater." *Zeitwende* 6 (1973):393–404.

————. "Luther und seine Mutter." *Luther. Zeitschrift der Luthergesellschaft* 44 (1973):123–30.

Bornkamm, Heinrich. "Luther und sein Vater: Bemerkungen zu Erik Erikson, *Young Man Luther.*" *Zeitschrift für Theologie und Kirche* 66 (1969):38–61.

Buchrucker, Armin. Review of *Young Man Luther. Lutherische Rundblick* 14 (1966):54–56.

Domhoff, G. W. "Two Luthers: The Traditional and the Heretical in Freudian Psychology." *The Psychoanalytic Review* 57 (1970):5–17.

Edwards, Mark. "Erikson, Experimental Psychology and Luther's Identity." In Homans, Peter, ed. *Childhood and Selfhood: Essays on Religion and Modernity in the Thought of Erik Erikson.* Lewisburg, Pa.: Bucknell University Press (forthcoming).

Faber, Heije. "Ein psychoanalyticus over Luther–I." *Nederlands Theologisch Tijdschrift* 20 (October 1965).

Greenslade, Stanley L. "*Young Man Luther: A Study in Psychoanalysis and History*—A Review." *Church Quarterly Review* 161 (July-September 1960):369–70.

197

Hamai, O. "Shoke no Luther no Shinri-kozo" ("The Young Luther's Psychological Structure"). *Jitsuzonshugi* 57 (Rishosha 1971):60–67.

Hill, C. "Luther and Freud." *Spectator* 203 (December 1959):831.

Kantzenbach, Friedrich W. "Martin Luther Psychoanalytisch. Liefert Erikson Umrisse eines neuen Lutherbildes?" *Lutherische Monatshefte* 10 (1971):86–90.

Kooiman, Willem J. "Een psychoanalyticus over Luther–II." *Nederlands Theologisch Tijdschrift* 20 (October 1965):38–48.

Lefevre, Perry. "Erikson's *Young Man Luther*: A Contribution to the Scientific Study of Religion." *Journal for the Scientific Study of Religion* 2, no. 2 (April 1963):248–52.

Lindbeck, George A. "Erikson's *Young Man Luther*: An Historical and Theological Reappraisal." *Soundings* 36 (Summer 1973):210–27.

Mack, J. E. "Psychoanalysis and Historical Biography." *Journal of the American Psychoanalytic Association* 19 (1971):143–79.

Meyer, Donald B. Review of *Young Man Luther. Psychoanalysis and History,* ed. Bruce Mazlish (Englewood Cliffs, N.J.: Prentice-Hall, 1960), pp. 291–97.

Peeters, H. F. M. Review of *Young Man Luther. Tijdschrift voor Gescheidenis* 18 (1968):524–26.

Scharfenberg, J. Review of *Young Man Luther. Theologica Practica* 4 (1969):399–402.

Snyder, R. "A Design of Growth for the Young Adult." *The Chicago Seminary Register* 49 (November 1959):2–13.

Woolcott, Philip. "Erikson's Luther: A Psychiatrist's View." *Journal for the Scientific Study of Religion* 2, no. 2 (April 1963):243–48.